191   PUMPKIN

Informal Entertaining Country Style

Other Cookbooks by Farm Journal

FARM JOURNAL'S COUNTRY COOKBOOK
FREEZING & CANNING COOKBOOK
FARM JOURNAL'S COMPLETE PIE COOKBOOK
AMERICA'S BEST VEGETABLE RECIPES
BUSY WOMAN'S COOKBOOK
LET'S START TO COOK
HOMEMADE BREAD
HOMEMADE CANDY
HOMEMADE COOKIES
HOMEMADE ICE CREAM AND CAKE

Informal Entertaining Country Style

Edited by
NELL B. NICHOLS

FARM JOURNAL FIELD FOOD EDITOR

Photography Supervised by
AL J. REAGAN

FARM JOURNAL ART STAFF

DOUBLEDAY & COMPANY, INC.

GARDEN CITY, NEW YORK

ISBN: 0-385-05470-4
Library of Congress Catalog Card Number 72–92207
Copyright © 1973 by FARM JOURNAL, INC.

Contents

See Index under Menus for individual meal plans

COLOR ILLUSTRATIONS

Color photographs by: *Faraghan Studio, Bruce Harlow, Hoedt Studio, Mel Richman.*

Informal Entertaining Country Style

INFORMAL ENTERTAINING
COUNTRY STYLE

The trend to easy, casual living is changing the lifestyle of all America. Growing interest even among urban dwellers in the good earth and its produce is making country-style cooking and hospitality the popular way to welcome guests. Sharing food informally and unpretentiously with the warmth and natural graciousness born from generations of farm neighborliness fills a need in our society today. And the time-tried dishes for which country women have developed a well-deserved reputation are served with enthusiasm.

Women all across the country, especially young hostesses, strive to capture the natural, casual charm of country entertaining. They ask many questions: What kind of menus do you use? What makes country food so good? Where do you get recipes? How do busy women find time to prepare them?

Country entertaining has changed, too, with changes in farming and in farm family life and interests. Over the years, farm women have adapted country-style entertaining to changing living conditions in a remarkable way. They have kept the warmth and ease with which guests are served but have prepared meals by more efficient timetables. They are experts at planning ahead—with the unpredictable schedules of farm life, they have had to be!

The main purpose of this book is to share their experiences and at the same time give the hostess who already entertains country style some new and exciting menus and recipes. It's really a hostess handbook because in addition to superior recipes there are tips on meal management.

In the country, people always have shared food—an important part of neighborliness, family life and community get-togethers. For the latter, the meals are likely to be "planned potluck"—actually a contradiction. But it is an improvement farm women have made over the old custom: "Bring a covered dish." This could result in a dozen bowls of coleslaw and only one main dish! Cooperative meals appropriated the name "potluck" even though every woman is assigned food to bring.

So now when cars stop in a farmyard, men and women, and often children, emerge carrying packages of different sizes and shapes, holding some of the most delicious homemade country food prepared today. These planned potlucks divide the work and cost of a dinner or supper party. And they practically eliminate much of the large-quantity cooking once done by clubs and other country groups.

Here's how the potlucks are planned. Take a recipe in this cookbook. Notice the number of servings it makes and then figure out how many times it would have to be made to get the total servings you need for the guests expected. This tells you the number of women required to prepare this dish. The hostess (or a committee) plans the entire menu this way. Large utensils for big-quantity cooking are no longer needed. But do select foods that travel well.

Much country hospitality is impromptu, which means having something on hand to heat and serve quickly. A farm business caller often arrives midmorning (and not always without a secondary motive—coffee break!). Or perhaps it is a neighbor down the road who has the earliest garden in the neighborhood and shares the first garden lettuce. Whoever it is will likely be invited to the kitchen table for hot coffee and heated homemade coffee bread, or whatever the freezer yields. The coffee break originated in the country!

Every farm woman can share tales of unexpected friends or relatives from a distance descending without notice. An advantage of modern travel: These guests often are equipped for camping so have their own beds, cooking facilities and some of their food. But meals are usually shared. The hospitable host may take over breakfast and bake pancakes for everyone on the outdoor grill.

Farm women are expert at stretching a meal to accommodate one or more unexpecteds. When the school bus stops at the front gate, the family schoolboy may bring friends, and suppertime approaches with the familiar question: "Mom, may David and John stay for supper?" Extra plates go on the table and the menu is quickly enlarged. Young people, especially teen-agers, are frequent unexpected guests in today's country homes.

Guest participation in cooking, serving or clean-up is a country custom. This is one reason why fondue suppers are a popular current way of entertaining. Fondue parties are easy to give; with one or more pots on the table, everyone cooks for himself. The informality promotes lively conversation.

These are a few of the occasions in this changing world in which country-style food lives up to its fabulous reputation as the best in America. Frequently the guests come family style and the hospitality and service are family style.

We compiled this cookbook with the help of homemakers who are experts in entertaining country style. In it we share tested recipes and menus, many of which they suggested. Here are some pointers for successful informal entertaining:

DEPEND ON GOOD HOME-COOKED FOODS to lift your meals and refreshments for guests above the commonplace. You can serve simple food if you prepare and season it with care. Then—if your guests are comfortable and feel welcome—they will enjoy what you serve them. Hamburgers with an extra touch, like our Home-made Burger Buns, can please more than a fancy dish.

PLAN AHEAD WHAT YOU WILL SERVE and stick to your menu. In this book we accompany our menus with a timetable—tips on what to do ahead and what to do on guest day—plus suggestions for serving. The women who contributed their favorite menus for country-style entertaining believe it is wise, whenever possible, to include few dishes that require last-minute cooking. If you have a freezer, make it work for you. Give the refrigerator its share of responsibility. This book makes maximum use of these appliances.

MAKE AND SERVE YEAST BREADS. They are the trump card for many country hostesses. Fortunately, breads keep successfully for months in the freezer. You can dramatize the serving of bread by placing it on a board and cutting and serving it at the table or buffet. This service is a direct takeover from the old-fashioned family table in the country kitchen. Our thrifty grandmothers served bread this way, not to glamorize it (good homemade bread was usual those days) but to avoid cutting more slices than would be eaten because they would dry out. With freezers and plastic wraps and bags, this is no problem today.

STOCK AT LEAST A FEW SHELVES in the cupboard or fruit closet with jellies, jams, preserves and other fruit spreads, spiced fruits, vegetable relishes and pickles. Use them to point up flavors in company meals and to add the magic country touch—especially if homemade. Another good idea borrowed from our grandmothers!

FEATURE GARDEN VEGETABLES AND FRESH FRUITS

when in plentiful supply. That's when they reach their flavor peak. One classic example of such a meal in this cookbook is the Iowa Corn Dinner. Sweet corn at the right stage of maturity, freshly picked and cooked promptly is always welcome. Notice, too, how Marinated Tomatoes, Fruit-Jar Tomato Relish, Fresh Cucumber/Onion Relish, Garden-Patch Salad and other garden treats show up in our menus.

FREEZE SOME OF SUMMER'S FLAVORS, if you have a freezer, to brighten guest meals out of season. One country hostess' favorite company dessert always ready in her freezer is a mixture of two—often more—packages of frozen fruits and berries. She places the frozen packages in a large bowl in the refrigerator to partially thaw by serving time. Then she tops the bowl with scoops of sherbet and invites guests to help themselves. The chance to help yourself makes the buffet style of serving so popular.

SERVE APPETIZERS IN THE LIVING ROOM before dinner or supper to lighten your last-minute activities. Make your husband a part of the hospitality by asking him to assume responsibility by serving and keeping guests happy during this course, while you are in the kitchen. If the children are old enough, they will enjoy helping their father to host. Our Christmas Snack Tree, from which guests have fun picking their snacks, is a great conversation piece. See also recipes for Sauerkraut Balls, Chicken Nuggets and spreads and dips.

MAKE ENTERTAINING A FAMILY ADVENTURE. Even small boys and girls can shell peas, pull radishes and do other simple chores. The teen-agers can do some of the cooking—even the baking. Don't call on them only for clean-up chores. Many hosts like to take an active role such as grilling meats, poultry and fish over coals for indoor or outdoor eating. We kept this in mind when we included recipes for Grilled Halibut Steaks, Barbecued Chicken Halves, Grilled Minute Steak Rolls, Grilled or Broiled Pot Roast and many other main-dish specialties. If your husband dislikes to carve roasts at the table, give him a second choice—to carve in the kitchen without spectators. An interested family greatly helps hospitality atmosphere, for which there is no substitute.

We hope this handbook on how to be a successful hostess country style will make your entertaining easier and more pleasant.

CHAPTER 1

Entertaining Before Noon

COFFEE BREAKS . . .
COFFEE PARTIES . . . BRUNCHES

The coffee break originated in pioneer country kitchens; today its popularity is universal. In the home, there is no more gracious and spontaneous way to extend a cordial welcome to midmorning guests. Regardless of how busy neighbors, friends and business callers are when they stop by on an errand, they will take at least a few minutes off to relax around the hospitable kitchen table and exchange ideas or news while they sip coffee and eat a tasty accompaniment.

Not all guests arrive unannounced, for women in town and country alike often telephone friends and invite them over for coffee. With advance notice, the hostess has time to make the coffee and bring out or fix something good to serve with it.

The perfect country coffee break creates the impression that the food is unplanned—the hostess serves what she has on hand and makes coffee. This carefree atmosphere contributes to the charm and success of the occasion. Thoughtful, busy guests like to believe they are not making extra work for their equally busy hostess. But most women actually do prepare appropriate food ahead to serve at coffeetime. They hide it in their freezers to bring out and run through the oven for a fast reheat.

Homemade breads excel as coffee companions. Try the recipes in this chapter for Square Doughnuts, Butter-Bright Pastries, Cottage Cheese Crescents and Golden Crown Coffee Cake—these are from country kitchens and will testify to the popularity of the country coffee break. You will also want to look in the Index under Breads for other homemade specialties that are great coffee go-withs.

Keep a special file of recipes for coffee accompaniments you can fix in a hurry. This is especially important for women without freezers. Quick Danish Pastry made with packaged rolls from the refrigerator and Pineapple Muffins are two good examples. Remember, too, how good homemade bread, toasted and buttered, tastes when served with jam, jelly or preserves—homemade, if you have them.

Coffee breaks sometimes evolve into full-fledged midmorning parties for invited guests. The scene shifts from the kitchen to the dining and living rooms and the menu expands to include fruit or fruit juice and often cake or cookies as well as bread. Our Mother's Day Coffee menu is an excellent example. If fresh strawberries are unavailable, substitute chilled fruit juice. Coffee parties also provide pleasing refreshments for afternoon entertaining.

Brunches are a more substantial way to entertain before noon. Regardless of what you call these late morning gatherings, the food consists of two meals in one, breakfast and luncheon. Youthful late sleepers call them breakfast (see Late Saturday Breakfast), but they skip lunch.

You can use the brunch menus in this chapter for informal suppers as well. Try Pancake Buffet and if you have a fondue pot, the Cook-at-Table Brunch menu. You'll find that many guests who fry their own French toast and eat it piping hot believe it tastes better than any they ever ate previously. Helping with the cooking and serving of food is a country tradition. It deserves much credit for the fame of country hospitality.

Recipes for all dishes starred (*) are in this cookbook.

NEIGHBORHOOD COFFEE

Square Doughnuts*   Coffee

Drop-in guests are an accepted country tradition. "Friends stop by so often," a Maryland farm woman says, "that I'm an expert at quickly putting on the coffeepot and running homemade bread of some kind in the oven to warm."

The kitchen usually is the setting for this midmorning or afternoon impromptu entertaining. No room in country homes is more friendly or attractive than the kitchen. Why not ask your visiting neighbors to sit down at the table and pour the coffee while you take the piping hot doughnuts from the oven and shake them in a bag containing sugar or dip them in a glaze?

TIMETABLE

Do-Ahead: You can fry the doughnuts, package and freeze them, but if you do, sugar or glaze them just before serving. (Like all fried foods, they have a comparatively short life in the freezer in comparison with other baked breads. The fat they contain may become rancid if they are held too long. The recommended maximum storage time is 2 months.)

On Guest Day: Spread a single layer of doughnuts in a big pan and warm in a slow oven (300°) about 20 minutes, or until hot. Then glaze or sugar them.

SERVING SUGGESTIONS

If you have mugs, serve the coffee in them. Coffee stays warm longer in any cup with straight sides. Bring out colorful paper napkins to brighten the scene. Guests will need them, for doughnuts are finger food.

SQUARE DOUGHNUTS

Try raisin doughnuts for a change—they're a pleasant surprise

¾ c. milk	1 pkg. active dry yeast
¼ c. sugar	1 egg, beaten
1 tsp. salt	3¼ to 3½ c. unsifted flour
¼ c. butter or regular margarine	Glaze
¼ c. lukewarm water (110 to 115°)	

Scald milk; stir in sugar, salt and butter. Cool until lukewarm.

Measure lukewarm water into a large warm mixing bowl (warm by rinsing out bowl with hot water). Sprinkle in the yeast and stir until yeast dissolves.

Add lukewarm milk mixture, egg and half the flour. Beat until smooth. Stir in enough remaining flour to make a soft dough. For lightness, add only enough flour to make a dough you can handle.

Turn dough onto a lightly floured board or pastry cloth. Knead until smooth and elastic, about 5 to 10 minutes. (If dough sticks to the hands, grease them lightly with shortening or oil.)

Place dough in a greased bowl, then turn the bottom side up. Cover with a damp cloth; let rise in a warm place until doubled, about 1 hour.

Punch down dough. On a lightly floured surface, roll about ½″ thick to make a rectangle 12×10″. With a sharp knife, cut in 2½″ squares (cut in rounds if you prefer round doughnuts); cut holes in centers with a 1″ cutter or bottletop. Place doughnuts about 2″ apart on oiled baking sheets or waxed paper. Cover with inverted baking pans (allow room for dough to rise), or with a cloth. Let rise until doubled, about 1 hour.

About 15 minutes before end of rising period, heat fat in deep fryer or electric skillet to 375°. (You will be more confident of temperature if you use a deep fat frying thermometer.)

Handle the doughnuts as gently as possible so they will not fall. Fry them, a few at a time, in deep fat 2 to 3 minutes, or until brown on both sides. Turn doughnuts only once. Drain on absorbent paper; dip while still warm, in a glaze or granulated sugar. (You can fry the center cutouts.) Makes about 20 doughnuts.

Variation

Raisin Doughnuts: Follow the recipe for Square Doughnuts, except use 2 pkgs. active dry yeast instead of 1 pkg., and stir in 1 c. chopped raisins with first half of the flour. Dough may rise slower.

Glazes for Doughnuts

Vanilla Glaze: Blend 2 c. confectioners sugar, ⅓ c. milk and 1 tsp. vanilla. Dip warm doughnuts into glaze and drain them on a rack over waxed paper. Reuse the glaze that drips off.

Spicy Glaze: Make like Vanilla Glaze, but omit the vanilla and add ½ tsp. ground cinnamon and ¼ tsp. ground nutmeg.

Orange Glaze: Follow recipe for Vanilla Glaze, but omit vanilla and substitute orange juice for milk.

To Glaze Doughnuts: Dip warm doughnuts in glaze and drain them on cooling racks over waxed paper. You can reuse the glaze that drips onto the waxed paper.

To Sugar Doughnuts: Drop drained, warm doughnuts into a paper bag of sugar and shake to coat. Or add 2 tsp. ground cinnamon to each ½ c. sugar when coating doughnuts.

SHORT-NOTICE COFFEE

Quick Danish Pastry*   Coffee

You could spend hours baking a go-with for coffee without getting results half as tasty as Quick Danish Pastry. You can make it from start to finish in a half hour. That is, you can if you have a can of crescent dinner rolls from the supermarket in your refrigerator and some fruit preserves in your cupboard. The North Dakota homemaker who first baked this coffee bread for a gathering of Girl Scout leaders, now considers it a standby when she plans to entertain and time is at a premium. We predict you'll do the same once you taste this treat and hear what your friends say about it.

TIMETABLE

On Guest Day: About 25 minutes before you wish to serve the coffee bread, put it in the oven. Make the coffee while it bakes.

SERVING SUGGESTIONS

The bread needs no accompaniment other than coffee. Be sure to serve it piping hot. If you wish to garnish the top of the bread, scatter dabs of the apricot preserves here and there on the sour cream topping just before returning bread to oven for the last 6 minutes of baking.

QUICK DANISH PASTRY

Crust is crisp and brown, in layers like Danish pastry—good

1 (8 oz.) can refrigerated crescent dinner rolls
½ c. apricot or peach preserves
1 egg, beaten

1 c. dairy sour cream
1 tblsp. sugar
1 tsp. vanilla

Press crescent rolls over bottom of ungreased 13×9×2″ pan to cover. Spread with preserves. Bake in hot oven (425°) 15 minutes. Remove from oven; turn temperature to slow (325°).

Combine egg, sour cream, sugar and vanilla; mix gently, but well. Spread over top of baked crust. Return to oven and bake 6 minutes. Cut in 4×3″ pieces and serve warm. Makes 12 servings.

MORNING COFFEE

Golden Crown Coffee Cake*   Coffee

When the chairman of the committee to which you belong telephones and asks if a special meeting can be held at your house next morning, chances are you'll immediately wonder what to serve with coffee. This coffee cake is a good one; it's easy to make. Time the baking so it will come out of the oven just before guests arrive. They'll sniff that marvelous aroma of yeast bread baking and be glad they came.

TIMETABLE

Do-Ahead: Make the dough for the coffee cake in the evening; cover and refrigerate.

On Guest Day: Put dough in the pan early in the morning. It will double in 1 to 1½ hours and be ready for baking.

SERVING SUGGESTIONS

If you and your guests sit around the table, serve the coffee cake on a large plate and let everyone pull off his servings. Pass butter for those who are not weight-watchers. And keep the coffee cups filled.

GOLDEN CROWN COFFEE CAKE

Made with same dough used for the refrigerator pan rolls in Harvest Festival Dinner menu in Chapter 4—an attractive coffee go-with

¾ c. sugar
2 tsp. ground cinnamon
½ c. chopped walnuts
½ c. seedless raisins

½ dough for Overnight Refrigerator Pan Rolls (see Index)
Melted butter

Combine sugar, cinnamon, walnuts and raisins.

Cut off pieces of dough about the size of a walnut. Roll each piece in melted butter, then in sugar-cinnamon mixture.

Arrange the first layer of dough pieces in a well-greased 9″ tube pan; place a second layer over the spaces. Continue building layers until all dough pieces are used. Sprinkle remaining sugar mixture over top.

Cover with a clean towel and let rise in warm place until doubled, 1 to 1½ hours. Bake in moderate oven (350°) 40 to 55 minutes. Take from oven, cool 10 minutes and then remove from pan. Makes 12 servings.

COFFEE FOR DROP-IN GUESTS

Pineapple Muffins*   Coffee

Take a pan of golden, fragrant muffins from the oven with your guests watching. Pour the coffee, pass the hot bread and butter and relax while you visit. A country coffee break is in session. The friendly custom started long ago in pioneer farm kitchens and it flourishes to this day. Usually the refreshments consist of coffee with one accompaniment, frequently from the freezer.

If you are too busy to stock your freezer with baked foods, or do not have one, depend on your cupboard to help you entertain unexpected drop-in guests. You can bake marvelous muffins with little fuss—and fast—from staple ingredients on hand. You can stir up the batter in a jiffy and get it in the oven. The muffins, when delivered to guests, are hot enough to melt, almost instantly, butter spread on them.

PINEAPPLE MUFFINS

Muffins are cake-like because of creaming method of mixing batter

2 c. sifted flour	¼ c. shortening
3 tsp. baking powder	1 egg, beaten
½ tsp. salt	1 c. crushed pineapple, undrained
½ c. sugar	

Sift together flour, baking powder and salt.

Cream sugar and shortening until light and fluffy. Add egg and beat well. Stir in undrained pineapple. Add dry ingredients and stir just enough to moisten flour. Do not beat.

Fill greased muffin-pan cups two thirds full. Bake in hot oven (400°) 20 to 25 minutes, or until golden. Remove from pans at once. Makes 12 to 15 medium muffins.

MOTHER'S DAY COFFEE

Strawberry Send-off
Superfine Sugar   Sour Cream/Brown Sugar Dip
Apricot/Almond Torte*
Orange Spice Cake*
Coffee   Tea

Inviting your mother, your husband's mother and their friends to share a few Maytime hours in your home shortly before Mother's Day contributes genuine pleasure to hostess and guests. The food for such celebrations is best if simple, but it must be exceptionally tasty. And a thoughtful hostess makes certain there is something, regardless of diets, for everyone to eat and enjoy.

Apricot/Almond Torte definitely meets the challenge of a special-occasion treat. Orange Spice Cake contains no egg yolk and with salad oil as the shortening, it's designed especially for guests restricted to low-cholesterol foods. The strawberry appetizer is as luscious as it looks. The hulls serve as handles when dunking the berries in the dips. Serve for the first course in the living room.

TIMETABLE

Do-Ahead: Bake the torte a day or two ahead, cool, wrap and freeze if you like, but glaze it shortly before serving. Bake the cake a day ahead, cool, wrap in foil and store overnight in a cool place. Frost when you glaze the torte.

On Guest Day: If the torte is frozen, thaw it in its heavy-duty aluminum foil wrap in a moderate oven (350°); it will thaw in 20 to 25 minutes. Remove from oven and glaze. Frost the cake. Fill a bowl with dairy sour cream and sprinkle liberally with brown sugar; fill a similar bowl with superfine sugar. Wash and drain choice ripe strawberries.

SERVING SUGGESTIONS

Arrange strawberries on tray in a wreath or any desired pattern around the twin bowls of dips and serve as an appetizer. Cut the torte and the cake and place on trays or large plates. Let everyone help herself. Give guests a choice of tea or coffee.

APRICOT/ALMOND TORTE

Elegant, yeast-flavored coffee bread made in three layers with sugar and almonds, and apricot preserves between, a glaze on top

1 pkg. active dry yeast	½ c. dairy sour cream
¼ c. warm water (110 to 115°)	1 c. chopped almonds
1⅓ c. butter, softened	¾ c. sugar
3½ c. flour	1 (12 oz.) jar apricot preserves
4 egg yolks	(about 1 c.)
½ tsp. almond extract	Glaze

Sprinkle yeast on warm water; stir to dissolve.

Combine butter and flour in large mixing bowl until mixture resembles coarse crumbs. Add egg yolks, beaten slightly, almond extract, sour cream and yeast. Mix until a dough forms. Do not let dough rise. Divide into 3 equal parts.

Roll out each third of dough on lightly floured surface to a 13×9″ rectangle. Fit one rectangle into bottom of greased 13×9×2″ pan.

Combine almonds and sugar; sprinkle over dough in pan. Top with second dough rectangle and spread with apricot preserves. Top with remaining dough. Bake at once in moderate oven (350°) 50 to 55 minutes. While warm, spread with Glaze. Makes 12 servings.

Glaze: Blend together ½ c. confectioners sugar, 2 to 3 tblsp. milk and 1 tsp. butter.

ORANGE SPICE CAKE

Orange peel and raisins enhance this spice cake. While tailored to fit low-cholesterol diets, it tastes too good to be limited to them

2 c. sugar	1 tsp. ground nutmeg
½ c. salad oil	2 c. buttermilk
1 tblsp. baking soda	1 tblsp. grated orange peel, or ½
3 c. flour	tsp. dehydrated orange peel
1 tsp. ground cinnamon	1 c. seedless raisins
½ tsp. ground cloves	Brown Sugar Frosting

Blend sugar and oil.

Sift together baking soda, flour and spices; add alternately with buttermilk to sugar-oil mixture, beating after each addition. Add orange peel and raisins. Pour into two greased 9″ round layer cake pans.

Bake in moderate oven (375°) 40 minutes, or until cake tests done. Frost with Brown Sugar Frosting. Makes about 12 servings.

Brown Sugar Frosting: Melt ½ c. regular margarine in saucepan; stir in 1 c. brown sugar, firmly packed. Heat to boiling, stirring constantly. Boil and stir over low heat for 2 minutes. Remove from heat; stir in ¼ c. milk. Return to heat and bring to a boil, stirring.

Remove from heat and gradually stir in 2 c. confectioners sugar. Place pan of frosting in a bowl of ice water and beat until of spreading consistency. If frosting becomes too stiff, heat it slightly, stirring all the time.

EVER-READY COFFEE PARTY

Butter-Bright Pastries*   Coffee

Most country women plan to have something tasty to serve friends who stop by at any time without advance warning. Home-baked bread is always welcome, and if it's yeast-leavened Butter-Bright Pastries, compliments are bountiful.

You can vary the pastries in many ways, as the recipe suggests. And you can keep them in the freezer in readiness for the days when the doorbell rings unexpectedly.

TIMETABLE

Do-Ahead: Bake the pastries several days or weeks ahead if you wish. Cool them, wrap in heavy-duty aluminum foil and freeze. You may prefer to glaze the pastries after freezing. It gives them a fresh-baked taste.

On Guest Day: Heat the frozen pastries in their wrap in a moderate oven (350°) 20 to 25 minutes. Or if you have time, you can let them thaw in their wrap at room temperature for 2 to 3 hours. If you add the icing after thawing, let your guests watch you spread it on the heated pastries. It will make them more eager than ever for a taste.

SERVING SUGGESTIONS

One of the friendliest places to serve the pastries is at the kitchen table with a full coffeepot nearby.

BUTTER-BRIGHT PASTRIES

Our Countryside Test Kitchens developed five excellent variations

2 pkgs. active dry yeast	4 to 4½ c. sifted flour
¼ c. warm water (110 to 115°)	2 eggs
⅓ c. sugar	1 c. butter
⅛ tsp. salt	Glaze
1 c. cold milk	

Dissolve yeast in warm water. Combine yeast mixture, sugar, salt and milk. Beat in 2 c. flour; add eggs, beating well. Stir in enough remaining flour to make a soft dough. Cover and refrigerate 15 minutes.

On a lightly floured surface, roll dough into an 18×15" rectangle. Cut ⅓ c. butter into small pieces. Dot surface of dough with butter pieces, leaving a 1" margin. Fold 18" side into thirds and then fold 15" side into thirds. Wrap in floured aluminum foil; chill 15 minutes. Repeat procedure twice, using remaining butter. (When you roll dough second and third times, turn dough so narrow side faces you.) Chill 15 more minutes.

Divide dough in fourths. Roll and cut into desired shapes (directions follow). Let rise until doubled. Bake in hot oven (400°) 8 minutes or until golden. Cool. Drizzle with Glaze. Makes 24 pastries.

Glaze: Combine 1 c. sifted confectioners sugar, 2 tblsp. butter, 2 tblsp. evaporated milk and ½ tsp. vanilla.

Crescents: Combine ¼ c. brown sugar, firmly packed, ¼ c. chopped nuts and ¼ tsp. ground cinnamon. Melt 2 tblsp. butter. Cut dough into 5×2×⅛" rectangles and spread with butter. Sprinkle with filling. Roll like a jelly roll. Shape into crescent with seam side down. Snip at 1" intervals.

Butterflies: Cut into 3×¼" squares. Fold opposite corners to the center and press down. After baking and adding Glaze, fill with assorted jams or jellies.

"S" Shapes: Cut into 8×1×¼" strips. Roll back and forth to form

evenly shaped sticks. Shape into an "S" with sides of "sticks" touching. After baking and adding Glaze, fill with assorted jams or jellies.

Whirls: Cut into 8×1×¼" strips. Roll back and forth to form evenly shaped sticks. Place one end in center and wind dough pinwheel fashion. Tuck loose end under. After baking and adding Glaze, fill with assorted jams or jellies.

Twists: Cut into 8×1×¼" strips. Roll to form evenly shaped sticks. Fold in half; cross ends over each other to form twists.

N O T E : If pastries are made more than one day before serving them, do not add glaze. Wrap the baked pastries in aluminum foil and freeze. To serve, heat frozen pastries in their wrap in a moderate oven (350°) 20 to 25 minutes. Add Glaze (and filling) before serving.

PLANNED COFFEE PARTY

· Cottage Cheese Crescents*   Coffee

Recipes for new delicacies to serve with coffee are a popular search project among thousands of women who like to have their friends stop by. One Wisconsin farm woman discovered an unusual bread her guests enjoy; try her Cottage Cheese Crescents.

TIMETABLE

Do-Ahead: Make the dough for the rolls a day ahead (or at least several hours) and refrigerate.

On Guest Day: Shape, bake, cool and glaze the rolls.

SERVING SUGGESTIONS

Cottage Cheese Crescents need no accompaniment other than cups of steaming coffee. You can serve currant or other tart jelly with them if you wish.

COTTAGE CHEESE CRESCENTS

No one will guess cottage cheese imparts the fascinating flavor

1 c. butter	⅛ tsp. salt
2 c. small curd creamed cottage	2 c. sifted flour
cheese	Vanilla Glaze

Have butter and cottage cheese at room temperature. Combine in bowl with salt and flour, and beat until smooth and elastic. Cover and chill for several hours, or overnight.

Divide dough into 4 equal parts. Roll 1 part in circle about ½″ thick, 6″ in diameter. Cut in 8 wedges. Roll up each wedge, starting at rounded edge. Place point side down on ungreased baking sheet and curve slightly. Repeat with remaining portions of dough.

Bake in moderate oven (350°) about 20 minutes. Cool on racks. Spread tops with Vanilla Glaze. Makes 32.

Vanilla Glaze: Mix 1½ tblsp. light cream or 1 tblsp. milk into 1 c. confectioners sugar and ½ tsp. vanilla until of spreading consistency.

N O T E : For a change, lightly brush circles of dough with melted butter and sprinkle with a little sugar-cinnamon mixture before rolling the wedges of dough into crescent shapes.

LATE SATURDAY BREAKFAST

Fruit Juice
Fluffy Omelet with Cheese Sauce*
Lacy Potato Cakes*
Coffee

When a daughter away at school returns home for the weekend, bringing a friend or two with her, an opportunity to get into the kitchen again usually appeals, but the timing is important. Up late on Friday night, the girls welcome a chance to "sleep in" Saturday morning until the family have breakfasted. While the girls call the meal they fix for themselves breakfast, it's really brunch. By evening they're ready for Mom's wonderful cooking.

The menu that pleases most consists of foods not served in the school dining hall. A fluffy omelet, for example, is a mighty fine country dish, but a difficult one to handle for a crowd. And crisp Lacy Potato Cakes, made by the recipe from a California girl of college age, are a good companion for omelet and other egg dishes. Something men and boys like too, so don't necessarily use the recipe for girls only!

TIMETABLE

Do-Ahead: If Mother has a loaf of homemade bread on hand, toast made with it and spread with butter and fruit or berry preserves from the fruit closet may prove irresistible even to ardent young weight-watchers.

On Guest Day: The hostess makes the cheese sauce and then the omelet, while a guest fixes the potato cakes.

SERVING SUGGESTIONS

The kitchen provides the homey setting girls home from school appreciate. Let them eat there too. They can bake potato cakes on an electric griddle or in an electric skillet placed on the kitchen table.

FLUFFY OMELET WITH CHEESE SAUCE

With fresh country eggs and the right techniques, this is a great dish

4 eggs, separated	1 tblsp. butter or regular
2 tblsp. water	margarine
¼ tsp. salt	Cheese Sauce

Beat egg whites until frothy. Add water and salt and beat until stiff, but not dry. Beat egg yolks until lemon-colored and very thick. Gently fold into the whites.

Heat butter in a 10″ skillet with ovenproof handle. Shake a few drops of water into the skillet. If they sizzle, pour in the egg mixture, spreading it evenly, but slightly higher around the edges. Reduce heat and cook *slowly* about 8 to 10 minutes, or until omelet is puffed up and set. Gently lift up one edge of it with a spatula; it should be golden on the underside.

Bake in a slow oven (325°) about 10 minutes, or until a knife inserted in omelet center comes out clean.

Loosen omelet around edges with spatula. Make a shallow cut across omelet shortly above center and parallel to skillet handle.

Tilt pan and fold the smaller, or upper half, over the lower half. With the aid of spatula and spoon, slip omelet onto hot platter. Spoon Cheese Sauce on it and serve at once. Makes 2 or 3 servings.

Cheese Sauce: Melt 2 tblsp. butter in saucepan over low heat. Blend in 2 tblsp. flour, ¼ tsp. salt and a dash of white pepper. Add 1 c. milk all at one time; cook and stir until mixture bubbles and thickens. Add 1 c. shredded sharp cheese and stir until it melts. Makes 1½ cups.

LACY POTATO CAKES

Potatoes and eggs team as well as peaches and cream in country meals. Make these for the entire family to enjoy

2 medium baking potatoes	Freshly ground pepper
1 tblsp. chopped fresh chives	Butter
1 tsp. salt	Salad oil

Peel potatoes, and shred coarsely into a medium mixing bowl. Add chives, salt and pepper and toss to mix. Heat equal parts butter and salad oil in a skillet over medium high heat until mixture stops foaming (should be hot, but not smoking).

Use 2 tblsp. of potato mixture for each cake and pan-fry 3 or 4 cakes at a time, flattening each to about 3″ in diameter with a spatula. Cook over medium-high heat 2 to 3 minutes on each side, or until golden. Serve at once. Use equal amounts of butter and oil as needed in baking the remainder of the cakes. Makes 9 or 10 potato cakes.

N O T E : This is an easy recipe to double.

PANCAKE BUFFET

Chilled Fruit Juice
Sour Cream Pancake Puffs*   Blueberry Pancakes
Maple Syrup   Pineapple Sauce*
Bacon Platter   Coffee

For a happy, relaxed way to entertain friends at brunch try this pancake buffet, featuring exceptionally light and tender sour cream pancakes. They'll disappear like magic—proof of how delicious they are. Flatter your guests by offering them a choice of pancakes;

the second kind could be made with a packaged mix. It might be blueberry cakes.

This meal plan gives the host a chance to star as the chef presiding over the electric griddle or skillet. Relief will come his way for some of the guests likely will ask to bake their own seconds, or, eventually, the hostess may take her turn at the griddle. You can handle up to 8 people with this meal.

TIMETABLE

On Guest Day: About an hour before mealtime, set up the buffet and combine juices for appetizer; refrigerate. One excellent choice is 1 (6 oz.) can frozen orange juice concentrate reconstituted with 3 cans cold water and mixed with 1 (1 lb. 13 oz.) can chilled apricot nectar. Make pancake batters and pour into pitchers or attractive bowls with ladles. While the bacon bakes and coffee drips or percolates, serve the fruit juice. Lay bacon, 2 or 3 strips per person, on rack in broiling pan; be sure not to overlap them. Bake in hot oven (400°) 10 minutes; allow 20 minutes for thick bacon slices. There's no turning or draining. Heat Pineapple Sauce.

SERVING SUGGESTIONS

Set pitcher of chilled fruit juice and juice glasses on a side table or coffee table so everyone can help himself. Float thin orange slices in pitcher. Place electric griddle (or electric skillet) on one end of buffet, with pancake batters nearby, the coffeemaker, cups, sugar and cream at the opposite end. Arrange serving plates, bacon, butter, Pineapple Sauce and maple syrup in between. You may wish also to serve other pancake toppings, such as honey and berry syrup from the supermarket. If you have a lazy susan, arrange pancake trimmings on it. The host asks the first guest to be served for her choice of pancakes and bakes them. She helps herself to the toppings and bacon; the hostess pours the coffee. This scene repeats until everyone has eaten his fill.

SOUR CREAM PANCAKE PUFFS

*Superlative dollar-size griddlecakes that contain 4 eggs and only ⅓
cup flour—they're light, tender and wonderfully delicious*

⅓ c. flour	¼ tsp. salt
3 tblsp. sugar	4 eggs
1 tsp. baking soda	2 c. dairy sour cream

Sift together flour, sugar, soda and salt.

Beat eggs; stir in sifted dry ingredients. Gently blend in sour
cream (a wire whip is a good tool to use).

Drop tablespoonfuls of batter onto greased griddle heated to 375°,
or hot enough to sizzle when a few drops of water are sprinkled
on it. When bubbles appear in pancakes, but before they break,
slip spatula halfway under each and turn to brown on other side.
Serve at once. Makes about 72 pancakes, or 8 servings.

PINEAPPLE SAUCE

This is best served warm—perfect accompaniment for pancakes

3 tblsp. butter or regular margarine	2 tblsp. brown sugar
1 (8¼ oz.) can crushed pineapple	

Melt butter in small saucepan. Add undrained crushed pineapple
and brown sugar. Heat about 5 minutes, or until sauce cooks down a
little. Makes about 1 cup.

N O T E : Add a dash of spice, if you like. Try ground nutmeg.

COOK-AT-TABLE BRUNCH

Chilled Fruit Juice
French Toast Nuggets*
Honey   Confectioners Sugar   Maple Syrup
Little Pig Sausages
Coffee

Spear a cube of crisp-crusted French bread on your fondue
fork, transform it into a golden nugget in the fondue pot, dunk in

honey or maple syrup, or sprinkle with confectioners sugar—m'm, good! Your guests will agree.

One or two guests in a group often come to brunch carrying an extra fondue pot. Fondue parties are popular in the country—guests, host and hostess enjoy sitting around the table, doing their own "cooking." It's part of the entertainment.

Always use a metal fondue pot (not earthenware—it may crack) when you cook with oil; it will handle high temperatures adequately. Provide one cooker for every four people if you can, so the oil will stay hot enough. The electric fondue cooker with more easily controlled heat helps to avoid temperature problems and is safer with crowds than the open burner. Or use your electric skillet. Buffet-style skillets are attractive and convenient for cooking at the table. They come in many colors, are deep, have two comfortable handles for carrying and temperatures are controlled.

Regardless of the kind of cooking utensil you use to make French toast, play safe and place a protective mat or tray under it to keep spatters and spills off the table.

TIMETABLE

Do-Ahead: The day before the brunch, cut a long loaf of French bread in about 50 bite-size pieces, every piece with crust on one side. Cover and keep in a cool place.

On Guest Day: Before the guests arrive, stir up the batter for dipping toast. A few minutes before serving time, pour orange juice or equal parts grapefruit and tangerine juices (reconstituted frozen juice concentrates) over cracked ice in a pitcher. Cook the sausages and make the coffee. Heat the oil in the fondue cooker.

SERVING SUGGESTIONS

Set the juice and juice glasses on the buffet or side table and ask guests to help themselves while you finish your chores. Arrange a bowl of the batter (or two bowls if you're using two fondue pots), bowls of bread pieces, honey, maple syrup and a shaker of confectioners sugar on the table. Provide a dinner fork, fondue fork and a serving plate for each person. Keep the sausages warm in a chafing dish or electric skillet alongside the fondue pot.

FRENCH TOAST NUGGETS

Anticipating amount of food needed is difficult but allow at least 8 bread cubes per person. Increase amount if appetites are ravenous

1 long loaf French bread (1 lb.)	¼ tsp. salt
2 eggs, well beaten	Salad oil
½ c. milk	

Cut bread in bite-size pieces, each with crust on one side.

Combine eggs, milk and salt until smooth. Pour into bowl.

Pour oil to depth of 2" (no more) in metal fondue cooker. Heat to 375° (using fat thermometer) on kitchen range; set over fondue burner. Or, if using an electric fondue pot, follow manufacturer's directions. Add 1 tsp. salt to hot oil to help reduce spatters. Adjust heat throughout cooking as needed to keep the oil at a satisfactory temperature.

Spear a piece of bread through the crust side with a fondue fork, dip in batter and let the excess drip off. Fry it in the hot oil until golden brown. Transfer to dinner fork and dunk in maple syrup or honey, or shake on confectioners sugar. Makes about 6 servings.

MAYTIME BRUNCH

Fruit-in-the-Pink*

Cheese Strata Soufflé*   Glazed Ham Strips

Hard Rolls

Coffee   Tea   Milk

Call this brunch or supper, as you like. The tempting food tastes equally good on a beautiful late Sunday morning in spring and early in the evening. It's a sit-down partnership meal with husband and wife involved in the cooking. The host grills the ham outdoors over coals and the hostess prepares the remainder of the food.

Use two slices of fully cooked center-cut smoked ham 1" thick. Score each side of ham slices ¼" deep, forming diamonds to help hold the barbecue sauce. Brush surface of ham with your favorite barbecue sauce or with ½ c. syrup drained from pickled peaches mixed with 1 c. brown sugar, firmly packed, and ¼ c. prepared horse-radish and brought to a boil. Lay slices on lightly greased grill over low to medium coals; the trick is to keep meat moist. Brush frequently with sauce and cook 10 to 15 minutes, or until underside is browned. Brush with sauce, turn and cook about 10 minutes longer. Keep warm on platter until serving.

TIMETABLE

Do-Ahead: Pour ginger ale over little red cinnamon candies (red hots) a day or several hours ahead. Stir occasionally and chill. Combine ingredients for casserole a day or a couple of days ahead, cover and refrigerate.

On Guest Day: Add pineapple to ginger ale-candy mixture at least 1 to 2 hours before serving time. About an hour before you want to serve the casserole, put it in the oven to bake. At that time, light the coals so the embers will be ready to cook the ham the last half hour before time to sit down to eat. Combine the fruit for the first course and serve.

SERVING SUGGESTIONS

Serve the fruit in chilled stemmed dessert glasses to display its lovely color. Cut the ham in strips and garnish the platter with water cress.

FRUIT-IN-THE-PINK

Candy teams with strawberries to tint and flavor this eye-opener

1 (7 oz.) bottle ginger ale	1 (1 lb. 4 oz.) can pineapple
¼ c. cinnamon candies (red hots)	chunks
	1 qt. strawberries

Pour ginger ale over cinnamon candies and let stand several hours. Pour over pineapple and chill at least 1 to 2 hours.

Add hulled, ripe strawberries and serve in chilled dessert glasses. Makes 8 servings.

CHEESE STRATA SOUFFLÉ

Blended seasonings, rich flavor distinguish this country-type soufflé

12 slices sandwich bread, crusts removed	¾ tsp. salt
	⅛ tsp. pepper
¾ lb. sharp Cheddar cheese, shredded	¼ tsp. dry mustard
	⅛ tsp. ground red pepper
6 eggs, beaten	½ tsp. seasoned salt
1¼ c. light cream	1 green onion, minced
1¼ c. milk	

Butter bread slices and dice. In greased 2-qt. baking dish arrange alternate layers of bread and cheese, beginning and ending with bread.

Combine eggs, cream, milk, seasonings and onion. Pour over bread and cheese. Cover and chill in refrigerator at least 1 hour, but better overnight or for a day or two.

Bake uncovered in moderate oven (350°) 1 hour, or until no particles adhere to a metal knife inserted into soufflé. Serve at once. Soufflé puffs up but falls somewhat if allowed to stand more than a few minutes. Makes 6 to 8 servings.

CHAPTER 2

Entertaining at Midday

. . . LUNCHEONS WITH FEMININE APPEAL

Country men are often called meat-and-potatoes men. Perhaps the old—and enduring—custom in farm communities of serving husbands the noon meal before wives drive off to join friends at luncheon helped to build this masculine reputation. And it established 1:00 to 1:30 afternoon time for country women's luncheons.

Although we planned most of the luncheon menus in this chapter primarily for women, you will find that some menus produce meals men accept—and praise. Our Autumn Picnic is one; success of this meal depends on the entire family's cooperation, including Father's. Certainly the Welcoming Lunch with its homemade bread, cheese, applesauce and coffee will please most men. But for the most part, our supper menus would be better menus for luncheons attended by men. Two of the menus, Vegetarian Luncheon and Accent-on-Youth Lunch, will please young people.

In the main, our menus feature salads and desserts designed for women. Melon Salad Plate presents a colorful picture plate. Plantation Chicken Salad in Women's Luncheon is another favorite. Our Buffet Luncheon is excellent for 8 to 10 guests. For a larger group, make as many recipes of the salad, hot rolls and dessert as you need.

Sit down in a comfortable chair and peruse this chapter while you make plans for luncheons in the months ahead. Choices from our menus will boost your reputation as a hostess—we guarantee it!

Recipes for all dishes starred (*) are in this cookbook.

SUMMER LUNCHEON

Melon Salad Plate*   Special Blue Cheese Dressing*
Parkerhouse Rolls   Hot Tea

Guests describe this luncheon, tailored to fit a hot, humid day, as both beautiful and refreshing. The hostess who prepares the meal keeps cool. All the cooking she needs to do is put rolls in the oven to warm and heat water for the tea. Water cress makes a charming garnish for the colorful melon and fruit, especially if its leaves are dark green. Romaine also adds a pleasing touch, and in summer is more widely available than the cress. Look for a head with as few blemishes as possible.

TIMETABLE

Do-Ahead: Wash water cress a day ahead. Place it in a glass jar containing a little water; let the stems, but not the leaves touch the water. Cover with plastic wrap and chill. If you use romaine instead of cress, hold it under running cold water, shake off excess and chill in a plastic bag.

On Guest Day: At least 3 hours before luncheon add ingredients to salad dressing and chill. Peel rind from melons and cut pulp in shapes, as recipe designates. Wash stemmed grapes and drain. Refrigerate different kinds of melon and grapes in separate containers. Pull rolls far enough apart to spread with butter; wrap them in foil. About 20 minutes before luncheon time, put them in a moderate oven (350°) to heat for 10 to 15 minutes. Arrange melons and grapes on plates and garnish. (If refrigerator space permits, first chill the plates.) Just before serving, put a dip of sherbet on each salad plate.

SERVING SUGGESTIONS

Place sprays of water cress around border of each salad. Or, if using romaine, cut off base of head, break off leaves, wash, pat dry with paper towels and use scissors to cut each leaf into a point. Tuck a few of these green petals under edge of salads. Pass salad dressing so guests may help themselves. Also pass the hot, buttered rolls.

MELON SALAD PLATE

You can substitute cottage cheese or chicken salad for lime sherbet

1 medium honeydew melon
4 c. watermelon chunks
4 c. cantaloupe balls
4 c. stemmed seedless green
  grapes

Salad greens
1 qt. lime sherbet
Special Blue Cheese Dressing

Peel rind from chilled melons and cut honeydew in 18 wedges. Place 3 of them on each salad plate to divide it in three sections of equal size. In one section, place watermelon chunks, cantaloupe balls in another and grapes in the third section. Garnish with water cress or romaine, or with other lettuce. Place a scoop of sherbet in center of salads. Serve with Special Blue Cheese Dressing. Makes 6 servings.

Special Blue Cheese Dressing: Shake 1 (8 oz.) bottle blue cheese salad dressing with ¼ c. orange juice and 1 tsp. lemon juice. Chill at least 3 hours before serving. Makes 1¼ cups.

WINTER LUNCHEON

Hot Chicken Salad Casserole*   Buttered Peas (optional)
Sautéed Cherry Tomatoes   Watermelon Pickles
Hot Rolls   Broiled Pink Grapefruit*

Some women prefer chicken salad hot, others prefer it cold, but just about everyone likes it both ways. The weather has much to do with the choice. For a luncheon in winter, when bitter-cold winds are blowing, the hot salad makes an appetizing, satisfying main dish. Team it with colorful foods, as in this menu, and you have a superb guest meal.

TIMETABLE

Do-Ahead: Cook chicken the day before the luncheon, cool and refrigerate. Or cook it several days ahead and freeze. In either case, after cooling, remove meat from bones, pour a little broth on to moisten and package the remaining broth separately.

On Guest Day: Assemble salad casserole at your convenience, cover and refrigerate. Thirty minutes before serving time put it in oven. Place the foil-wrapped rolls in oven alongside salad for the last 10 to 15 minutes. Cook frozen peas by package directions.

Melt 2 tblsp. butter in skillet, add 1 pint cherry tomatoes, washed, stems removed and each tomato pricked several times to prevent skin breaking when heated. Cook and stir gently over medium heat just long enough to heat thoroughly, about 3 minutes. Sprinkle with seasoned salt, if desired. Broil grapefruit between main and dessert courses, while removing dishes, filling water glasses and coffee cups, but watch it. It's easy to brown the tops too much.

SERVING SUGGESTIONS

Serve plates in kitchen and carry to table. On each warm luncheon plate, arrange a mound of the hot salad, a ramekin filled with the peas and a few of the cherry tomatoes. Pass the rolls and watermelon pickles. Garnish each grapefruit half with a fresh strawberry or a maraschino cherry.

HOT CHICKEN SALAD CASSEROLE

Requires no attention while baking—delicious for lunch in winter

2 c. chopped cooked chicken	3 tblsp. chopped onion
2 c. chopped celery (green if available)	½ tsp. salt
	2 tblsp. lemon juice
½ c. chopped salted almonds (blanched)	½ c. mayonnaise
	⅓ c. grated Swiss cheese
2 tblsp. chopped pimiento	2½ c. crushed potato chips
⅓ c. chopped green pepper	

Blend together chicken, celery, nuts, pimiento, green pepper, onion, salt, lemon juice and mayonnaise. Turn into a buttered 2-qt. casserole. Top with cheese and potato chips.

Bake in moderate oven (350°) about 25 minutes, until cheese melts. Makes 6 servings.

BROILED PINK GRAPEFRUIT

Treat your guests to this pretty, tasty, easy, light dessert

3 pink grapefruit	6 tblsp. flaked coconut
6 tblsp. dark brown sugar	

Cut each grapefruit in half; remove seeds. Loosen sections with grapefruit knife and cut out center. Sprinkle each half with 1 tblsp. brown sugar. Place in shallow pan.

Broil 4 to 6" from heat until hot or until juice bubbles, 5 to 10 minutes. Sprinkle 1 tblsp. coconut on each half and broil 1 minute longer, or just long enough to lightly brown coconut. Serve hot. Makes 6 servings.

WOMEN'S LUNCHEON

Plantation Chicken Salad*   Whole Wheat Refrigerator Rolls*
        Cranberry Sherbet*   Hot Tea or Coffee

The salad country hostesses most often serve to their women friends is chicken. There are almost as many versions of this classic in a neighborhood as there are homes. Plantation Chicken Salad, a southern special, certainly deserves the praise it always generates. You will note that it contains hard-cooked eggs and that chopped sweet pickles and other seasonings, discreetly added, point up flavors. Team the salad with piping hot, homemade whole wheat rolls and cranberry sherbet and you have a feast for the palate and the eyes.

In days gone by, cranberry or lemon sherbet in stemmed crystal dessert dishes accompanied the main course of country chicken and turkey dinners. Revive the custom by serving the sherbet alongside the chicken salad, and you'll please your guests with the harmonious blending of flavors. Often something so old in meal planning has the freshness of something new. After all, holding on to the best of the old and adding the best of the new is the key to successful meal planning.

TIMETABLE

Do-Ahead: Cook the chicken a day ahead, cool. Remove from bones, cut in cubes, and chill chicken and broth separately. (Freeze the broth for future use.) Make the dough for the refrigerator rolls and chill overnight. Make the sherbet, or buy it if you prefer.

On Guest Day: Make the chicken salad, cover and chill at least 2 hours. Shape dough for rolls and let rise until double in bulk; it will take from 1½ to 2 hours. Bake them the last 15 minutes before time to serve the luncheon. Arrange chicken salad in lettuce cups and garnish. Make the tea or coffee.

SERVING SUGGESTIONS

Garnish salad with sliced hard-cooked eggs and thin slices of pimiento-stuffed olives. Either serve the sherbet with the salad or as the dessert.

PLANTATION CHICKEN SALAD

Seasonings added with a light hand round out the salad's flavor

3 c. cubed cooked chicken	¼ tsp. onion salt
1½ c. diced celery	¾ tsp. salt
3 hard-cooked eggs, quartered	Salad dressing
3 tblsp. chopped sweet pickle	Lettuce
¼ tsp. poultry seasoning	

Combine all ingredients, except salad dressing and lettuce, in a bowl. Moisten with salad dressing and toss to mix. Cover and chill. Serve on lettuce. Makes 6 to 8 servings.

WHOLE WHEAT REFRIGERATOR ROLLS

Dough keeps up to 5 days if refrigerator temperature is 45° or below

2 pkgs. active dry yeast	½ c. sugar
½ c. warm water (110 to 115°)	2 eggs, beaten
1 c. milk, scalded	2 c. whole wheat flour
⅓ c. shortening	4 c. sifted flour (about)
2 tsp. salt	

Sprinkle yeast on warm water; stir to dissolve.

To the hot milk, add shortening, salt and sugar; stir until shortening melts and sugar dissolves. Cool to lukewarm.

Add eggs and yeast to lukewarm milk mixture and mix thoroughly. Beat in whole wheat flour. Gradually add all-purpose white flour to make a soft dough that leaves the sides of bowl. Place on lightly floured board. Let rest 10 minutes. Knead until smooth and elastic, about 8 minutes. Place in lightly greased bowl, turn dough over to grease top; cover and refrigerate overnight.

Punch down dough, and take out half of it. (Cover and return other half to refrigerator to use later.) Divide in small 1″ balls;

place 3 in each greased muffin-pan cup. Balls should half-fill cups. Let rise until doubled. Bake in hot oven (400°) 12 to 15 minutes. Half of dough makes 18 cloverleaf rolls.

CRANBERRY SHERBET

Recommended for its tart-sweet flavor and its brilliant red color

1½ tsp. unflavored gelatin (½ envelope)	Dash of salt
	2 c. cranberry juice cocktail
¾ c. sugar	2 tblsp. lemon juice

Mix gelatin with sugar and salt in saucepan; add 1 c. cranberry juice cocktail. Stir and cook over medium heat until gelatin and sugar dissolve. Remove from heat.

Add remaining 1 c. cranberry juice cocktail and lemon juice. Pour into refrigerator tray and freeze until firm. Break in chunks and turn into mixer bowl. Beat until smooth. Return to tray and freeze at least several hours. Makes 6 to 8 servings.

COOPERATIVE CLUB LUNCHEON

Special Chicken Salad*   Cucumber Swirl*
Assorted Sandwich Triangles
Coffee or Tea

One of the signs of the times is the way in which women's organizations share the preparation of refreshments for their meetings. In one Florida committee group of 8 members, 7 of them bring a sandwich each and the hostess provides a choice of two salads and coffee or tea.

Each sandwich has been cut diagonally in half and the halves cut again to make little triangles. Sandwiches are arranged on a large plate or tray, and making the selections is fun. You don't know what you'll draw, but as one of the women says: "All of us try to bring our best sandwiches."

Usually the hostess molds one salad and makes a protein-rich chicken, fish or meat salad also. This menu features a pretty, marbled molded salad and the old country special, chicken salad, with a new note—bright orange sections.

TIMETABLE

Do-Ahead: The hostess cooks the chicken for the salad unless she has it in the freezer. And she molds the gelatin salad (Cucumber Swirl) a day ahead.

On Guest Day: Fix the chicken salad, cover and chill for a minimum of 2 hours before serving. Wash lettuce leaves for placing under salads, drain and chill them in a plastic bag.

SERVING SUGGESTIONS

Serve the luncheon buffet style, or if you prefer, place salads on individual serving plates. Pass the sandwiches.

SPECIAL CHICKEN SALAD

Tiny orange sections add color, a juicy note and they enliven flavors

6 c. cubed cooked chicken	2 tsp. onion juice
1½ c. sliced celery	2 (11 oz.) cans mandarin oranges,
¾ c. mayonnaise or salad dressing	drained
1¼ tsp. salt	Lettuce
Dash of pepper	

Combine chicken and celery in bowl. In another bowl mix mayonnaise, salt, pepper and onion juice. Pour over chicken-celery mixture and toss to mix. Cover and chill at least 2 hours to blend flavors.

At serving time, fold in orange sections. Serve on lettuce. Makes 8 servings.

CUCUMBER SWIRL

Delight guests with this decorative marbled salad—marvelous flavor

2 (3 oz.) pkgs. lime flavor gelatin	2 tblsp. mayonnaise
3 c. hot water	2 to 3 tblsp. milk
¼ tsp. salt	1½ tsp. prepared horse-radish
¼ c. lemon juice	¼ c. finely snipped fresh chives or
1 c. grated cucumber, drained	thinly cut green onion
2 (3 oz.) pkgs. cream cheese,	
softened at room temperature	

Dissolve gelatin in hot water (scant measurement); cool. Add salt, lemon juice and cucumber, and stir. Chill until partially set, or until mixture molds slightly when dropped from a spoon.

Combine cream cheese, mayonnaise, milk, horse-radish and chives to make a smooth mixture. Swirl gently into the gelatin mixture for marbled effect. Pour into a 9″ square pan and chill until firm. To serve, cut in squares. Makes 8 to 10 servings.

THREE-PIECE LUNCHEON

Chicken Treasure*
Hot Buttered Rolls
Black Cherry Salad*

You'll find it easy to be both cook and hostess if you use this three-piece menu when you give a luncheon for members of your Homemakers Club or some other group of women friends. The casserole, which is a treasure chest of fine flavors, combines the meat (chicken) and vegetable (asparagus). The salad does double duty and also serves for dessert. If you prefer, you can have a fresh fruit salad instead of molded. And it's easy to change the menu into a dinner for men and women—we tell you how.

TIMETABLE

Do-Ahead: Cook chicken breasts a day ahead, cool, remove meat from bones and refrigerate chicken and broth separately. Make the salad a day ahead and chill.

On Guest Day: About 1¼ hours before serving time, prepare casserole. Bake it the last 45 minutes before luncheon. About 10 minutes before serving time, put foil-wrapped rolls in oven to heat. Serve the salad on individual plates and make the coffee.

SERVING SUGGESTIONS

Unmold salad on lettuce and garnish each serving either with a spoonful of salad dressing or mayonnaise.

N O T E : To convert luncheon to a dinner, serve chilled cranberry juice cocktail for an appetizer in small glasses containing a spoonful of lemon sherbet. Pass nibblers. Add buttered lima beans to menu.

Cook 3 (10 oz.) pkgs. frozen limas by package directions; drain. Add ¼ c. melted butter, 1 to 2 tblsp. lemon juice and ½ tsp. dill weed; stir to mix. Serve the cherry mold, topped with spoonfuls of salad dressing, in the main course. For dessert, have a chocolate-frosted sour cream yellow cake, using packaged mixes for cake and frosting.

CHICKEN TREASURE

Mayonnaise contributes rich flavor to this chicken-asparagus bake

4 whole chicken breasts	2 c. chicken broth
Water	1 tsp. lemon juice
⅓ c. butter or regular margarine	1 c. mayonnaise
½ c. flour	2 (15 oz.) cans green asparagus
1 tsp. salt	½ c. toasted bread crumbs
1 c. milk	

Simmer chicken in boiling salted water to cover 1 hour, or until tender. Save broth (you'll need 2 c.). Spread chicken on plate to cool. Discard bones, fat and skin; pull chicken into bite-size pieces.

Melt butter and stir in flour and salt; stir to mix. Add milk and chicken broth; cook until creamy and thick, stirring constantly.

Beat lemon juice and mayonnaise together and stir into the creamy sauce. Remove from heat and stir well.

Lightly grease a 2½-qt. casserole and layer chicken and asparagus alternately in it. Pour sauce over and top with bread crumbs. Bake in moderate oven (375°) 45 minutes, or until mixture bubbles in center. Makes 8 to 10 servings.

BLACK CHERRY SALAD

Celery and nuts add crunchy texture to this black-red fruit salad

1 (1 lb.) can dark sweet cherries	1 (8½ oz.) can crushed pineapple
Juice drained from cherries	½ c. thinly sliced celery
Water	½ c. chopped walnuts
1 (3 oz.) pkg. dark cherry flavor gelatin	Romaine or other lettuce

Drain cherries; measure juice and add enough water to make 1¾ c. Heat half of liquid and add to gelatin; stir until gelatin is dissolved. Add remaining liquid (mixture of water and cherry juice). Chill until mixture starts to thicken.

Meanwhile, cut cherries in halves and combine with drained

pineapple, celery and nuts. Fold into gelatin and turn into individual molds. Chill until firm.

To serve, unmold on romaine or other lettuce. Makes 9 servings.

JULY LUNCHEON

Peachy Cherry Salad Mold*
Whole Wheat Berry Muffins*
Iced Tea

When wild fruits ripen, country women like to share with their friends these free gifts from their land. Juneberries come to Montana tables in July. After the family enjoys the first fresh berries of the year, plain with sugar and cream, they begin to find their way into recipes like these whole wheat muffins. (If you don't have Juneberries try blueberries, or another berry—muffins are also delicious plain, of course.)

Serve a salad worthy of the muffins for luncheon. In this menu, lovely gold and red Peachy Cherry Salad Mold comes highly recommended.

TIMETABLE

Do-Ahead: Make the salad a day ahead. Wash and drain lettuce to serve under it and chill in a plastic bag.

On Guest Day: Make muffins at the last minute and serve them so hot that butter spread on them melts almost instantly.

PEACHY CHERRY SALAD MOLD

Cut the servings so each contains a peach half in orange gelatin

1 (3 oz.) pkg. black cherry flavor gelatin	2 tblsp. chopped nuts
1 c. boiling water	1 (3 oz.) pkg. orange flavor gelatin
1 c. cold water	1½ c. boiling water
1 (3 oz.) pkg. cream cheese	½ c. peach syrup
2 tblsp. orange marmalade	2 tblsp. lemon juice
1 (1 lb. 13 oz.) can cling peach halves	Dash of salt
	Lettuce

Dissolve cherry gelatin in 1 c. boiling water. Add 1 c. cold water. Pour into an $11 \times 7 \times 1\frac{1}{2}''$ glass dish; chill until partially thickened.

Mix together cream cheese and orange marmalade.

Drain peach halves, reserving syrup (you should have ½ c.). Fill cavities in peach halves with cream cheese mixture. Sprinkle with nuts. Arrange peaches cut side up in partially thickened gelatin. Return to refrigerator; chill until almost set.

Dissolve orange gelatin in 1½ c. boiling water; add peach syrup, lemon juice and salt. Cool until partially set. Pour over peaches in cherry gelatin. Chill until set. Cut in squares and serve on lettuce. Makes 8 servings.

WHOLE WHEAT BERRY MUFFINS

If you do not add berries to these muffins you may wish to use only 3 tblsp. each brown and white sugars for a slightly less sweet bread

1 c. flour
½ tsp. salt
¼ c. sugar
¼ c. brown sugar, firmly packed
3 tsp. baking powder
1 c. whole wheat flour

1 egg, well beaten
1 c. milk
¼ c. melted butter or regular
  margarine
1 c. fresh Juneberries or
  blueberries

Sift all-purpose flour, salt, sugars and baking powder into a bowl. Stir in the whole wheat flour.

Add egg to milk and add with melted butter all at one time to flour mixture. Use care not to overmix batter. Batter will not be smooth. Fold in berries.

Pour batter into greased muffin-pan cups, filling two thirds full. Bake in hot oven (400°) 20 to 25 minutes. Remove from pan immediately and serve hot. Makes 12 medium muffins.

SALAD LUNCHEON

Carrot/Coconut Salad*
Cheese Muffins*   Toasted Party Rye Bread
Almond Butter Crunch*

When a salad is the main dish in a meal, it needs to look beautiful, taste wonderful and satisfy appetites. Carrot/Coconut Salad meets these requirements. And it stands alone; you serve no salad dressing with it. Hostesses rate this a perfect choice for the buffet supper. In this luncheon you can serve the salad in a big ring at the table or you can chill it in individual molds.

Hot breads lift guest meals above the commonplace. This menu pampers the guests by offering them two kinds, muffins and toasted rye bread slices. You can skip a dessert, but a piece of Almond Butter Crunch provides a much enjoyed sweet-tooth ending. If you prefer, you can pass candy mints or assorted salted nuts.

TIMETABLE

Do-Ahead: Make the almond treat a day or two ahead, put it in an airtight container and store in a cool place. The delicacy often gets sticky in an hour or less if not protected from air exposure. Make salad a day ahead and refrigerate.

On Guest Day: Butter slices of party rye bread, spread on baking sheet and toast in a slow oven (325°) until crisp, 10 to 12 minutes. Get the muffins in the oven about 10 minutes before lunchtime. Stir up the batter at the last minute—no need to use your electric mixer because you can mix it by hand in 2 to 3 minutes. Remove muffins from pans as soon as baked; serve piping hot. If they must wait, remove them and place on their sides in the muffin cups; keep warm in a very low oven.

SERVING SUGGESTIONS

Garnish salad with green leaves; make a wreath of them around base of ring or tuck a jaunty bouquet of them in center opening. Use water cress, curly endive or lettuce—even spinach. Pass muffins in napkin-lined basket or roll warmer, rye toast on a large plate. When making Almond Butter Crunch, go artistic and form it into flower shapes. Arrange clusters of toasted almond halves in petal fashion on baking sheet. With a teaspoon drop hot candy mixture on them.

CARROT/COCONUT SALAD

It's pale yellow with orange flecks; lemon juice gives it extra zip

4 c. finely grated carrots	2 c. boiling water
2 tsp. grated lemon peel	2 (3 oz.) pks. lemon flavor gelatin
¼ c. lemon juice	2 c. cold water
1 c. flaked coconut	1 c. dairy sour cream
¼ tsp. salt	Greens

Mix carrots, lemon peel, lemon juice, coconut and salt in a large bowl; toss. Cover and set aside.

Stir boiling water into gelatin; stir until it dissolves. Add cold water. Cover and refrigerate until mixture mounds when dropped from a spoon. Fold in carrot mixture and sour cream.

Turn into a 2-qt. ring mold. Chill until set. To serve, unmold on large plate and garnish with salad greens. Makes 10 to 12 servings.

CHEESE MUFFINS

Key secret to success with muffins is to avoid overmixing the batter

2 c. sifted flour	1 egg, beaten
3 tsp. baking powder	1 c. milk
½ tsp. salt	¼ c. salad oil
¼ c. sugar	½ c. grated sharp Cheddar cheese

Sift flour, baking powder, salt and sugar into a big bowl. Make a well in the center.

Combine egg, milk and salad oil; stir to mix. Pour all at once into the well in flour mixture. Mix quickly with fork or spoon until flour is moistened, but do not beat. The batter will contain some lumps. Fold in cheese with a few strokes.

Pour into greased muffin-pan cups, filling them two thirds full. Bake in hot oven (400°) 20 to 25 minutes, until muffins are golden. Serve at once. Makes 12 medium muffins.

ALMOND BUTTER CRUNCH

Candied nuts add texture contrast—shape like stars at Christmastime

1½ c. blanched almond halves	1 tblsp. light corn syrup
¾ c. butter	3 tblsp. water
1½ c. sugar	

To halve almonds, pour boiling water over nuts and simmer 2 minutes. Drain and split in halves.

Toast almonds on baking sheet in slow oven (300°) until golden brown.

Melt butter in 2-qt. heavy saucepan; add sugar, corn syrup and water. Cook to soft crack stage (290°) without stirring.

Remove from heat and pour in thin stream over nuts on baking sheet. Cool. Break into pieces. Makes about 1½ pounds.

Variation

Christmas Stars: Arrange clusters of 5 toasted almond halves in star patterns on baking sheets. Drop teaspoonfuls of hot candy on clusters of almonds. Cool.

SUPERB SPRING LUNCHEON

Ham/Asparagus Roll-Ups*
Summer Squash Parmesan*
Relish Tray
Orange Pinwheels*
Grapefruit Halves

No need to suggest to the country hostess that she feature seasonal foods in company meals; it's a traditional habit. What better time to serve asparagus than when it takes almost daily cutting to keep up with the delicate spears that shoot up overnight?

In this menu asparagus teams with smoky-flavored ham and bakes briefly in a special mustard sauce. To maintain the pace for fascinating food, cook thin slices of young, green-skinned zucchini and yellow crookneck squash in the same saucepan. The vegetable combination is much more exciting than either vegetable cooked singly.

The orange rolls are an illustration of what makes country guest meals famous—homemade yeast bread. Center each chilled grapefruit half with a particularly lush fresh strawberry.

You can serve a replica of this luncheon when snow drifts and arctic winds blow, by using canned asparagus and frozen squash. And you will find another garnish for the grapefruit. It might be maple syrup, or possibly frozen strawberries. Not that such a luncheon equals the springtime meals, but it is highly acceptable.

You can expand this menu into a full-fledged spring dinner that both women and men will enjoy. Just add parslied new potatoes to the bill of fare and substitute fresh strawberry-rhubarb pie for the grapefruit. You may want to buy (and heat) rolls if you're baking pies.

TIMETABLE

On Guest Day: Start the rolls early—before you wash the breakfast dishes. It takes 3 hours to make and bake them, but you do not have to stand over them. While the dough doubles, attend to other preparations. Assemble relishes and chill. Make the mustard sauce. Pull the green onions for the main dish and relish tray when you cut the asparagus. Cook asparagus and wrap the ham around it. If refrigerator space permits, cut grapefruit in half, cut out centers, loosen sections from membrane, but leave them in the yellow shells; chill. Stem, wash, crush, sweeten and chill berries. While the roll-ups bake, cook squash.

SERVING SUGGESTIONS

Serve the plates for this sit-down meal in the kitchen, but pass the relishes and second helpings (maybe thirds) of the rolls. Spoon strawberries over grapefruit at serving time, and if you have fresh mint, garnish with a few fragrant leaves.

HAM/ASPARAGUS ROLL-UPS

Give the sauce credit for its part in seasoning this pretty main dish. You can easily double this recipe to serve more guests

24 cooked fresh asparagus spears (or canned)
6 slices boiled ham, ¼″ thick

Creamy Mustard Sauce
¼ c. chopped green onions

Place 4 asparagus spears on each ham slice. Roll up cornucopia fashion and secure with toothpicks.

Pour Creamy Mustard Sauce into shallow baking dish. Lay roll-ups in sauce. Bake in moderate oven (350°) 20 to 25 minutes. Just before serving, garnish with onions. Makes 6 servings.

Creamy Mustard Sauce: Heat ¾ c. light cream in top of double boiler. Beat 1 egg yolk with ¼ c. light cream. Mix ½ c. sugar, 4 tsp. dry mustard, ¼ tsp. salt and 1 tblsp. flour; add to egg yolk mixture.

Stir into heated cream in double boiler; cook, stirring constantly, until mixture thickens. Heat 1/3 c. vinegar; blend into sauce and beat.

SUMMER SQUASH PARMESAN

Quick-cooking squash require no peeling—just washing and slicing

4 c. thinly sliced unpeeled, fresh or frozen summer squash	2 tblsp. butter
	1/2 tsp. salt
1 small onion, sliced	1/8 tsp. pepper
1 tblsp. water	3 tblsp. Parmesan cheese

Put all ingredients except cheese in a skillet. Cover and cook 1 minute over high heat. Uncover, continue to cook over low heat, turning with spatula, until barely tender.

Sprinkle with cheese and serve. Makes 6 to 8 servings.

ORANGE PINWHEELS

Feather-light yeast dough rolled around orange filling and baked

Dough:	3 tblsp. soft butter
1 pkg. active dry yeast	4 to 4 1/2 c. flour
1/4 c. warm water (110 to 115°)	*Orange Filling:*
3/4 c. milk	1/3 c. soft butter
1/4 c. sugar	1/2 c. sugar
1 tsp. salt	2 tsp. grated orange peel
3 eggs	

To make dough, dissolve yeast in warm water in mixing bowl.

Scald milk; cool to lukewarm. Add milk, sugar, salt, eggs, butter and half the flour to yeast mixture. Stir with a spoon until smooth. Mix in enough of remaining flour to make a soft dough. (The consistency of the dough is important. When you first make these rolls, you may have difficulty handling the soft dough, but it's the softness that makes these rolls so very light and tender.)

Knead on a lightly floured board until smooth and elastic, about 5 minutes. Place in a greased bowl; turn dough over to grease top. Cover with a clean towel; let rise in a warm place until doubled, about 1 1/2 hours. Punch down; let rise until amost doubled, about 30 minutes.

Roll dough in a 15×9" rectangle. Mix ingredients for Orange Filling and spread over the dough. Roll as for jelly roll, pinching edges together. Cut roll in 1" slices.

Place cut side down in a greased 13×9×2″ pan. Cover and let rise until doubled, 35 to 40 minutes. Bake in moderate oven (375°) 25 minutes, or until lightly browned. Makes 18.

MAYTIME LUNCHEON

Chilled Pineapple Juice
Baked Asparagus/Cheese Sandwiches*
Celery Hearts   Radish Roses   Cucumber Pickle Slices
Angel Food Cake   Pink Party Topping*

Spring delivers tender stalks of asparagus to country kitchens either from home gardens or markets. Appetites start to crave other seasonal treats soon to appear, such as strawberries and red raspberries to serve with tall, stately angel food cakes. Why not cash in on this prevailing mood and entertain friends at a lovely luncheon? This menu will help you do it easily.

The pink berry topping for the snowy angel food cake uses frozen strawberries or raspberries, universally available, but if you have even a few plump fresh berries, generously garnish with them to glamorize the cake.

TIMETABLE

Do-Ahead: Bake the angel food cake a day ahead, or several days ahead and freeze. Combine in a bowl the ingredients for the cake topping (except for whipped cream), cover and chill overnight.

On Guest Day: You can fix and bake the sandwich in less than an hour. While it bakes, wash celery and radishes, make radish roses and chill in ice water. At dessert time, cut cake, whip cream and fold it into topping and put the two together for a wonderful ending to a delightful meal.

SERVING SUGGESTIONS

Serve chilled pineapple juice in small glasses for an appetizer to sip in the living room or at the dining table. Garnish with perky mint sprigs. Arrange sandwich servings on individual plates in kitchen with celery hearts, radish roses and pickles.

BAKED ASPARAGUS/CHEESE SANDWICHES

You may need to bake two dishes of the hot sandwiches—depends on how many people you're having for lunch

6 thick (¾″) slices firm-textured bread (like home-baked)	1 tsp. salt
	⅛ tsp. pepper
6 (3½″ square) slices process Swiss cheese	¼ tsp. ground nutmeg
	1 tblsp. finely chopped onion
4 eggs	18 cooked asparagus spears
2 c. milk	½ c. shredded Cheddar cheese

Trim crusts from bread slices. Arrange bread slices in bottom of 13×9×2″ pan or glass dish. Top each bread slice with a slice of process Swiss cheese.

In a bowl, beat eggs slightly; add milk, stir in seasonings and onion. Pour this mixture over sandwiches and bake in slow oven (325°) 25 minutes.

Remove from oven. Top each bread slice with 3 cooked asparagus spears. Sprinkle on shredded Cheddar cheese. Return dish to oven and continue to bake 10 to 15 minutes, until custard sets and top is golden. Allow to stand 5 minutes before serving. Makes 6 servings.

PINK PARTY TOPPING

Pretty pink fluffy sauce on cake slices is so good and so easy to fix

1 c. miniature marshmallows	1 c. heavy cream, whipped
1 (10 oz.) pkg. frozen red raspberries or strawberries	

Pour marshmallows and frozen berries in a bowl. Cover; refrigerate overnight. Before serving, fold in whipped cream. Serve on angel food cake slices. Makes 3 cups.

BUFFET LUNCHEON

Hearty Buffet Salad*
Bran Refrigerator Rolls*
Assorted Olives
Blancmange Ring with Fresh Peaches (or Berries)*

This luncheon menu is of blue-ribbon caliber—select it when you entertain a group of friends whom you want to impress and please. The bowl salad, with ingredients arranged as the serving suggestions describe, makes a pretty buffet. And it's neither too light to qualify as a main dish salad nor too heavy to refresh. The homemade bran rolls, yeast-leavened, are the perfect go-with. And the molded dessert ring holds fresh peaches, sliced and lightly sugared.

TIMETABLE

Do-Ahead: Cook the turkey a day ahead and refrigerate. The salad recipe starts with the turkey cooked and cut in julienne strips. Make the dough for the rolls and cover; fix the dessert mold. Chill both the dough and mold. Wash the salad greens, drain and refrigerate each kind in a plastic bag.

On Guest Day: Shape the dough for rolls, let rise and bake. It will be easier to do this first in the day and reheat the rolls at mealtime in order to serve them piping hot. Cook the bacon.

Chop the three kinds of lettuce, chives and water cress; do not mix. Chop finely the tomatoes, avocado (sprinkle with a little lemon juice if it must wait) and bacon. To arrange salad, alternate layers of the different kinds of lettuce and water cress in a *big* (wide) salad bowl. On top place alternate rows of the chopped foods for a striking effect. Take time to build this salad by the culinary artist's pattern (allow about 30 minutes!).

If you use fresh peaches with the dessert mold, peel, slice and lightly sugar them. Then sprinkle with ascorbic acid powder, the kind you use when freezing peaches, dissolved in a little cold water to retain color. Follow label directions, or use 2 tsp. of powder to 3 tblsp. water for 1 qt. fruit. Or sprinkle with lemon juice. Cover peaches and keep in refrigerator until time to serve the dessert. Serve them in center and around base of the mold. Heat the rolls, wrapped in foil, in a moderate oven (350°) 10 to 15 minutes.

SERVING SUGGESTIONS

The menu is designed for food to be served buffet style. Don't worry about garnishes—the food is so beautiful that decorating is unnecessary. An attractive way to build the salad, after adding alternate layers of the different kinds of lettuce and water cress, heaping the greens a little in the center, is to place a row of turkey strips at the center across the bowl. On one side arrange rows of chopped tomato, egg and bacon, with rows of grated cheese, cubed avocado and chopped chives on the other side.

After guests see the spectacular salad, sprinkle one side, including all toppings, with salad dressing and toss lightly; repeat with the other half later. This helps to maintain part of the attractive design while serving.

HEARTY BUFFET SALAD

You can use chicken instead of turkey for this handsome salad

½ head lettuce	½ lb. bacon, cooked crisp
1 small bunch red lettuce or chicory	3 c. julienne strips cooked turkey or chicken breast
1 head romaine	½ c. finely grated Cheddar or crumbled blue cheese
½ bunch water cress	
2 medium tomatoes, peeled	2 tblsp. finely chopped fresh chives
1 medium avocado, peeled	
3 hard-cooked eggs	1 c. garlic French dressing

With a sharp knife, chop each of the greens very fine. Spread in layers in large salad bowl, heaping up slightly in center.

Finely chop tomatoes, avocado, eggs and bacon. Arrange the turkey, tomatoes, avocado, eggs, bacon, cheese and chives in rows in pretty, contrasting colors over top of the greens. (See Serving Suggestions.)

Sprinkle part of salad dressing across only one end at a time, toss lightly and serve from that section. Makes 3½ quarts salad, or 8 to 10 large servings.

BRAN REFRIGERATOR ROLLS

Cloverleaf yeast rolls provide a charming homemade country touch

½ c. shortening	1 pkg. active dry yeast
⅓ c. sugar	½ c. warm water (110 to 115°)
¾ tsp. salt	1 egg, beaten
½ c. boiling water	3 to 3¼ c. sifted flour
½ c. ready-to-eat bran cereal	

Combine shortening, sugar and salt with boiling water; stir until shortening is softened. Add bran, stir and cool to lukewarm.

In the meantime dissolve yeast in warm water; stir into cooled bran mixture. Blend in egg. Stir in enough flour to make a soft dough and mix thoroughly. Cover, and store in refrigerator.

When needed, remove dough from refrigerator and allow to stand in warm place (85°) 15 minutes. Form dough into small balls. Place in groups of 3 in greased muffin-pan cups. Allow to rise until almost doubled.

Bake in hot oven (425°) 15 to 20 minutes. Makes 12 to 18 rolls.

N O T E : Recipe may be doubled or tripled for more servings.

BLANCMANGE RING WITH FRESH PEACHES (OR BERRIES)

An old-fashioned pudding presented in a new-fashioned way

1½ envelopes unflavored gelatin (1½ tblsp.)	3¾ c. cold milk
¼ c. cold water	¼ tsp. almond extract
2 (3¾ oz.) pkgs. vanilla instant pudding	4 c. fresh peach slices
	1 c. heavy cream, whipped and sweetened to taste

Soften gelatin in cold water; set in pan of boiling water to dissolve.

Combine vanilla pudding and cold milk according to package directions, then stir in dissolved gelatin and almond extract. Pour into oiled 1-qt. ring mold and chill until set.

Unmold ring onto large serving platter. Fill center with peach slices and arrange remaining fruit around edge. Garnish with whipped cream. Makes 8 to 10 servings.

N O T E : You can use 4 c. fresh berries instead of the peaches.

AUTUMN PICNIC

Rancho Beans*   Spaghetti Bake*
Dutch Slaw*
Sliced Tomatoes
Homemade Cucumber Pickles
Sourdough Bread*
Pears   Chocolate Fudge
Coffee   Milk

Aspen trees changing from green to gold on western mountain sides signal it's time for those last fall picnics—winter's on the way. This is when a ranch wife will call a neighbor and invite her family to join them for lunch at noon in the cottonwood grove by the stream. Usually such an impromptu picnic turns into a cooperative meal: "I'll bring my beef-spaghetti casserole and the girls will make a batch of fudge."

Food for the noon meal needs to be easy to fix and to carry in car or jeep, substantial enough to satisfy hungry people and so good that memories will brighten winter days. This menu meets the requirements regardless of where the two families dine, in the shadow of the Rocky Mountains or in Vermont where the hills are a riot of fall color.

Rancho Beans, the recipe contributed by a Montana homemaker, and Spaghetti Bake, a favorite picnic food of a Vermont family, provide a hearty and delicious choice which a cooperative meal affords. Dutch Slaw (from Illinois) fits perfectly into the meal, plus the last of the season's homegrown tomatoes, sliced and sprinkled with a bottled salad seasoning.

Sourdough Bread and a jar of homemade pickles are tasty testimony of time well spent in advance in the country kitchen. Juicy fresh pears, a pan of smooth chocolate fudge and vacuum containers of hot coffee and cold milk round out the meal.

TIMETABLE

Do-Ahead: Only the bread and pickles were ready when picnic day dawned.

On Guest Day: All the other foods are prepared or collected by the participating families.

SERVING SUGGESTIONS

Picnic baskets hold plates, cups, spoons, forks and knives along with napkins and a tablecover to spread on a portable table or the ground. The casseroles, wrapped in several layers of newspapers, retain their heat on the short drive to the picnic spot.

RANCHO BEANS

Well seasoned beef-and-bean hot dish that men especially like

1 lb. lean ground beef	2 tsp. cider vinegar
1 envelope dry onion soup mix	2 (1 lb.) cans pork and beans in
1 c. ketchup	tomato sauce
2 tblsp. prepared mustard	1 (1 lb.) can kidney beans
½ c. water	

Stir and brown beef in large skillet over medium heat. Add the remaining ingredients; mix well. Heat thoroughly. Pour into 3-qt. casserole and bake in hot oven (400°) about 30 minutes, until bubbling hot in center. Makes 8 to 10 servings.

SPAGHETTI BAKE

Seasonings are mild in this tasty beef-spaghetti casserole

1 lb. ground beef	1 soup can water (1¼ c.)
¾ c. finely chopped onion	1 (8 oz.) can tomato sauce
½ c. finely chopped green pepper	½ tsp. salt
1 can condensed cream of	1 clove garlic, minced
mushroom soup	1 (8 oz.) pkg. spaghetti
1 can condensed tomato soup	1 c. shredded sharp process cheese

Combine beef, onion and green pepper in skillet. Stir and cook to lightly brown meat. Add soups, water, tomato sauce, salt and garlic. Heat.

Meanwhile, cook spaghetti by package directions; drain. Blend ½ c. cheese and spaghetti into soup mixture. Turn into greased 3-qt. casserole. Top with remaining ½ c. cheese.

Bake in moderate oven (350°) about 45 minutes, until bubbling hot in center. Makes 8 to 10 servings.

DUTCH SLAW

Bacon and lemon juice do wonders flavor-wise for cabbage slaw

¾ c. chopped bacon
2 tblsp. lemon juice
½ tsp. salt
½ tsp. dry mustard
½ c. salad dressing or mayonnaise

2 c. finely shredded cabbage
¼ c. chopped green pepper
2 tblsp. chopped parsley
1 medium onion, finely chopped

Cook bacon in skillet to a light golden brown. Remove from heat; add lemon juice, salt and mustard. Mix in the salad dressing. Add vegetables and toss. Makes about 3 cups.

SOURDOUGH BREAD

It takes time to make this, but keeping the starter in the refrigerator will shorten the procedure. Toast it for a treat

1 c. warm water (110 to 115°)
1 pkg. active dry yeast
2 tblsp. sugar

2 tsp. salt
1½ c. Sourdough Starter
5 c. flour

Put warm water, yeast, sugar and salt in blender and blend at low speed until yeast is dissolved (or in large bowl and beat at low speed on mixer). Add starter (if you don't have some in your refrigerator, see recipe which follows). Continue blending to mix. Turn the control high and gradually blend in 1½ c. flour, using rubber spatula to scrape down sides of blender.

When smooth, pour into bowl and gradually add 2½ c. flour, mixing with spoon until smooth. Cover bowl with damp towel and let stand in a warm place until doubled, about 1½ hours.

Turn onto lightly floured surface and work in about 1 c. more of remaining flour, or enough so that the dough no longer is sticky. Knead until elastic and satiny; shape into large round loaf (or in two long oval loaves).

Sprinkle a little cornmeal on ungreased baking sheet and place loaf on it. Cover lightly with a towel and let rise again in warm place until doubled, or about 1½ hours.

Put shallow pan of water on lower shelf in oven. Preheat oven to hot (400°). With razor blade, make diagonal slashes on loaf about 2″ apart.

Bake 40 to 50 minutes until crust is a dark brown. Cool on rack. Makes 1 big round loaf.

N O T E : If you freeze bread, for a picnic, thaw it, wrapped in heavy-duty foil in moderate oven (350°) about 30 minutes. Slice, butter and put together in sandwich style.

SOURDOUGH STARTER

This is the magic that gives sourdough its characteristic flavor

2 c. warm water (110 to 115°)   2 c. flour
1 pkg. active dry yeast

Put ingredients in blender, cover and blend on low speed until smooth, or blend in large bowl of electric mixer. Pour into a 2-qt. mixing bowl, cover with cheesecloth and leave in a warm place 48 hours, stirring two or three times. Then pour into jar with a tight-fitting lid and refrigerate.

To use, stir starter and pour off 1½ c. or the amount the bread recipe specifies. Add 1 c. flour and 1 c. warm water (110 to 115°) to the remaining starter, using blender or electric mixer to blend smooth.

Cover with cheesecloth and let stand at room temperature for 5 to 6 hours, or until mixture bubbles. Then pour into jar, cover tightly and refrigerate. Always add an equal amount of flour and water after using some of the starter.

WELCOMING LUNCH

Homemade 100% Whole Wheat Bread*
Whipped Butter
Sharp Cheddar Cheese   Applesauce
Coffee   Milk

Visitors, traveling by car, often arrive between meals. The farm hostess and host, always suspecting that their guests may be hungry, welcome them with a lunch. Frequently the food is spread on a neat table in a cheerful kitchen. This traditional country custom rates the same popularity it enjoyed in horse-and-buggy days. Everyone in the house gathers around the table to share in the talk and simple feast.

The super star in this menu is the rich-flavored, nut-brown whole wheat bread. It glorifies the other foods. You'll want to bake these loaves soon.

TIMETABLE

Do-Ahead: All the food is ready before the friend-filled car shows up in the driveway. You can fix the butter a day or a few days ahead and store it in covered bowls in the refrigerator to serve with pancakes, waffles, hot rolls, biscuits, muffins and all hot breads. To fix the spread, whip 1 lb. butter with electric mixer on medium speed, scraping down sides of bowl several times with rubber spatula. Beat until light and fluffy. It will almost double in volume.

SERVING SUGGESTIONS

Add glamor to this homespun food by the way you serve it. Place the loaf of bread on a bread board and slice it at the table. Set a bowl of butter nearby and alongside place the cheese on cutting board with knife. Bring out a big bowl of freshly made or home-canned applesauce and let your guests ladle it into their sauce dishes. Have the coffee or teapot (your guests' preference) and a pitcher of cold milk ready to pour.

HOMEMADE 100% WHOLE WHEAT BREAD

This bread created by the hostess' own hands makes lunch special

1 pkg. active dry yeast	4 tsp. salt
¼ c. warm water (110 to 115°)	2 c. milk, scalded
¼ c. sugar	5 c. stone-ground whole wheat
¼ c. molasses	flour
2 tblsp. shortening	

Sprinkle yeast on warm water; stir to dissolve.

Add sugar, molasses, shortening and salt to warm milk; stir to blend. Pour into large mixing bowl and cool until lukewarm. Stir in yeast.

Add flour, beating until well mixed. Turn dough out onto lightly floured surface; knead until smooth and elastic, 8 to 10 minutes. Place in lightly greased bowl, turn dough over to grease top. Cover and let rise in warm place until doubled. Punch down dough and divide in half; shape into loaves.

Place in two lightly greased 9×5×3" or 8½×4½×2½" loaf

pans. Let rise until doubled. Bake in hot oven (400°) 20 to 25 minutes. Makes 2 (1½ lb.) loaves.

VEGETARIAN LUNCHEON

Hearty Mushroom/Barley Soup*   Garden Sandwiches*
Homemade Mayonnaise*
Fresh Apple Cake*

If your college-age daughter decides to invite friends to lunch, don't be surprised if she selects a vegetarian menu. Times change; mothers fretted for years because their children often balked at eating their full vegetable quota. Now these foods enjoy great popularity with many young people. You don't need to be a vegetarian, though, to like this meal, for it's flavorful and satisfying.

The sandwiches are made with a filling of several vegetables, held together with mayonnaise (homemade is nice!) and whole wheat bread. The soup has a pleasing blend of flavors, and the moist, apple spice cake is as easy to eat as it is to make. A crisp topping bakes right on the cake.

TIMETABLE

Do-Ahead: Make the mayonnaise a day or two ahead and refrigerate. Make the sandwich filling (all but adding tomatoes) the day before the luncheon.

On Guest Day: Bake the cake. Start making soup about 1½ hours before lunchtime. While the soup vegetables cook, make the sandwiches. If you want 6 instead of 12 sandwiches, halve the recipe.

SERVING SUGGESTIONS

Serve sandwiches pointed ends toward center of plate to show off the color of sandwich filling. If you have fresh dill, sprinkle a bit into the bowls of soup just before serving.

HEARTY MUSHROOM/BARLEY SOUP

Almost filling enough for a meal if served with a tossed green salad

10 to 12 fresh mushrooms	2 qts. boiling water
⅓ c. large pearl barley	1½ tblsp. butter
2 tsp. salt	¼ c. diced onion
¼ tsp. pepper	2 tblsp. flour
1½ tblsp. butter	½ c. milk
½ c. diced celery	Chopped fresh dill
½ c. diced carrots	

Wash mushrooms under gently flowing cold water; wipe dry and slice. Add mushrooms, barley, salt, pepper, 1½ tblsp. butter, celery and carrots to boiling water. Cover and simmer gently 1 hour, or until barley is tender. Stir every 20 minutes while cooking.

Meanwhile melt 1½ tblsp. butter in skillet; add onion and sauté until transparent (do not brown). Add flour and blend well. Add milk; cook and stir to make a smooth sauce. Add to soup, mixing well. Serve hot, garnished with dill. Makes about 6 servings.

GARDEN SANDWICHES

Texture contrast, flavor and gala color of filling appeal to almost everyone—it's a pleasing, attractive way to put vegetables in meals

2 c. frozen peas	1 c. cut-up peeled, firm tomatoes
2 c. cut-up peeled carrots	Homemade Mayonnaise
2 c. finely cut celery	24 slices bread

Cook peas by package directions in salted water, only cook less time; they should be slightly *undercooked.*

Cut carrots in small squares, the size of peas, and slightly undercook. Cut celery in pieces of the same size; do not cook.

Mix peas, carrots and celery to distribute vegetables evenly. Cover and refrigerate overnight.

At serving time, cut tomatoes in pieces the size of peas; add to vegetable mixture and toss lightly with just enough homemade or other mayonnaise to moisten vegetable mixture.

Spread on 12 whole wheat or other bread slices; top with remaining bread slices. Cut sandwiches diagonally in fourths. Makes 12 sandwiches.

HOMEMADE MAYONNAISE

Keep a jar of this in the refrigerator. It improves many salads

2 tblsp. flour	1¼ c. hot water
3 tblsp. cornstarch	1 egg
2 tblsp. sugar	2 c. salad oil
½ tsp. dry mustard	2 tblsp. lemon juice
1 tsp. salt	2 tblsp. vinegar

Mix flour, cornstarch, sugar, dry mustard and salt in saucepan. Add hot water; stir and cook to a thick paste. Cool.

Add egg to cooled mixture and beat well. Continue to beat while slowly and alternately adding oil, lemon juice and vinegar. Makes about 1 quart.

N O T E : If you wish to make mayonnaise in blender, start with the cooked paste when cooled. Put it in blender and add the other ingredients as directed in recipe.

FRESH APPLE CAKE

This is a moist spice cake with crisp top. It contains chopped apples

½ c. shortening	1 tsp. ground cinnamon
½ c. brown sugar, firmly packed	¾ tsp. ground nutmeg
1 c. sugar	½ tsp. ground cloves
2 eggs	1 c. buttermilk
2 tsp. baking soda	2 c. finely diced apples
2¼ c. flour	Topping

Cream together shortening and sugars until light and fluffy. Add eggs, one at a time, beating well after each addition.

Sift together baking soda, flour and spices. Add alternately with buttermilk to creamed mixture. Fold in apples. Pour into a greased and floured 13×9×2″ baking pan. Sprinkle with Topping.

Bake in moderate oven (350°) 45 to 50 minutes. Makes 12 servings.

Topping: Mix together ¼ c. brown sugar, firmly packed, ¼ c. sugar, ½ c. chopped nuts and 1½ tsp. ground cinnamon.

ACCENT-ON-YOUTH LUNCH

Egg Salad Dip   Crackers
Miniature Drumsticks   Corn Chips
Chilled Pineapple Juice   Baked Tuna Sandwiches*
Overnight Vegetable Salad*   Alabama French-Style Dressing*
Chocolate Ice Cream Float

The success of this meal depends to a large extent on making plenty of sandwiches. They're so good you may want to bake more than one batch. Active teen-age boys and girls often arrive at the table with ravenous appetites. Boys may say what they like is quantity, but when they and girls plan menus for their guests, they have decided ideas about what to serve and how a food tastes.

If the teen-ager has only a guest or two, the remainder of the family can join them at the table. So this menu is for a family lunch or supper, with the spotlight on youth favorites.

Egg salad, usually served as a sandwich filling, makes a great spread for crackers. The large joints of chicken wings (broiler-fryers), which resemble little drumsticks, rolled in seasoned flour and pan-fried in a little salad oil until golden, also win praise from young people. And always there are nibblers who like to munch on peanuts, potato and corn chips and other crisp foods.

TIMETABLE

Do-Ahead: Make sandwiches a day ahead and chill; they'll be ready to dip in batter and bake. Make the vegetable salad at least a day ahead, cover and chill. It stays in good condition for several days.

On Guest Day: Fry the chicken at any time convenient. Drain on paper toweling. Start dipping and baking sandwiches about an hour before time to serve them, especially if you bake two batches. Set out appetizers on buffet or on table in living room. Let the teen-age host or hostess fix and serve the dessert at serving time. For each cup of cold milk, beat in 2 tblsp. chocolate syrup and a small scoop of vanilla ice cream. Use the electric blender for the mixing if you have one. Serve in glasses with scoops of ice cream on top.

SERVING SUGGESTIONS

Serve the plates in the kitchen. Arrange a double sandwich (2 slices bread) on each plate and place the salad, well drained, in lettuce cups alongside. Have extra warm sandwiches waiting in a very low oven to pass for second helpings. If you wish to dress up the drumsticks, put paper frills on them (the kind used on lamb chops). A ketchup dip for the chicken wins the approval of most youngsters. If you wish to make it, stir (do not beat) 2 tblsp. prepared mustard into 1 c. ketchup. Serve in small bowls. Frost the egg salad in the bowl with dairy sour cream and sprinkle a finely chopped hard-cooked egg over the top for a party look. Serve teaspoons or iced beverage spoons with the dessert, the size depending on the size of the serving glasses.

BAKED TUNA SANDWICHES

Hot sandwiches are crusty and brown on outside with moist filling

1 can condensed cream of chicken soup	¾ c. milk
	8 slices white bread
1 tblsp. minced onion	2 eggs, beaten
2 tblsp. chopped pimiento	3 tblsp. milk
2 (7 oz.) cans water pack tuna, flaked	2 c. crushed potato chips
	½ c. chopped pecans
3 tblsp. flour	

Mix soup, onion, pimiento and tuna in saucepan. Blend flour with ¼ c. milk and add with remaining ½ c. milk to soup mixture. Cook, stirring, until thick. Cool; then chill.

Remove crusts from bread. Place 4 slices in bottom of any shallow baking pan. Spread with tuna mixture. Top with remaining bread slices. Cover and refrigerate overnight or at least several hours.

Blend eggs with 3 tblsp. milk. Cut each sandwich in half. Dip both sides into egg mixture, then in potato chips. Spread on greased baking sheet sprinkled with pecans. Bake in moderate oven (350°) 25 to 30 minutes. Makes 4 sandwiches (8 halves).

OVERNIGHT VEGETABLE SALAD

A tasty way to include a satisfactory quota of vegetables in a meal

1 (1 lb.) can peas, drained
2 (1 lb.) cans whole green beans
½ c. sliced pimiento-stuffed olives
4 carrots, cut in 1″ matchsticks
4 oz. slivered almonds

4 c. celery cut in 1″ matchsticks
6 green onions, thinly sliced
  (about ¾ c.)
1½ c. Alabama French-Style
  Dressing

Combine all ingredients, except dressing. Toss with Alabama French-Style Dressing. Cover and refrigerate overnight. Salad will keep several days in refrigerator. Makes about 3 quarts.

ALABAMA FRENCH-STYLE DRESSING

Keep handy in refrigerator—good served on green and fruit salads

1 c. salad oil
¼ c. vinegar
1 tsp. Worcestershire sauce
½ tsp. paprika
2 tsp. salt

1 clove garlic, crushed
⅓ c. orange juice
¼ c. lemon juice
⅓ c. confectioners sugar
½ tsp. dry mustard

Combine all ingredients; shake to mix well. Chill. Shake before using. Makes about 2 cups.

CHAPTER 3

Entertaining at Supper

. . . GREAT EVENING MEALS

When you ask country women the difference between a company supper and dinner, you get a variety of answers. But on one point everyone agrees . . . it is easier to invite friends to supper than dinner because the menu is less pretentious. For example, steaming hot, homemade Pleasant Valley Cheese/Vegetable Soup, a recipe in this chapter, takes the main-dish role in one of our supper menus.

Supper is expected to be a lighter meal than dinner and contains fewer foods, which makes it easier to get. Boys' Burger Supper, Chili Supper, Cook-In, Eat-Out Supper and Fondue Supper are hearty. And you'll notice that many of our suppers are more considerate of a tight food budget than those for company dinners. For instance, Barbecued Turkey Wings taste great and cost less than other turkey pieces.

The menus that follow are exceedingly good family meals, with a few touches that create a company atmosphere. Fruit-Jar Tomato Relish, for example, is really a fresh-from-the-garden, mixed vegetable salad you fix a day ahead in a glass fruit jar and chill until serving time. The varicolored layers add charm to the dish. Eliminates tossing a salad at the last minute, too.

So does Garden-Patch Salad, which consists of an expertly seasoned gelatin mixture that holds color-bright vegetables. It represents the many fix-ahead salads in this chapter that make clever and delicious use of vegetables when they are in bountiful supply. Consider Easygoing Summer Supper to share with friends on a sultry evening when cooking appeals to no one. Notice how again gelatin traps a variety of garden vegetables in a salad that refreshes.

The recipe for Chili con Carne in the Chili Supper comes from a ranch kitchen in southern Colorado, an area in which Spanish-Americans have farmed for many generations. The unusual addition is hominy, which makes a delicious difference.

There are many other distinctive recipes in this chapter. Grilled

Halibut Steaks and Grilled Minute Steak Rolls (the beef is rolled around butter) are two wonderful examples . . . and the handsome Salmon Loaf with Shrimp Sauce.

Look through this chapter and you'll make other discoveries for easy, successful entertaining.

Recipes for all dishes starred (*) are in this cookbook.

BOYS' BURGER SUPPER

Peanuts in Shell

Ground Beef Patties   Homemade Burger Buns*

Tomatoes   Dill and Sweet Pickles   Onions   Cheese

Ketchup   Mustard

Mom's Best Baked Beans*

Caramel Fondue* with Dippers

Milk   Soft Drinks

Forget your creative urge when your senior and junior high school sons entertain their friends. Give them hamburgers and make them happy. If you want to add a special touch, bake the buns yourself. The boys will appreciate the homemade taste. Set out the trimmings and let everyone build his own burger.

To help satisfy hungry boys fix our recipe for dressed up canned baked beans; heat them to blend flavors. End the meal with a dessert fondue with chunks of fruit and marshmallows to dip. Such a menu pleases 99 out of 100 boys, and especially if bowls of peanuts in shell are on hand to satisfy the nibblers.

TIMETABLE

Do-Ahead: Bake the buns the day before (or several days ahead and freeze them).

On Guest Day: If buns are frozen, thaw them at room temperature in their wrap; this will take from 2 to 3 hours. Put the beans in the oven about an hour before serving time. Shortly before supper, slice the tomatoes, pickles, onions and cheese (unless you buy packaged slices). Cook the beef patties the last half hour before mealtime. Use an electric grill or a skillet, or broil them if you prefer. Make them about ½″ smaller than buns. While the boys eat, get the fondue ready. Cut the unpeeled apples and bananas in bite-size chunks;

sprinkle with lemon juice diluted with water to prevent discoloration if they have long to wait. Set out a bowl of marshmallows. Make a second batch of Caramel Fondue and keep warm in double boiler over hot water so you'll be ready to replenish it if needed. Or use two fondue pots if there are more than four or five boys.

SERVING SUGGESTIONS

Serve the supper buffet style indoors or out, as weather and situation dictate. Place the hot burgers in the buns and arrange them on a platter alongside serving plates (these can be paper). On a tray arrange alternate rows of tomato, onion, pickle and cheese slices. Set a bottle of ketchup and a jar of prepared mustard nearby. If you have a bean pot, bake and serve the beans in it; a casserole will do. Place drinking glasses and bottles of soft drinks, inserted in an ice-filled bucket, within easy reach. And don't forget the pitcher of milk, for many boys are great milk drinkers. When the main course is eaten, bring out the fondue, set it over the burner (or at low heat if using an electric pot or skillet—which is safer), and then carry out the dippers—marshmallows, apples and bananas. Provide bowls or trays to hold peanut shells.

HOMEMADE BURGER BUNS

Boys prefer plain buns, so you may omit sesame and poppy seeds

2 pkgs. active dry yeast	2 c. water
¼ c. sugar	2 eggs, beaten
½ c. warm water (110 to 115°)	½ c. salad oil or melted
6 c. sifted flour	shortening
½ c. nonfat dry milk (not	1 egg, beaten
reconstituted)	Milk
1 tblsp. salt	Sesame or poppy seeds (optional)

Combine yeast, sugar and water; let stand until yeast softens. Stir to dissolve.

Sift together flour, dry milk and salt into large bowl. Make a well in center and pour in the water, yeast, 2 beaten eggs and oil. Mix well; cover and let rise in a warm place 1 hour.

Turn dough onto well-floured board (dough may be sticky), turn a few times to coat dough well with flour. Pinch off pieces about the size of an egg; place smooth side up about 3″ apart on greased baking sheet. Brush with mixture of 1 beaten egg (or egg yolk) and a little milk; then sprinkle with sesame or poppy seeds, if desired.

Let rise 20 minutes. Bake in hot oven (425°) 8 to 12 minutes, or until done. Makes about 30 buns.

MOM'S BEST BAKED BEANS

You can fix these beans in an uncovered skillet in about 20 minutes. Bring them to a boil, then simmer gently, stirring occasionally

6 bacon slices
1 c. finely chopped onions
⅓ c. ketchup

2 tsp. prepared mustard
3 (about 1 lb. 3 oz.) cans pork and beans

Cut bacon in small pieces with kitchen scissors; cook with onions in skillet, stirring until bacon is crisp. Stir in ketchup, mustard and beans. Pour into ungreased 2-qt. casserole or bean pot and bake uncovered in moderate oven (350°) 40 to 45 minutes. Serves 8.

CARAMEL FONDUE

Caramel sauce coats the dippers with a delicious glaze. Keep it warm; if it gets too hot fondue runs off dippers and also may scorch

1 (14 oz.) pkg. vanilla caramels
⅓ c. water
Dash of salt

Marshmallows, apple and banana pieces

Place caramels and water in top of double boiler and heat over water until melted. Stir in salt. Pour sauce into fondue pot and set over fondue burner. (If boys are young teens, stick around for safety's sake—boys will be boys.) Keep warm (not hot) over low heat. If sauce gets too thick, stir in a little warm water.

Let boys spear marshmallow or bite-size chunks of unpeeled apple or banana (if fruit has been dipped in lemon juice diluted with water, it should be dry and at room temperature) on fondue forks or bamboo skewers and dip into the fondue. Makes 1⅓ cups sauce, about 4 servings.

TEEN-AGE SUPPER

Sardine/Egg Spread*
Crackers   Cherry Tomatoes
Orange Fizz
Southwestern Ham Rolls*
Speedy Bean Skillet*
Choco/Date Squares*
Snack Bowl*

The girl who planned this menu thinks young. That's not surprising for she's sweet sixteen. Proof of her wisdom in selecting the right foods was the speed with which the supper disappeared after the high school crowd arrived. And it's a meal a girl can get without her mother's help.

TIMETABLE

Do-Ahead: Either make the cookies a day ahead, cool and place in tightly covered container, or bake them the morning of the supper.

On Guest Day: Fix the ham rolls, wrap in foil and refrigerate. Make the sardine spread at any time convenient; cover and chill. Put the ham rolls in the oven to heat 1 hour before supper. Put the beans on to heat about 20 minutes before you want to serve them. Reconstitute frozen orange juice for the Orange Fizz, pour into a pitcher and chill. Finish the Orange Fizz just before serving: Usually a boy will volunteer to open the chilled ginger ale and add an equal amount of it to the orange juice, while one of the girls adds a spoonful of orange sherbet to each glass. Young guests like to help their hostess.

SERVING SUGGESTIONS

Serve the food buffet style. Bring out the Sardine/Egg Spread in a bowl along with a tray of crackers and knives for spreading. To give the spread color, scatter snipped fresh parsley over it. Set out a bowl of cherry tomatoes; have a shaker of seasoned salt nearby. Serve the orange drink with straws. Serve the ham rolls in their foil wrap; the beans in an attractive casserole. And to end the feast, serve the Snack Bowl and Choco/Date Squares.

SARDINE/EGG SPREAD

Ingredients for this tasty appetizer usually are on hand

2 (3¾ oz.) cans sardines in oil
2 hard-cooked eggs, finely
  chopped

¼ c. mayonnaise
2 to 3 tblsp. lemon juice
¼ c. finely chopped pecans

Drain oil from sardines. Place them in a bowl and mash with a fork. Add remaining ingredients and blend well. Makes 2 cups.

SOUTHWESTERN HAM ROLLS

If you prefer a milder filling, split buns, insert a slice each of baked ham and process American cheese, wrap in foil; chill. To serve, heat in moderate oven (350°) 25 minutes; serve in foil, opened at top

1 (12 oz.) can chopped ham, or
  2 c. cubed cooked ham
¾ lb. grated or cubed sharp
  Cheddar cheese
1 large onion, chopped
1 (4½ oz.) can chopped ripe
  olives

1 (4 oz.) can whole green chili
  peppers
1 (8 oz.) can tomato sauce
2 tblsp. vinegar
Hard rolls (10 to 12)

Mix all the ingredients, except the rolls.

Slice off tops of hard rolls, scoop out inside (save for crumbs) and fill with ham-cheese mixture. Replace tops on rolls and wrap individually in foil. Bake in very slow oven (275°) 1 hour. Makes 10 to 12 servings.

SPEEDY BEAN SKILLET

A bean bowl accented with franks pleases the boys and fills them up

2 tblsp. butter or regular
  margarine
1 c. diced peeled tomatoes

¼ tsp. crushed orégano leaves
2 (1 lb.) cans beans and franks in
  tomato sauce

Melt butter in skillet; add tomatoes and orégano. Cook a couple of minutes to blend flavors. Stir in beans. Heat, stirring frequently, until piping hot. Makes 6 servings.

CHOCO/DATE SQUARES

Cookies made with ready-to-eat cereals rate high with young people

1 c. chopped dates	2 c. crisp rice cereal
½ c. butter or regular margarine	6 squares semisweet chocolate
⅓ c. sugar	

Combine dates, butter and sugar in saucepan; heat until butter is melted and dates are tender; remove from heat and add crisp rice cereal. Mix well with spoon.

Press mixture into 8″ square pan and cool.

Melt chocolate over very low heat and spread over date cookies. When completely cool, cut in small squares. Makes about 24 small cookies.

SNACK BOWL

The teen-age crowd goes for fruit-nut-candy mixes

2 c. light or dark raisins	2 c. candy-coated chocolate
2 c. salted redskin peanuts	pieces

Stir ingredients to distribute evenly. Serve in attractive glass bowl. Makes 6 cups.

EASYGOING SUMMER SUPPER

Platter of Cold Cuts   Vegetable Salad Mold*
Buttered Hot Rolls
Lemon Sherbet   Brownies

Collect some fresh vegetables in a salad that you can make ahead and you have a good start on a delightful summer company meal. The salad in this menu is a California special inspired by the famous cold Spanish vegetable soup, gazpacho. Add a generous platter of cold meats that have variety in color, flavor and texture—slices of liver sausage, salami and large bologna, for instance—and Swiss cheese. If you have a meat loaf in the freezer, by all means include slices of that.

Add buttered hot rolls and you have the main course planned. If the weather isn't too hot, bake a batch of baking powder biscuits in-

stead of warming ready-made rolls. It's fast work with packaged biscuit mix. Generations of farm women have relied on hot bread to
give meals a special appeal. You'll want to open a jar of berry jam
or peach preserves. And do remember how good honey is on hot,
buttered biscuits.

For dessert, we give you two suggestions: lemon sherbet with some
kind of chocolate cookies, or chilled small cantaloupe halves with a
scoop of lime sherbet in the center.

N O T E : To convert this supper into a dinner, add sweet corn on the
cob to the menu.

TIMETABLE

Do-Ahead: Make salad a day ahead, or at least in the morning for
evening serving. For serving more than 5, make two molds of salad.

On Guest Day: Shortly before suppertime, heat buttered rolls
(wrapped in foil) in moderate oven (350°) 10 to 15 minutes. Arrange cold cuts and cheese on platter. Unmold the salad on lettuce
or other greens.

SERVING SUGGESTIONS

Garnish ends and center of cold meat platter with spiced crab apples, your best sweet pickles or small clusters of seedless green
grapes. Or use perky sprigs of parsley. Serve salad at table or individual servings on salad plates lined with crisp lettuce. Pass salad
dressing to make it optional. Try to serve the rolls piping hot in a
napkin-lined and covered basket, or in a roll warmer.

VEGETABLE SALAD MOLD

Western hostesses use hot green chili peppers in this but you can use the more widely available and milder green pepper

1 envelope unflavored gelatin
1½ c. tomato juice
1 large ripe tomato, peeled
2 tblsp. vinegar or pickle juice
1 medium cucumber, peeled and
   finely chopped
1 peeled and seeded green chili
   pepper, finely chopped, or about
   ¼ c. chopped sweet green
   pepper

½ c. finely chopped celery
¼ c. finely chopped onion
1 tsp. garlic salt
⅛ tsp. pepper
¼ tsp. orégano leaves
Greens

Soften gelatin in ¼ c. tomato juice 5 minutes.

Meanwhile, heat 1 c. tomato juice; add the gelatin mixture and stir to dissolve.

Chop fresh tomato, saving the juice. Combine vinegar, remaining ¼ c. tomato juice and juice from tomato (add water if necessary to make ½ c. liquid). Add fresh tomato and add to hot gelatin mixture with cucumber, green chili, celery, onion, garlic salt, pepper and orégano. Pour into 1-qt. mold. Chill until firm. To serve, unmold on greens. Makes about 6 servings.

WESTERN BUFFET SUPPER

California Chicken*   Baked Almond Rice*
Garden-Patch Salad*
Hot Roll Ring*   Berry Preserves
Orange-Glazed Cake*

You can almost hear the Pacific breakers when you serve and eat this wonderful meal . . . it consists of the kinds of food highly esteemed in California. The chicken has an exciting Americanized oriental taste. This comes from the soy sauce and faint sweet-sour flavor of pineapple juice and sugar. It is a main dish that can wait in the oven a bit without deteriorating when dinner is delayed.

Rice cooked in the oven in a *tightly* covered casserole is easy, fluffy and flavorful with almonds, butter and chicken broth. It bakes at the same temperature as the chicken.

Amazing how good the salad tastes. It assumes the role of vegetables in the menu. The ring of little hot rolls always fascinates— guests like to pull off a roll, drop a bit of melted butter and a sweet spread on it. You'd better bake two rings!

The Orange-Glazed Cake tops off the meal in great country style. All that's needed to make the supper a huge success is a big pot of hot coffee.

TIMETABLE

Do-Ahead: Get the salad in the refrigerator a day ahead. You can bake the cake and rolls a day or several days ahead, wrap in foil and freeze.

On Guest Day: All you have to cook is the chicken dish, which needs an hour in the oven, and the rice, which bakes only half an hour. You do baste the chicken four times while it cooks, but the taste results are worth the effort. If the rolls are baked ahead, reheat them in a moderate oven (350°) 20 to 25 minutes if frozen, 10 to 15 minutes if at room temperature. Remove foil wrapping after heating.

SERVING SUGGESTIONS

Raid your cupboard for your most delectable jam, preserves or marmalade. If you have a divided relish dish, you can generate a lot of praise by offering more than one kind.

CALIFORNIA CHICKEN

Excellent dish to serve a crowd. Double or triple the recipe. It's important to be faithful in the basting while the chicken cooks

⅔ c. flour	4 whole chicken breasts, split,
1 tsp. salt	skinned and boned
½ tsp. celery salt	¼ c. melted butter
½ tsp. garlic salt	1 c. pineapple juice
½ tsp. ground nutmeg	½ c. soy sauce
	2 tblsp. sugar

Mix together flour, salt, celery salt, garlic salt and nutmeg; dredge chicken in mixture. Brown chicken in melted butter in skillet. Transfer to roasting pan.

Combine pineapple juice, soy sauce and sugar; mix well and pour over chicken. Bake uncovered in moderate oven (350°) 1 hour, basting every 15 minutes. Makes 4 servings.

BAKED ALMOND RICE

Ideal way to cook rice for an oven meal. It's easy and tastes good

3 c. boiling chicken broth or
   water
1½ c. regular rice, uncooked
1¼ tsp. salt

¾ c. slivered almonds
3 tblsp. butter or regular
   margarine

Mix broth, rice and salt in ungreased 3-qt. casserole (or a 13×9×2″ baking pan). Cover *tightly*—use aluminum foil to cover pan. Bake in moderate oven (350°) 25 to 30 minutes, until liquid is absorbed and rice is tender.

Meanwhile, lightly brown almonds in butter. Add to hot, cooked rice and toss to mix. Makes 6 to 8 servings.

GARDEN-PATCH SALAD

Lemon gelatin accented with tarragon vinegar holds six vegetables

2 (3 oz.) pkgs. lemon flavor
   gelatin
2 c. hot water
1½ c. cold water
¼ c. tarragon vinegar
½ tsp. salt
2 c. finely chopped cabbage

½ c. thinly sliced carrots
½ c. chopped celery
¼ c. chopped green pepper
¼ c. thinly sliced radishes
2 tblsp. thinly sliced green onion,
   including some of green top
2 tblsp. pickle relish

Dissolve gelatin in hot water. Add cold water, vinegar and salt; pour into 2-qt. mold or an 11×7×1½″ glass dish and chill until mixture is partially set (the consistency of unbeaten egg white).

Add vegetables and pickle relish to gelatin and chill until firm. Serve with salad dressing if you like. Makes 8 to 10 servings.

HOT ROLL RING

Have a bowl of melted butter in open center of the ring—spoon it on

1 (13¾ oz.) pkg. hot roll mix
¾ c. warm water

1 egg
⅓ c. melted butter

Follow package directions for mixing dough with water and egg. Place dough in lightly greased bowl, invert to grease top; cover and let rise until doubled.

Roll dough ¼" thick on lightly floured board. The rectangle will be about 16×12". Cut in diamond-shaped pieces about 3×2". Dip each piece in melted butter and arrange in ungreased 9" ring mold, overlapping pieces. Let rise until doubled, about 30 minutes.

Bake in moderate oven (375°) 20 to 25 minutes. Remove from oven, unmold while very warm and brush lightly with butter. Serve top side up. Makes one 9" ring, 40 diamonds or rolls.

ORANGE-GLAZED CAKE

A pour-on orange glaze dresses up and flavors this raisin-nut cake

½ c. shortening	½ tsp. salt
1 c. brown sugar, firmly packed	½ tsp. baking soda
2 eggs	1 c. buttermilk
1 tsp. lemon extract	1 c. seedless raisins
½ tsp. maple flavoring	½ c. chopped walnuts
2 c. sifted cake flour	Peel of 1 orange
1 tsp. baking powder	Orange Glaze

Cream shortening and brown sugar thoroughly. Add eggs one at a time, beating well after each addition. Add flavorings.

Sift together flour, baking powder, salt and soda. Add alternately with buttermilk to creamed mixture. Put raisins, walnuts and orange peel through food chopper and stir into cake batter. Pour into greased 9" square cake pan.

Bake in moderate oven (350°) 40 minutes. Remove from oven and let stand in pan 5 minutes. Pour Orange Glaze over cake while it is still in pan. Cool on rack.

Orange Glaze: Combine 1 c. sugar and ⅓ c. orange juice; stir to dissolve. Pour over warm cake.

SUPPER DELICIOUS

Broiled Ham/Pineapple Patties*
Tart Barbecue Sauce*
Maple Sweet Potatoes*
Tossed Green Salad
Nutmeg Cake*
Green Grapes with Sour Cream and Brown Sugar

If you've been looking for a distinctively different supper that's exceptionally delicious, use this menu. The patties of smoky ham and ground beef with juicy pineapple rings on top have both eye and taste appeal. The fruity basting sauce heightens flavor.

The golden cake powdered with confectioners sugar is out of this world in flavor. And it's so easily baked. Chilled green grapes in a sour cream and brown sugar sauce are an eating experience your guests will not forget.

TIMETABLE

Do-Ahead: Bake the cake a day ahead if you like. Make the basting sauce for the meat patties; cool, cover and chill. Wash, drain and chill salad greens in plastic bag.

On Guest Day: Prepare seedless green grapes several hours before suppertime. Remove from stems, wash, drain and place in an 8″ square baking pan. Cover with dairy sour cream and sprinkle generously with brown sugar. Start cooking the meat patties about 25 minutes before time to serve. Meanwhile, glaze canned sweet potatoes. Toss the salad just before serving.

SERVING SUGGESTIONS

This is a sit-down dinner. At dessert time, spoon the grapes into stemmed dessert glasses, or in goblets, filling half full. Serve on plate with cake alongside.

BROILED HAM/PINEAPPLE PATTIES

An unusual feature of these patties is that they contain ground beef and ham. Fruit juices and chopped vegetables make sauce special

1½ lbs. ground cooked ham	6 slices pineapple
½ lb. ground beef	Tart Barbecue Sauce

Mix together ground ham and beef. Shape into 6 patties about ¾″ thick. Press a pineapple slice firmly into the top of each patty. Place patties, pineapple side down, on cold broiler grid.

Broil 12 to 15 minutes on one side, brushing occasionally with Tart Barbecue Sauce. Carefully turn and broil 4 to 6 minutes on other side, brushing occasionally with sauce. Makes 6 servings.

TART BARBECUE SAUCE

Blend of flavors that can't be surpassed for ham and pineapple

1 onion, grated	1 tsp. prepared mustard
2 tblsp. salad oil	½ c. pineapple juice
¼ c. lemon juice	½ c. chopped celery
2 tblsp. brown sugar	½ c. finely chopped green pepper
1 c. ketchup	2 tblsp. Worcestershire sauce

Combine all ingredients in medium-size saucepan. Stir to blend. Cover and simmer gently 30 to 40 minutes, stirring occasionally. Makes about 1½ cups.

MAPLE SWEET POTATOES

Maple syrup enhances flavor and gives attractive glaze

1 c. maple-blended syrup	2 (17 oz.) cans vacuum pack
½ c. butter or regular margarine	sweet potatoes, drained

Combine syrup and butter in 2-qt. saucepan; bring to a boil and cook until thickened.

Add sweet potatoes; simmer until hot, basting occasionally with glaze. Makes 8 servings.

NUTMEG CAKE

Surprisingly easy cake to make and surprisingly good eating

1 pkg. yellow cake mix (for
  2-layer cake)
¾ c. salad oil
¾ c. dry sherry or sauterne
4 eggs

1 (3¾ oz.) pkg. vanilla instant
  pudding
¾ tsp. ground nutmeg
Confectioners sugar

Combine cake mix, oil and wine in mixing bowl. Blend thoroughly. Add eggs, one at a time, mixing well after each addition. Add vanilla pudding and nutmeg; beat 3 minutes at medium speed on mixer.

Pour into greased and floured 10″ tube or fluted tube pan. Bake in moderate oven (350°) about 45 minutes, or until cake tests done. Cool on rack.

When cool, remove cake carefully from pan and lightly dust with confectioners sugar.

GARDEN SUPPER

Melon Appetizer
Crab/Zucchini Casserole*
Buttered Peas
Cucumber Bowl*
Lemon/Raspberry Parfait*

This meal is not served in the garden, but comes from there. It features one of the most prolific vegetables, zucchini. When your vines are producing more of the squash than you know how to use, entertain your friends at this supper. The zucchini combined with crabmeat and Swiss cheese is so delicious that you'll want to serve it again and again. Your guests will ask for the recipe and if they don't have a garden will hope for a handout of the plentiful zucchini. The casserole is filling and its red (diced tomato) and brown top gives it eye appeal.

The cucumbers make a perfect accompaniment. You can substitute asparagus for peas, if you wish.

Start the meal with cubes of watermelon, cantaloupe and honeydew. Squeeze lime or lemon juice over them. For dessert, serve chilled lemon tapioca cream pudding, a country favorite, teamed with raspberries.

TIMETABLE

On Guest Day: Prepare the cucumbers at any time during the day and chill. Make the tapioca and chill; assemble the dessert at serving time. About 35 minutes before dinnertime, put the casserole in the oven to bake. Meanwhile, cook and season the peas.

CRAB/ZUCCHINI CASSEROLE

For a women's luncheon you can bake this in buttered scallop shells

1¼ lbs. zucchini (about 5 small)	2 cloves garlic, crushed
1 medium onion, chopped	1 (7½ oz.) can crabmeat
1 stick butter (¼ lb.)	1⅓ c. small sticks of Swiss cheese
½ tsp. salt	1 tsp. sweet basil leaves
Dash of pepper	1 c. fresh bread crumbs
3 medium tomatoes, peeled	

Wash unpeeled zucchini, cut in ½″ slices. Sauté with chopped onion in two thirds stick of butter, but do not brown. Add salt and pepper.

Cut tomatoes coarsely.

Sauté garlic and crabmeat briefly in remaining one third stick of butter. Discard garlic. Fold crabmeat into zucchini-onion mixture. Add cheese (in matchlike strips), tomatoes, basil and bread crumbs. Pour into a greased 2-qt. casserole.

Bake, uncovered, in moderate oven (350°) 30 to 35 minutes. Makes 8 servings.

CUCUMBER BOWL

Dill weed, wine vinegar and thorough chilling make this special

4 medium cucumbers, peeled and thinly sliced	1 tsp. salt
	1 tsp. wine vinegar
1½ c. dairy sour cream	½ tsp. dill weed
2 tblsp. salad oil	Chopped fresh parsley or chives
2 tsp. sugar	

Slice cucumbers into a bowl.

Mix sour cream, salad oil, sugar, salt and vinegar. Pour over cucumbers. Toss gently to mix. Sprinkle with dill weed. Cover and chill at least 1 hour, or a few hours.

To serve country style, leave in bowl and sprinkle with chopped parsley or chives. Makes 8 servings.

LEMON/RASPBERRY PARFAIT

If you don't have parfait glasses serve in stemmed dessert glasses; place a layer of raspberries in the bottom of glass and on top

¼ c. quick-cooking tapioca	Grated peel of 1 lemon
¾ c. sugar	½ c. heavy cream
¼ tsp. salt	1 c. sweetened red raspberries, or
2¼ c. water	1 (10 oz.) pkg. frozen
¼ c. lemon juice	raspberries

Combine tapioca, sugar, salt and water in saucepan; let stand 5 minutes. Bring just to a boil over medium heat, stirring occasionally. Remove from heat and stir in lemon juice and peel; cool.

Whip cream and fold into tapioca mixture. Chill. Spoon alternate layers tapioca and raspberries in parfait glasses, ending with raspberries. Makes 6 servings.

IMPROMPTU FISH BARBECUE

Grilled Halibut Steaks*
Tomato/Macaroni Salad*
Hard Rolls
Honeyed Fruit Compote*
Homemade Cookies
Hot Coffee   Iced Tea

Impromptu entertaining radiates an easygoing charm of its own. You telephone the invitations on the day of the party when you are in a social mood and no rain is predicted. Advance preparations are impossible, but you can make do with what you have or can get in a hurry. Few ways of sharing food with friends excel the spontaneous cookout.

Actually, with this menu, all you cook is the macaroni for the salad, and the fish. You (or your husband) can pick up the halibut steaks and any other needed supplies at the supermarket. Of course he will check the charcoal supply.

The substantial salad, enlivened by ripe tomatoes, complements the fish. All you need to round out the meal is a compote of melons and fruits. If you have homemade cookies in the freezer or cookie jar, by all means bring out a plate full. (Perhaps you have a daughter who can bake a batch of cookies for you.)

TIMETABLE

On Guest Day: Cook the macaroni and fix the salad as early in the day as you can, to give flavors a chance to blend. Add the tomato quarters just before serving. Make the fruit compote at least an hour, or several hours ahead, cover and chill. When the host has the coals at the right stage for cooking the fish, bring the other foods to the table. Fish cooks in about 10 minutes.

SERVING SUGGESTIONS

Eat indoors or out, whichever place seems more inviting.

GRILLED HALIBUT STEAKS

The smoky flavor makes fish taste good; lemon, parsley add color

8 halibut steaks (about ¼ lb. each)	Salt
2 small cloves garlic, cut in halves	Paprika
6 tblsp. salad oil	4 to 6 tblsp. Toasted Sesame
6 tblsp. lemon juice	Seeds (see Index)

Rub halibut on both sides with cut garlic clove; brush with salad oil. Sprinkle with lemon juice (bottled lemon juice is easy to use) and salt. Place on grill about 4" above medium-hot coals.

Cook about 5 minutes; turn. Sprinkle top of steaks with paprika and Toasted Sesame Seeds. Cook 5 minutes longer, or until the fish is done. Test for doneness with a fork; if the fish flakes easily, it is ready to serve. Serve at once with lemon wedges and chopped parsley. Makes 8 servings.

TOMATO/MACARONI SALAD

Young boys coming to the barbecue? If so, use bow-tie macaroni

½ lb. bow-tie or seashell macaroni
1 c. diced celery
1 green pepper, chopped
2 tblsp. finely chopped onions
3 tblsp. finely chopped fresh
   parsley, or 1½ tblsp. dried
   parsley flakes
1¼ tsp. salt

¼ tsp. pepper
½ tsp. celery seeds
¼ c. mayonnaise
⅓ c. creamy French dressing
4 large tomatoes, peeled and cut
   in wedges and sprinkled lightly
   with salt
Lettuce

Cook macaroni in boiling salted water by package directions; rinse under cold water, drain and cool. Combine macaroni and all ingredients except tomatoes and lettuce. Cover and chill until serving time. Fold in tomato wedges, serve on lettuce. Makes 8 servings.

HONEYED FRUIT COMPOTE

Serve in a big bowl and let everyone help himself. Set a filled cookie jar on table. Refill coffee cups and iced tea glasses

1 cantaloupe
1 honeydew or casaba melon
2 large peaches
2 Bartlett pears

1 c. strained honey
1 (1 lb.) can apricots (about 2 c.)
1 c. juice from apricots (about)

Cut each melon in half, remove seeds and peel off rind and unedible portions. Cut each melon half in eighths. Peel peaches, remove pits and cut in serving-size pieces. Cut pears in halves (no need to peel) and remove cores; cut in serving-size pieces.

Add honey to canned apricots. Stir in liquid drained from apricots. Mix all the ingredients together with a light hand, cover and let stand 30 minutes to 1 hour. Let guests help themselves. Makes 8 servings.

SUNDAY SUPPER

Seafood Supper Soup*
Toasted French Bread Slices
Assorted Relishes
Easy Pear Torte*
Hot Tea or Coffee

Keep the ingredients for this meal in your kitchen and you'll always be ready for a good family meal to share with guests. When friends telephone late on a dreary Sunday afternoon and suggest dropping in for a brief visit, rise to the occasion and invite them to stay for an early supper. That's true country hospitality.

TIMETABLE

Do-Ahead: Before your guests arrive, get the torte in the oven. It's easy, fast, delicious and different. Check the freezer to find out if you have a jar of hard sauce. If not, bring out the mixer and beat up the fluffy sauce in a jiffy. Put in refrigerator. Take fish filets from freezer to thaw partially so you can cut them in slices. Thaw the frozen bread in its foil wrap. And if there is time, start opening cans from the cupboard shelf and some of your choice relishes.

On Guest Day: For the finishing touches, put the soup on to cook, open the bread and spread it on the grid to toast later in the broiling oven. (Be glad you sliced the loaf before you wrapped and froze it.) Arrange some of your choice pickles and a spiced fruit on a tray. Take the torte from the oven and toast the bread. Make tea or coffee.

SERVING SUGGESTIONS

Carry the relishes and toast to the table. Ladle the steaming soup into bowls in the kitchen, or if you prefer, turn it into a tureen and serve it at the table. A good way to brighten the evening for friends.

SEAFOOD SUPPER SOUP

After one spoonful you'll know people do not have to live near an ocean to enjoy tasty seafood dishes. Expert seasonings help

1 (1 lb. 12 oz.) can tomatoes, cut up
2 c. water
1 (7½ oz.) can minced clams
1 medium onion, chopped
½ c. chopped celery
¼ c. chopped green pepper
1 clove garlic, minced
1 tsp. salt
¼ tsp. thyme leaves, crushed
⅛ tsp. pepper
1 lb. frozen fish filets, partially thawed
1 (10 oz.) pkg. frozen green beans
Parmesan cheese

In a large kettle, combine tomatoes, water, clams, onion, celery, green pepper (maybe some you froze), garlic, salt, thyme and pepper. Cover; bring to a boil and simmer gently 15 minutes.

Meanwhile, cut block of fish filets in half lengthwise, then crosswise in ½" slices. Add to kettle along with green beans. Bring to a boil and simmer 15 minutes, or until green beans are tender. Pass Parmesan cheese at table to sprinkle over top. Makes 6 servings.

EASY PEAR TORTE

Dried fruits have been important in country cooking from pioneer days. Many heirloom dishes depend on them for flavor. This is a combination of the old and the new. It is surprisingly delicious

¼ c. butter or regular margarine
¾ c. sugar
3 eggs
1 tsp. vanilla
¼ tsp. ground cinnamon
1 pie crust stick, finely crumbled
1 c. snipped dried pears
½ c. snipped dates
½ c. chopped nuts
Fluffy Hard Sauce

Cream butter with sugar; add eggs, vanilla and cinnamon and beat well. Stir in crumbled pie crust stick, pears, dates and nuts.

Spread in greased 9" pie pan. Bake in slow oven (325°) 45 to 50 minutes. Serve warm, cut in wedges and topped with Fluffy Hard Sauce. Makes 6 servings.

Fluffy Hard Sauce: Cream ½ c. butter or regular margarine with 2 c. sifted confectioners sugar until fluffy. Add 1 tsp. vanilla and 1 egg yolk; beat well. Fold in 1 egg white, stiffly beaten. Chill.

FRESH-AS-A-DAISY SUPPER

Artichoke/Tuna Casserole*
Marinated Tomatoes*   Bread Sticks
Lemon Angel Pie*

A hostess who serves this meal to friends calls it her fresh-as-a-daisy menu. This, she insists, is the way she feels when she greets her company—after getting the supper. And it describes the way the food tastes and looks.

The menu wanders off the beaten path a bit: Artichoke hearts and cashews are not everyday ingredients but they lift the tuna, rice and cream of celery soup casserole above the commonplace. Chilling thick, ripe tomato slices in salad dressing gives them time to absorb and blend flavors. This is an old trick in country kitchens, where layers of sliced tomatoes, cucumbers and onions often chill several hours in seasoned vinegar.

Lemon Angel Pie, correctly named, is not a new dessert, especially to anyone who ever has lived in or visited Milwaukee or other areas along Lake Michigan's shores to the north where people of German ancestry live. Our version is a revised one, which is superlative, we think—queen of make-ahead desserts.

TIMETABLE

Do-Ahead: Make the dessert a day ahead (all but adding whipped cream) and refrigerate.

On Guest Day: Pour the salad dressing over the tomatoes and chill several hours, or until very cold. You can also fix the casserole several hours ahead and refrigerate. It needs to bake at least 1½ hours to heat (until the center bubbles). While it bakes, you have ample time to set the table and arrange a centerpiece.

SERVING SUGGESTIONS

This meal needs no garnishes because the food itself has eyes appeal—the browned casserole, the ripe red tomatoes, buttercup-yellow pie filling in a brown-tipped meringue shell.

NOTE: To convert this supper or luncheon into a dinner, add buttered asparagus or peas to the menu and substitute hot buttered rolls for the bread sticks.

ARTICHOKE/TUNA CASSEROLE

This is a very pretty dish—one you'll add to your list of favorites.
You can substitute 1/3 cup fresh lemon juice for the 1/2 cup wine

2 (10 oz.) pkgs. frozen artichoke hearts

2 cans condensed cream of celery soup

1/2 c. dry white wine or 1/3 c. lemon juice

2 (7 oz.) cans tuna, drained and flaked

3/4 c. coarsely chopped cashew nuts

3/4 c. regular rice (uncooked)

1 c. water

1 tsp. salt

2/3 c. bread crumbs

1 1/2 tblsp. melted butter

Cook artichoke hearts as directed on package; drain.

Combine soup and wine in a small saucepan; bring to a boil, stirring occasionally.

Layer half the artichokes, tuna, cashews and soup mixture in a 2-qt. casserole. Add all the rice, water and salt. Repeat with layers of remaining artichokes, tuna, cashews and soup mixture.

Toss bread crumbs with melted butter and sprinkle over casserole. Cover and bake in slow oven (325°) 1 to 1 1/2 hours. Makes 6 to 8 servings.

MARINATED TOMATOES

Stir tomatoes in the marinade a few times to distribute flavor

5 large ripe tomatoes

1/4 c. salad oil

1 1/2 c. red wine vinegar

1/2 clove garlic, minced

1/4 tsp. salt

1/2 tsp. orégano leaves

1/4 tsp. pepper

Greens (optional)

Peel tomatoes, cut in thick slices and put in bowl.

Combine remaining ingredients, except greens, and pour over tomatoes. Cover and chill thoroughly. Serve on greens, or if you prefer, in bowl. Makes 6 to 8 servings.

LEMON ANGEL PIE

This meringue shell is a versatile dessert base—for a change from lemon, fill meringue at serving time with vanilla ice cream and top with fresh strawberries or sliced fresh peaches, sugared lightly

Meringue Shell:
    3 egg whites (⅓ to ½ c.)
    ¼ tsp. cream of tartar
    ¾ c. sugar
Lemon Filling:
    ¾ c. sugar
    3 tblsp. cornstarch

¼ tsp. salt
3 egg yolks, slightly beaten
¼ c. water
1 tblsp. butter or regular
    margarine
1¼ tsp. grated lemon peel
⅓ c. fresh lemon juice
1 c. heavy cream, whipped

To make shell, beat egg whites with cream of tartar until frothy. Gradually beat in sugar, 1 tblsp. at a time. Beat until glossy and very stiff (do not underbeat). Use your electric mixer.

Spread on heavy brown paper covering baking sheet to make a 9″ round, building up sides with spoon to make a rim as for a pie shell. Bake in very slow oven (275°) 1½ hours; turn off heat and leave meringue in oven, door closed, for 1 hour. Remove and cool completely away from drafts.

Meanwhile, prepare filling. Blend sugar, cornstarch and salt in saucepan. Combine egg yolks with water; gradually stir into mixture in saucepan. Cook over medium heat, stirring constantly, until mixture thickens and comes to a boil. Boil 1 minute, stirring. Remove from heat and stir in butter, lemon peel and juice. Cool to room temperature.

Spread cooled filling in meringue shell and refrigerate overnight, or at least 12 hours. Top with whipped cream before serving. Makes 8 servings.

SUPPER SPECIAL

Salmon Loaf with Shrimp Sauce*
Buttered Peas and Carrots
Hot Rolls
Homemade Pickles
Pineapple/Cheese Salad*

When you return home from an afternoon meeting, bringing guests for supper, you want to serve a superior meal with a minimum of work at the last minute. This menu has that kind of timetable. While many recipe files contain directions for making salmon loaves, this one we consider champion of them all. Seasoned expertly and subtly, it tastes extra good.

The fruit salad is substantial enough to serve as both salad and dessert.

TIMETABLE

Do-Ahead: Make the salad a day ahead; chill.

On Guest Day: Before you leave home, fix salmon, place in loaf pan ready to bake, cover and chill. On your return home, or a little more than an hour before suppertime, put the salmon loaf in the oven. You can forget about it. Since the loaf is chilled, you may need to bake it a few minutes longer than the recipe specifies. After the salmon bakes 30 minutes, set the table, cut the salad in individual servings, cook the carrots and frozen peas separately, drain if necessary, combine and season with butter. Heat the shrimp sauce and make the coffee or tea.

SERVING SUGGESTIONS

This is a sit-down dinner. Slice the salmon loaf at the table or cut it in the kitchen and arrange slices on platter. Garnish platter with celery leaves or parsley and lemon slices (see photo).

SALMON LOAF WITH SHRIMP SAUCE

Loaf slices hold their shape and display that lovely salmon color

2 (1 lb.) cans salmon	½ to 1 tsp. ground thyme
¼ c. finely minced onion	2 c. coarse cracker crumbs
¼ c. chopped parsley	½ c. milk (about)
¼ c. lemon juice	4 eggs, well beaten
½ tsp. salt	¼ c. melted butter
½ tsp. pepper	Shrimp Sauce

Drain salmon, saving liquid.

Flake salmon into bowl; add onion, parsley, lemon juice, seasonings and cracker crumbs; mix lightly.

Add salmon liquid plus enough milk to make 1 cup; add eggs and melted butter. Mix lightly.

Spoon into greased 2-qt. loaf pan or casserole. Bake in moderate oven (350°) 1 hour or until loaf is set in center. Spoon Shrimp Sauce over top. Makes 8 servings.

Shrimp Sauce: Heat 1 can condensed cream of shrimp soup according to directions on label. Add ¼ c. milk, stir until smooth.

PINEAPPLE/CHEESE SALAD

Decorative, flavorful topping chills on salad—no dressing needed

2 pkgs. lemon flavor gelatin	½ c. sugar
2 c. boiling water	3 tblsp. cornstarch
2 c. cold water	2 (8¼ oz.) cans crushed pineapple
6 bananas, peeled and sliced	1 c. heavy cream
2 c. miniature or cut-up marshmallows	1 c. shredded Cheddar cheese

Dissolve gelatin in boiling water; add cold water and chill until syrupy. Stir in sliced bananas and marshmallows. Pour into 13×9× 2″ pan. Chill until set.

Mix sugar and cornstarch; add to undrained pineapple. Cook over medium heat, stirring constantly, until thickened. Cool.

Whip cream and fold into cooled pineapple mixture along with half the shredded cheese. Spread mixture on congealed lemon gelatin.

Sprinkle remainder of shredded cheese over top. Chill overnight. Cut into squares. Makes 12 to 15 servings.

INLAND CLAM CHOWDER SUPPER

Famous Clam Chowder*
Hearts of Lettuce and Tomato Salad
Vinegar and Oil Dressing
Sourdough Bread
Elegant Chocolate Log

To dramatize the food in this menu and tempt guests, serve it at the table. They never will dream that this might rightfully be called a kind-to-the-budget supper. Canned clams are a good buy. The Elegant Chocolate Log reflects a graceful elegance that gave the dessert its name.

This is the kind of simple supper members of a family like to come home to at the end of a busy, frustrating day, and especially on a rainy, chilly evening. Guests fortunate enough to share it feel that the hostess merely put extra plates on the table for them and went to no extra work. That gives an at-home feeling.

TIMETABLE

Do-Ahead: See Index for Elegant Chocolate Log recipe (featured in "February Dessert Party" menu) and directions for baking it ahead and freezing; also for baking it on guest day. Also see Index for Sourdough Bread and directions for baking it—included in Autumn Picnic menu.

On Guest Day: If you have made the dessert and bread previously, you can get this supper ready in less than an hour from start to finish.

SERVING SUGGESTIONS

Serve the chowder from a soup tureen or large bowl at the table to add glamor to the homespun dish. Slice and serve the lovely dessert at the table.

FAMOUS CLAM CHOWDER

Taste a spoonful of this flavorful inland clam chowder and you'll know why it's famous and always brings compliments from guests

2 (6½ oz.) cans minced clams	¾ c. flour
1 c. finely chopped onions	1 qt. dairy half-and-half
1 c. finely diced celery	1½ tsp. salt
2 c. very finely diced potatoes	Few grains white pepper
¾ c. butter	2 tblsp. red wine vinegar

Drain juice from clams and add to vegetables in small saucepan. Add enough water to barely cover vegetables. Simmer, covered, over medium heat until just tender.

In the meantime, melt butter; add flour, blend and cook, stirring for 2 to 3 minutes. Add dairy half-and-half; cook and stir with wire whisk until smooth and thick.

Add undrained vegetables and clams and heat through. Add salt, pepper and vinegar. Makes 8 servings.

SUPPER IN LILAC TIME

Pleasant Valley Cheese/Vegetable Soup*   Assorted Crackers
Radishes   Wilted Garden Lettuce*
Rhubarb Crisp*

A perfect setting for this supper is a chilly, Sunday evening in spring when the fragrant breath of lilacs along the drive greets arriving guests. If you have a garden, now is the time to make the most of the early vegetables and foods that complement them, such as cheese and bacon. Start off with a hearty soup and wind up with slender, red-pink rhubarb stalks, cut up, sweetened and baked in a simple dessert. Punctuate the meal with tiny, crisp, red radishes fresh from the earth and a big bowl of delicate leaf lettuce tossed with hot bacon-vinegar dressing. What country feast could be better?

TIMETABLE

Make-Ahead: You did your advance work when you planted your garden!

Sugared or glazed Square Doughnuts (recipe, **page 7**) will be the talk of your coffee party. They're easy to make. Use a knife to cut dough in squares and any small cutter for centers. Also try our Raisin Doughnuts.

What better welcome to spring than fresh-cut asparagus for luncheon? Baked Asparagus/Cheese Sandwiches—bread and cheese in velvety egg custard, topped with tender spears—are superior (recipe, page 44).

Keep the ingredients for Salmon Loaf with Shrimp Sauce (recipe, **page 84**) on hand in your pantry and you're deliciously ready for guests. This well-flavored loaf with its easy sauce makes a first-rate company dish.

It's the seasonings that make Summer Chicken with Peas and New Potatoes so delicious (recipe, page 128)—lemon juice, green onions, sour cream, parsley, thyme and lots of freshly ground pepper in this gourmet special.

On Guest Day: Gather the radishes and green onions, cut the lettuce and rhubarb, wash and prepare them. If they must wait more than an hour, chill them in plastic bags. Make the soup at any convenient time during the afternoon, or just before supper. The important point is never to let it boil in the making or reheating. Put the dessert in the oven to bake about 30 minutes before you wish to serve supper. It will be ready when the main course is finished. Dress the lettuce at the last minute.

SERVING SUGGESTIONS

Serve the lettuce in individual salad bowls or on plates. Or pass it in a big bowl and let everyone help himself. If you have a tureen, you can ladle the soup into bowls at the table while guests serve themselves lettuce.

PLEASANT VALLEY CHEESE/VEGETABLE SOUP

Rich, substantial, delicious and attractive—serve it piping hot

1 c. finely cut celery	1½ lbs. process American cheese,
½ c. finely cut carrot	cut up
¼ c. finely chopped onion	½ c. butter or regular margarine
2 tblsp. instant chicken bouillon	½ c. flour
crystals	½ tsp. dry mustard
1 qt. water	Salt (optional)
1 qt. milk	

Place celery, carrot, onion, bouillon and water in saucepan. Cook until vegetables are tender.

Meanwhile, scald the milk but do not let it boil. Add cheese, stir until melted.

Melt butter. Add flour and mustard; mix until smooth. Stir into cheese-milk mixture and heat. Stir in hot vegetables and the water in which they cooked. Check for salt. Serve hot. Makes 2 quarts.

WILTED GARDEN LETTUCE

For a pretty, springtime garnish top with 2 hard-cooked eggs, chopped

3 qts. bite-size pieces leaf lettuce	5 slices bacon, diced
1 tsp. salt	¼ c. vinegar
2 tsp. sugar	2 tblsp. water
2 green onions, sliced	

Place torn lettuce in a 3-qt. bowl. Sprinkle with salt, sugar and onions (use some of the green tops).

Cook bacon until crisp (not brittle). Drain bacon on paper towels. To bacon drippings add vinegar and water. Heat to boiling point and at once pour over lettuce. Toss until all the lettuce is slightly wilted. Check for salt. Sprinkle with bacon and serve immediately. Makes 8 servings.

RHUBARB CRISP

Serve topped with vanilla ice cream or pass pitcher of light cream

4 c. cut-up rhubarb	1 tsp. ground cinnamon
½ tsp. salt	2 tsp. grated orange peel
1⅓ to 2 c. sugar	⅓ c. butter or regular margarine
¾ c. flour	

Put rhubarb in ungreased 10×6×1½" baking dish. Sprinkle with salt.

Combine sugar (amount depends on tartness of rhubarb), flour, cinnamon, orange peel and butter in small bowl and mix until crumbly. Sprinkle evenly over rhubarb.

Bake in moderate oven (350°) about 45 minutes, or until topping is golden brown. Serve warm in bowls. Makes about 6 servings.

NOTE: For more servings, make the recipe 2 times.

CHILI SUPPER

Chili con Carne*	Assorted Crackers
Carrot Sticks	Pickles
Fruit Salad/Dessert*	Iced Tea

In thousands of western homes chili con carne rates high on the list of favorite main dishes to serve to company. It is to the west what baked beans are to New England. Americans shorten the name of this cross between a stew and a soup to chili. It's a shortcut version of Mexico's chili con carne in which the first step in preparation is to cook beef in water until almost tender, cut in tiny cubes and pan-fry them in a little fat. And beans accompany the dish, but are not a part of it. Speedy ground beef substitutes in our country kitchens for the precooked meat. The beef and the hearty ingredients, including beans, simmer together gently in an electric skillet.

Our recipe comes from a ranch in Rio Grande County, Colorado, the home of Mexican-Americans who are the fourth generation of the family (the fifth if you count the children) to live on the same land. An unusual feature of the main dish is the inclusion of hominy. It imparts that special taste south-of-the-border cornmeal gives to certain dishes.

Try this menu when your youngsters are having supper guests. You may wish to use less chili powder than the recipe specifies, but do taste the chili before you ladle it into serving bowls to make certain it is "hot" enough. If it isn't, stir in a little more of the lively powder. Serve the main dish with cooling fruit. Our Fruit Salad/ Dessert fills the bill. The salad dressing is the traditional kind country women like to cook for fruit salads and keep in the refrigerator. It adds a special-occasion taste.

TIMETABLE

Do-Ahead: Make the salad dressing a day ahead and chill, but fold the whipped cream into it at serving time.

On Guest Day: You can get the supper in an hour. While the chili simmers, make the salad and fix the iced tea.

SERVING SUGGESTIONS

Serve the chili in bowls, the salad/dessert on lettuce-lined individual salad plates, or pass it in a lettuce-lined bowl. Add sprigs of fresh mint to tall glasses of iced tea; accompany them with lemon slices or wedges.

CHILI CON CARNE

Double this recipe to serve a crowd of twelve; triple or quadruple for a bigger crowd—you'll have good results

1 lb. ground beef
¾ to 1 c. chopped onions
1 (1 lb. 13 oz.) can tomatoes
1 (1 lb.) can hominy
1 (15½ oz.) can red, pinto or
  kidney beans

1 tsp. salt
2 tblsp. chili powder
¼ tsp. ground cumin seeds
  (optional)

Cook and stir beef and onions until beef is lightly browned and onions are almost tender. Pour off fat. Add remaining ingredients and simmer, covered, about 30 minutes. Check seasonings, especially salt. Serve piping hot. (If chili is not as thick as you like it, simmer, uncovered, an additional 15 minutes.) Makes 6 servings.

FRUIT SALAD/DESSERT

Combine shortly before serving to prevent discoloration of fruits

4 unpeeled red apples, diced	½ c. heavy cream, whipped
¼ c. lemon juice	6 tblsp. Fruit Salad Dressing
1 (14¼ oz.) can sliced pineapple, diced	Lettuce
	⅓ c. chopped walnuts
4 bananas, sliced	

Toss diced apples with lemon juice; let stand while preparing other fruits.

Drain apples and combine with pineapple and bananas. Fold whipped cream into Fruit Salad Dressing; fold into fruits. Serve on lettuce and sprinkle with nuts. Makes 6 servings.

Fruit Salad Dressing: Mix ⅓ c. orange juice, ⅓ c. pineapple juice and 2 tblsp. lemon juice. Add 2 eggs, beaten slightly, then add ½ c. sugar and ¼ tsp. salt. Cook in top of double boiler 3 to 5 minutes, until dressing thickens. Cool; cover and refrigerate. Use as directed in Fruit Salad/Dessert recipe, folding in whipped cream before serving. Store covered in refrigerator and use as needed, adding whipped cream as desired. Makes about 2½ c. salad dressing with 1 c. heavy cream, whipped, folded in.

MINUTE STEAK BARBECUE

Grilled Minute Steak Rolls*
Hominy/Bean Barbecue*   Fruit-Jar Tomato Relish*
Buttered French Bread
Watermelon Wedges
Hot Coffee

While this barbecue menu is on the new side, it scores success with guests. The foods are familiar favorites handled in an unusual way.

Take the scored cube or minute beef steaks for example: The

trick is to wrap the beef around sticks of cold, hard butter and grill quickly over coals. The vegetable relish reminds you in flavor of the floating vegetable salads in old-time country kitchens. They consisted of vegetables, usually tomatoes, cucumbers and onions, in a sweet-sour vinegar sauce. For this meal you make the salad in a glass fruit jar.

The hearty casserole, which bakes without attention, almost always brings ovations. Among the ingredients is a pioneer special, hominy. And what could be better to wind up the meal on a summer evening than cold watermelon? Watermelon with bowls of buttered, salted, warm popped corn—a great taste combination.

TIMETABLE

Do-Ahead: Make the vegetable relish a day ahead and chill.

On Guest Day: In the morning combine foods in casserole ready to bake; cover and refrigerate. Slice the French bread at your convenience, butter, reassemble loaf and wrap in heavy foil. Wrap cold minute steaks around butter as recipe directs and chill until about 15 minutes before suppertime, when the coals should be ready for grilling the steaks over them. During the last 10 to 12 minutes before mealtime, put the bread in its foil wrap alongside the casserole to heat.

SERVING SUGGESTIONS

If you want to show off the striped relish, serve it in the glass jar picnic style. It will intrigue your guests. If you have an electric corn popper, ask the children to pop a big bowl of corn, add salt and melted butter and deliver it warm to the picnic table to serve with the melon.

GRILLED MINUTE STEAK ROLLS

These steaks cost less than those usually grilled but they taste superb

8 minute steaks (cube beef)	Pepper
½ tsp. marjoram leaves, crushed	5 tblsp. cold, hard butter (about)
Garlic salt	

Sprinkle steaks with marjoram, garlic salt and pepper. Cut butter in 8 sticks of equal size. Place 1 stick on each steak and roll, turning ends to completely cover butter. Skewer to keep closed.

Broil over medium coals, turning often, until steak is browned on the outside, but rare inside, about 10 to 12 minutes. Makes 8 servings.

HOMINY/BEAN BARBECUE

This substantial dish features four American originals: beans, hominy, tomatoes, chili peppers—they all come from cans

6 slices bacon, chopped	¼ c. chopped canned green chili
1 c. chopped onion	peppers
2 (20 oz.) cans yellow hominy, drained	2 tblsp. cider vinegar
2 (15½ oz.) cans kidney beans, drained	2 tsp. Worcestershire sauce
	2 tsp. prepared mustard
1 (15 oz.) can tomato sauce	1 tsp. salt

Cook bacon in skillet until crisp. Remove and set aside. Pour off all but 2 tblsp. drippings.

Add onion to skillet and cook until tender, but do not brown. Combine onion and bacon with remaining ingredients. Pour into a greased 2-qt. casserole; cover and bake in moderate oven (350°) 1½ hours. Makes 8 servings.

FRUIT-JAR TOMATO RELISH

Seeing and tasting is believing how pretty and good this relish is

2 tomatoes, peeled and chopped	2 tblsp. wine vinegar
1 cucumber, peeled and chopped	1 tblsp. snipped fresh parsley
1 green pepper, seeds removed and chopped	1 small clove garlic, minced
	½ tsp. salt
¼ c. chopped onion	Dash of pepper
¼ c. olive or salad oil	

In a 1-qt. glass jar, alternate layers of tomatoes, cucumber, green pepper and onion to make stripes when viewed from the side.

Combine remaining ingredients and pour over vegetables; cover and chill overnight. Turn jar upside down during part of the chilling to marinate vegetables evenly. Makes 1 quart.

COOK-IN, EAT-OUT SUPPER

Green Soup*   Crackers
Lasagne Roll-ups*
Garlic Green Beans   Fiesta Salad Bowl
Warm French Bread
Strawberry-Almond Sundaes

Cook indoors and eat under the maple tree in the yard. Or drive the family, guests and supper to a favorite picnic spot on the farm. How about the pond so the children, after eating, can fish while the adults visit?

This menu is for a meal you can serve indoors or out, whichever you think your guests will enjoy more. No doubt the weather will dictate where to dine, saving you from making a decision. The supper is better adapted to serving near the house so you can return to the kitchen to get the dessert.

But you can easily alter the menu for the situation. Eliminate the soup, change the dessert to fresh fruit—such as apples, pears, grapes or whatever is available—and add a jar of homemade cookies, a vacuum container of iced tea or hot coffee and bottles of ice cold milk. No one will wish for more.

TIMETABLE

Do-Ahead: You can, if you like, combine the casserole ingredients a day ahead and refrigerate.

On Guest Day: Wash the salad greens. Be sure to include some young, tender spinach leaves with the lettuce. Drain well and chill in plastic bags. Cut a 1-lb. long loaf of French bread in 1″ slices, butter, reassemble, wrap in heavy-duty aluminum foil. About 45 minutes before serving time, put the lasagne in oven to bake. Heat the foil-wrapped bread alongside the last 20 minutes. Make the soup. Toss the greens in a big bowl with Italian salad dressing and, if eating indoors, serve in individual bowls. Garnish tops of salads. If toting salad outdoors, place garnishes on top of big bowl of salad.

Cook 2 (10 oz.) pkgs. frozen green beans by package directions, drain and dress with garlic butter. To make it, melt ¼ c. butter and add 1 clove garlic, crushed. Heat, but do not brown garlic. Discard garlic and pour butter over beans. Make the dessert at serving time. Prepare the Strawberry-Almond Sundaes at the last minute. Drizzle bottled strawberry-flavored syrup over vanilla ice cream in sherbet glasses and top each serving with a few toasted slivered almonds.

SERVING SUGGESTIONS

If serving soup in the yard, carry it out in a tureen or bowl and ladle into cups or bowls. Set up a portable table for a buffet and let everyone help himself. Use slivers of pickled beets, bits of green pepper, shredded carrots, green or ripe olives and peeled tomato quarters, lightly salted on both sides, for the salad garnish. Serve the sundaes in dessert bowls.

GREEN SOUP

Easy to fix, refreshing and pretty. Garnish with chopped chives

2 c. frozen peas, thawed	2 tsp. onion juice
2 (14 oz.) cans chicken broth	Dash of curry powder (optional)

Put peas through a sieve or food mill, or whirl in blender. Add broth and heat to simmering point. Add onion juice and curry powder. Check for salt. Makes 8 servings.

LASAGNE ROLL-UPS

A delicious new way to fix and serve lasagne—freezes well too!

Meat Sauce:
- 1½ lbs. ground beef
- ⅓ c. salad oil
- ⅓ c. finely chopped onion
- 1½ cloves garlic, minced
- 2 tsp. salt
- ¼ tsp. pepper
- 2 whole cloves
- ½ bay leaf
- 3 (1 lb. 1½ oz.) cans plum tomatoes, sieved
- 2 (6 oz.) cans tomato paste
- 1¼ c. water
- 1 tsp. orégano leaves, crushed
- ¼ tsp. monosodium glutamate
- 2 tsp. sugar

Filling:
- 2 lbs. ricotta cheese
- ½ tsp. salt
- ⅛ tsp. pepper
- ½ tsp. ground nutmeg
- ¼ lb. mozzarella cheese, shredded
- 4 tblsp. grated Parmesan or Romano cheese
- 1 tblsp. chopped fresh parsley
- 1 (1 lb.) pkg. lasagne noodles

Partially brown ground beef in oil. Add onion, garlic, salt, pepper, cloves and bay leaf. Continue to brown over medium heat for 10 minutes or until well browned.

Stir in tomatoes, tomato paste, water, orégano, monosodium glutamate and sugar. Let come to a boil, then simmer gently, loosely covered, for about 1 hour; stir occasionally.

In the meantime, whip ricotta cheese. Add salt, pepper, nutmeg, mozzarella cheese, grated cheese and parsley. Set aside.

Cook lasagne noodles according to package directions. Rinse with cold water; drain well. Lay noodles on clean dish towels.

On each noodle, spread ¼ c. filling. Fold over 1″ and continue to fold, making a slightly flat roll.

Place 1 c. meat sauce in each of 2 (2-qt.) rectangular baking dishes. Place roll-ups, seam side down, in baking dishes. Add ⅓ c. hot water to each dish and enough meat sauce to almost cover roll-ups. Reserve rest of sauce.

Bake in moderate oven (350°) 45 minutes, or until sauce bubbles in center of dish.

Serve with rest of sauce and grated cheese. Makes 16 party rolls (8 main dish servings, or 16, if served as meat accompaniment).

OUTDOOR SUPPER

Cornucopias*   Pineapple Sparkler   Popcorn Bowl
Tamale Pie Santa Fe*   Fresh Cucumber Relish*
Quartered Tomatoes   Warm Vienna Bread
Sundae Ice Cream Cones

When the weather is right—neither too hot nor too cold—call friends and invite them to supper. Serve the meal on the porch or patio, or set up card tables and chairs on the lawn. This easy meal requires no make-ahead preparations—good for spur-of-the-moment entertaining.

Provide an appetizer course to put everyone in a social mood. For the Pineapple Sparkler, reconstitute frozen pineapple juice concentrate with chilled ginger ale instead of water. Or substitute frozen orange juice concentrate for the pineapple. Fix the cornucopias with slices of cold meat; pop some corn and sprinkle with seasoned salt.

Ice cream cones fit the occasion. Some guests at outdoor meals prefer mobile desserts—finger food they can eat while moving around to look at the garden or flowers in bloom.

TIMETABLE

On Guest Day: Make the cucumber relish early in the day and chill. Cut the loaf of bread in ½" slices, spread with butter, reassemble loaf and wrap in heavy-duty aluminum foil. Put the tamale pie in the oven about 30 minutes before serving time; then add the bread alongside to heat the last 15 or 20 minutes. Keep warm until served. While you fix the cornucopias, encourage your husband or children to pop the corn, add melted butter and sprinkle with seasoned salt. The dessert can be made up quickly just before serving.

SERVING SUGGESTIONS

Depend on the family or willing friends to help carry the platter of cornucopias and crackers, pitcher of Pineapple Sparkler and the big bowl of popcorn outdoors to the assembled guests. Set up the main-course buffet in the house and let everyone carry his food outdoors. Or if you prefer, arrange the buffet on the porch or patio, or in the yard.

When it's dessert time, excuse yourself and invite guests to follow and pick up their dessert. Fill ice cream cones with chocolate ice cream, dip the top of the ice cream in fudge sauce. (Vanilla ice cream and butterscotch sauce are also a good combo.) If desired, sprinkle frosted ice cream tops with chopped nuts. Repeat until everyone is served. Set out a pot of coffee so that guests can fill their own cups or mugs for a finish.

Cornucopias: Cut thin bologna or salami slices in halves; roll each semicircle around a tiny stuffed olive or pickled onion to make a cornucopia. Fasten with a toothpick and fill with a dab of softened cream cheese.

TAMALE PIE SANTA FE

Inviting crust on top of this tasty meat pie is yellow and crisp

1½ lbs. ground beef	2 tsp. salt
1½ tsp. salt	½ tsp. chili powder
½ tsp. orégano leaves	2 tblsp. butter or regular
½ tsp. pepper	margarine
⅔ c. finely chopped onion	1 c. yellow cornmeal
1 (1 lb.) can tomatoes	½ c. shredded process American
1 (12 oz.) can Mexicorn, drained	cheese
2 c. water	

In a 10" skillet brown beef lightly; drain off excess fat. Add 1½ tsp. salt, orégano, pepper, onion and tomatoes. Stir to mix; bring to a boil. Simmer 10 minutes or until excess liquid evaporates and mixture thickens. Stir in corn; cook just to heat. Pour into greased 2½-qt. casserole.

For topping, mix water, 2 tsp. salt, chili powder, butter and cornmeal in saucepan. Cook until mixture thickens, stirring frequently. With spoon and rubber spatula, gently drop spoonfuls on top of hot mixture in casserole. Spread thinly over the top.

Bake, uncovered, in moderate oven (375°) 30 minutes. Sprinkle cheese over top and bake 10 to 15 minutes longer, or until cheese melts. Makes 8 servings.

FRESH CUCUMBER RELISH

Garnish with small chilled tomato quarters or whole cherry tomatoes for bright color. The cooling cucumber-tomato flavors always please

3 medium cucumbers	1 tsp. dill seeds
¼ c. minced onion	1½ tsp. salt
¼ c. cider vinegar	½ tsp. pepper

Peel cucumbers and chop fine. Let stand a few minutes; drain. Add remaining ingredients; chill several hours so flavors will blend. Makes about 2 cups.

BARBECUE SUPPER

Barbecued Turkey Wings*
Savory Baked Beans   Scalloped Corn
Tossed Green Salad
Homemade French Bread*
Fresh Lemon Ice Cream*
Coconut Cookies

This menu for a supper with cooked turkey, brushed with barbecue sauce and grilled over coals until hot and crusty, will help keep down food costs. At the same time it will enable you to serve a superior meal.

Using turkey wings (many markets now carry turkey parts) stretches food dollars. You can barbecue turkey thighs instead of wings if you prefer them.

To round out the meal, toss a big green salad, bake long loaves of French bread, add your own seasonings to canned baked beans and fix a casserole of Scalloped Corn (we feature it in the menu "A Dinner to Tote"—see Index for recipe). And for dessert freeze a gallon of Fresh Lemon Ice Cream and offer a choice of cold milk or coffee for the beverage. Have plenty of all foods and your guests will rate you a genius with food. Not a thought of economy will cross their minds.

TIMETABLE

Do-Ahead: Most of the food preparation takes place a day ahead. That's the time to cook the turkey wings or thighs in salted water until tender, drain and chill. Make the barbecue sauce; refrigerate. Also wash, drain and store the lettuce in plastic bags; chill. Bake the bread a day or several days ahead and freeze.

On Guest Day: About 4 hours before suppertime, start freezing the ice cream and let it ripen in the freezer. At least 30 minutes before time to serve supper, have the coals ready for grilling the turkey and heat casseroles of corn and baked beans in a moderate oven (350°). Heat the foil-wrapped bread in oven 25 to 30 minutes if frozen. Meanwhile, get the beverages ready and toss the salad.

BARBECUED TURKEY WINGS

Different and delicious way to cook turkey—serve it sizzling hot

10 turkey wings (or 5 turkey thighs)	½ tsp. chili powder
	2 tblsp. instant minced onion
¾ c. water	2 tblsp. vinegar
¾ c. ketchup	1 tblsp. Worcestershire sauce
1 tsp. salt	

Separate wing pieces at joints and discard wing tips. Cook turkey wings in small amount of boiling salted water 1 to 1½ hours, or until tender. Or cook in pressure cooker according to manufacturer's directions. Drain cooked turkey and chill.

Combine water, ketchup, salt, chili powder, onion, vinegar and Worcestershire sauce in small saucepan; cover and simmer about 45 minutes. Store in covered jar in refrigerator to use as needed.

Place turkey pieces over hot coals and broil 15 minutes; turn. Brush with barbecue sauce and continue cooking 15 minutes more, basting frequently, or until turkey is hot and crusty. Makes about 5 servings.

N O T E : This recipe can be doubled for more servings.

HOMEMADE FRENCH BREAD

Everyone's favorite—it's crusty and crunchy with a shiny glaze

2 pkgs. active dry yeast	1 tblsp. salt
½ c. warm water (110 to 115°)	⅓ c. salad oil
2 c. hot water	6 c. flour, stirred before measuring
3 tblsp. sugar	1 egg white, slightly beaten

Dissolve yeast in warm water.

Combine 2 c. hot water, sugar, salt, oil and 3 c. flour; stir well. Stir in yeast. Add remaining flour, stirring well with a heavy spoon. Leave spoon in batter and allow dough to rest 10 minutes. Stir down batter, let dough rest another 10 minutes. Repeat this process 3 more times (making 5 times in all).

Turn dough onto lightly floured board. Knead only enough to coat dough with flour so it can be handled, then divide it into two equal parts. Roll each part into a 12×9″ rectangle; roll up like a jelly roll, starting on the long side. Arrange lengthwise on greased baking sheet, seam side down, allowing room for both loaves. Let rise in warm place 30 minutes.

With a very sharp knife cut 3 diagonal gashes in the top of each loaf; brush with egg white. Bake in hot oven (400°) about 30 minutes, or until crusty brown. (For added crustiness, put a pan of hot water on floor of oven during baking.) Makes 2 loaves.

FRESH LEMON ICE CREAM

Light, refreshing dessert—perfect to serve on a hot summer night

2 qts. milk	2 tsp. lemon extract
1 c. heavy cream	4 c. sugar
¾ c. lemon juice (3 large)	

Combine all ingredients in a 1-gal. ice cream freezer can, filling about three fourths full. Adjust dasher and cover. Pack crushed ice and rock salt around can, using 6 parts ice to 1 part salt.

Turn dasher slowly until the ice melts enough to make a brine. Add more ice and salt, mixed in the proper proportion, to maintain the ice level. Turn the handle fast and steadily until it turns hard. Then remove ice until the level is below the lid of can; take off lid and remove the dasher.

Plug the hole in lid and cover can with several thicknesses of waxed paper or foil to make a tight fit for the lid. Pack more ice-salt mixture, using 4 parts ice to 1 part salt, around can and filling the freezer. Cover with a blanket, canvas or other heavy cloth, or with newspaper. Let the ice cream ripen 4 hours before serving. Or put it in the home freezer for an hour. Makes 1 gallon.

NOTE: If you use an electric ice cream freezer, follow the manufacturer's directions.

MAIN-DISH QUICHE SUPPER

Hot Tomato Bouillon   Crackers
Quiche*
Tossed Green Salad
Fruit Compote
Candy Mints

Quiche is a French gourmet dish that will delight a group of women as the main dish at a luncheon—or the family plus guests at supper. We give you a basic recipe with three delicious substantial fillings. Make all three and cut small wedges—guests enjoy tasting all three and comparing preferences. The pastry and ingredients can all be ready and combined with cream and eggs just before putting in the oven.

TIMETABLE

Do-Ahead: You can make the pastry a day before you entertain. Fit it into the pan, cover with plastic wrap and refrigerate. (Or if you wish, make it a week or more ahead and keep, unbaked, in freezer.) Wash and drain salad greens and chill in a plastic bag.

On Guest Day: About an hour before supper, make filling, pour into pastry-lined pan and bake. You can get the ham and cheese cut up or spinach cooked and ready earlier in the day. Make the fruit compote and chill. Use your favorite combinations of fruits. Grapefruit sections, sliced bananas and frozen peaches are delicious—especially when topped with frozen red raspberries. Heat the bouillon. A good way to make it is to combine 1 (1 lb.) can tomato juice and a can of condensed beef broth. Point up flavors with a dash of celery salt. Toss the salad just before the Quiche is ready to serve.

SERVING SUGGESTIONS

If you do not use a colorful fruit such as raspberries in the compote, decorate each serving with a maraschino cherry and pour on a little of the cherry juice. Serve very cold in dessert glasses.

QUICHE

The crust is rich with butter, filling is rich with cream

1½ c. sifted flour	Filling
¼ tsp. salt	3 eggs
½ c. butter	1 c. heavy cream
1 egg, slightly beaten	

Sift together flour and salt. Cut in butter with pastry blender until mixture resembles coarse cornmeal. Add the slightly beaten egg and toss with a fork to mix. Gather dough into a ball and chill.

Roll dough out on a well-floured board. Fit into 10" pie pan, or a 10" fluted tart pan. Measure depth of pan and trim pastry 1" wider. Fold dough over and press it firmly against the pan sides. Arrange the filling ingredients (directions follow) in the crust.

To make custard, beat the 3 eggs; beat in cream. (See Fillings for seasonings.) Pour over filling in crust.

Bake in hot oven (425°) 10 minutes; reduce heat to slow (325°) and continue baking about 30 minutes, or until custard is set. To test for doneness, insert a knife in center of pie. If it comes out almost clean, remove pie from oven. It will set completely in a few minutes. Cut in wedges and serve warm. Makes 6 to 8 servings.

Fillings

Ham/Cheese Filling: Sprinkle ¼ lb. shredded Cheddar cheese and ¾ c. finely diced cooked ham in the crust. Blend 1 tsp. Worcestershire sauce, ¼ tsp. salt, ¼ tsp. dry mustard and ⅛ tsp. pepper into the custard. Pour over the cheese-ham mixture. If you like, sprinkle 1 tsp. caraway seeds over the pie before baking.

Chicken/Cheese Filling: Sprinkle ¼ c. grated Parmesan cheese in the crust. Top with 1 c. finely diced cooked chicken and 2 small green onions with tops, finely chopped. Add ¼ tsp. salt, ⅛ tsp. dry mustard and ⅛ tsp. pepper to the custard and pour it over the chicken-onion mixture. Sprinkle top of pie with ¼ c. sliced almonds and ¼ c. grated Parmesan cheese and bake.

Cheese/Spinach Filling: Cook 1 (10 oz.) pkg. frozen chopped spinach (or 1 c. finely chopped fresh spinach leaves) until tender. Drain and squeeze dry. Cook 4 small green onions with tops, thinly sliced, in 1 tblsp. butter until soft. Remove from heat and combine with the spinach and ¼ c. finely chopped (or snipped with scissors) parsley. Blend ½ tsp. salt, ½ tsp. rubbed sage and ⅛ tsp. pepper into the custard and stir into it the spinach mixture. Pour into the crust. Sprinkle top of pie with ¼ c. grated Parmesan cheese and bake.

COUNTRY KITCHEN SUPPER

Chilled Cocktail Vegetable Juice   Baked Cheese Fondue*
Apple/Grape Salad*   Brownies à la Mode

Most good hostesses treasure at least a few recipes for old-fashioned dishes too taste-rewarding to forget. They appreciate the enthusiasm their guests almost always show over old-time favorites that remind them of what their mothers used to make. Baked Cheese Fondue, an American original, is an excellent example. Created in country kitchens when women considered it their duty to salvage scraps of bread no longer fresh, and cheese somewhat hardened, it bears little resemblance to European-type fondues which skip the oven and cook in pots—also much in vogue in America now.

A California woman who entertains often says that Baked Cheese Fondue, which she sometimes calls cheese pudding, is a main dish her friends enjoy. You may prefer to think of it as a substantial, three-decker sandwich. We share her recipe with you.

Why not save the dessert to serve at the end of the evening just before guests leave? It gives them a well-fed feeling as they step out into the night to return home—and it's a country custom.

TIMETABLE

Do-Ahead: Get the main dish ready to bake a day ahead and refrigerate. Bake the brownies.

On Guest Day: Put the canned vegetable juice in refrigerator to chill; it is expertly seasoned and is flavorful served as it comes from the can. Put the fondue in the oven an hour before you wish to serve supper. Make and chill the salad, using tart, red apples and whatever grapes are available. If they are not seedless, cut them in halves and remove seeds.

SERVING SUGGESTIONS

This is a good supper to serve buffet style, especially if you bake the fondue in a glass baking dish. Arrange salad in lettuce-lined bowl and garnish the top with nuts and wedges of unpeeled red apples sprinkled with lemon juice to prevent discoloration. Or serve on the supper plates. Cut the brownies in somewhat larger pieces than usual, or bake them in a pie pan and cut in pie-shaped pieces. Top with vanilla or coffee ice cream at serving time.

BAKED CHEESE FONDUE

It's as American as the Fourth of July—and you can have it all ready in advance, except for the baking

18 slices dry bread	8 eggs
Butter or regular margarine	5 c. milk
Salt	1½ tsp. dry mustard
Pepper	2 tsp. Worcestershire sauce
2 lbs. process sharp cheese, shredded	

Butter bread slices. Arrange 6 slices, buttered side up, in greased 13×9×2″ ovenproof glass dish. Sprinkle lightly with salt and pepper and one third of cheese. Press down and add another layer of buttered bread and cheese, and press down; repeat. (You will have three layers and the pan will be full.)

Beat eggs; add milk, dry mustard and Worcestershire sauce. Pour over the bread-cheese layers in pan. Cover with foil and let stand in refrigerator at least 8 hours, or overnight.

Baked uncovered in moderate oven (350°) about 1 hour, or until a knife inserted in center comes out clean. Serve at once. Makes 8 or 9 servings.

APPLE/GRAPE SALAD

Apples, grapes and black walnuts unite in this great farm salad

6 tart unpeeled red apples, diced
2 tblsp. lemon juice
1½ c. diced celery
1½ c. halved and seeded Tokay or
   Emperor grapes

1 c. miniature marshmallows
¾ c. salad dressing
½ c. broken black walnuts or
   hickory nuts
Lettuce

Sprinkle diced apples with lemon juice. Combine with celery, grapes, marshmallows and salad dressing. Cover and chill. At serving time add the nuts. Serve on lettuce. Makes 8 servings.

NOTE: You can use pecans, toasted almonds or walnuts if black walnuts or hickory nuts are not available. Some country salad makers use ½ c. salad dressing with ¼ c. heavy cream, whipped, folded into the salad.

FONDUE SUPPER

Cheese Fondue*
French Bread   Rye Bread
Lettuce Salad Cups*
Fresh Fruit
Butterscotch Wafers*
Coffee

Nothing surpasses gathering with several favorite friends around a pot of cheese fondue, to add warmth and brightness to a freezing-cold winter evening. And this supper featuring hearty food is a meal a busy woman, even though she may work away from home, can prepare quickly after she returns late afternoon. It is important, however, to do some of the food preparation ahead. Our timetable is a guide.

Many treasured recipes for cheese fondue, patterned after the Swiss classic, circulate around the countryside, but most of them— like the one we give you—are Americanized. You can follow this menu even if you wish to use your own favorite fondue recipe. It may be one from the manufacturer's leaflet that came with your fondue pot.

This menu features some pleasing variations from those for most fondue suppers. Long-loaf rye, as well as French bread, awaits dunking, and fresh fruit, such as apples, pears and/or grapes contribute flavors that complement cheese. You can omit the wafers, which are really refrigerator cookies, but they contribute a typical country-style, homemade, sweet addition almost everyone enjoys. Perhaps your young cook can help by baking the cookies for you. If you do serve them, you'll notice that practically everyone happily eats a crunchy wafer or two as he sips the last cup of coffee.

TIMETABLE

Do-Ahead: Prepare rolls of cookie dough a couple of days ahead, wrap tightly in waxed paper or plastic wrap and refrigerate. Or freeze the rolls several days or weeks ahead. If you bake the wafers the evening before guest day, cool them and store in an airtight container. Fresh-from-the-oven cookies, of course, always score a hit, but day-old ones also taste good.

Wash and drain the salad greens and chill in plastic bags. Make the salad dressing and store, tightly covered, in refrigerator.

On Guest Day: Cut bread in bite-size pieces with crust on one side of each if possible; place in baskets. Cover with napkins to prevent drying. If you are hurried, assign this chore to your husband, an older child or to a guest. Wash and drain chilled fruits and divide grapes into small clusters. Arrange on a tray. Slice and bake as many cookies as you think you will need (you may have baked them the previous evening). Make the fondue after guests arrive and toss the salad at the last minute.

SERVING SUGGESTIONS

Center fondue pot on table and place individual salads at each plate. Set baskets or bowls of bread within easy reach of everyone. Bring the tray of fruit and plate of wafers to the table when you pour the second cup of coffee.

CHEESE FONDUE

This fondue is made with one kind of cheese—aged natural Swiss

French bread (long loaf)	1 clove garlic
Rye bread (long loaf)	1¼ c. dry white wine
1 lb. natural Swiss cheese,	1 tblsp. lemon juice
shredded (about 4 c.)	Dash of pepper
1½ tsp. cornstarch	

Cut bread in bite-size pieces with crust on one side.

Combine cheese and cornstarch and mix.

Rub inside of metal fondue cooker or heavy skillet with cut garlic clove. Pour in wine and lemon juice. Heat on low to medium heat until air bubbles rise and cover surface of wine-lemon juice mixture. Do not let come to a boil.

Add about ½ c. cheese at a time, stirring vigorously all the time with a wooden spoon. Keep on low to medium heat; do not let mixture boil. When cheese melts, add another ½ c. cheese, stirring constantly. Be sure to let each addition of cheese melt before adding another. Repeat until all the cheese is added and melted. Stir in pepper. Place fondue on heating unit if using electric fondue pot in case the fondue was not made on it. Keep warm over low heat. If making fondue in skillet, pour into the fondue pot's ceramic cooker and set over burner. Keep over low heat.

Spear bread pieces through the crust side with fondue fork and swirl in fondue. The swirling is important because it keeps the cheese mixture moving so it will not thicken and stick to bottom of cooker. Transfer dipped bread to dinner fork and eat. Makes 4 to 6 servings.

LETTUCE SALAD CUPS

Salad adds color, crispness and piquant flavor to the supper

1 large head iceberg lettuce	⅛ tsp. pepper
⅓ c. salad oil	⅛ tsp. dry mustard
2 tblsp. wine vinegar	2 c. bite-size spinach
1 tsp. paprika	12 cherry tomatoes
½ tsp. seasoned salt	

Remove outer leaves of lettuce to use for lettuce cups. Arrange cups in individual salad bowls. Shred remaining lettuce.

In a large salad bowl make the salad dressing by beating together with fork or wire whisk, salad oil, vinegar, paprika, seasoned salt, pepper and dry mustard. Add lettuce and spinach and toss well.

Cut tomatoes in halves and fold gently into salad. Makes 6 to 8 servings.

BUTTERSCOTCH WAFERS

Keep rolls of dough in freezer and you'll be ready to fast-bake wafers

1 c. softened butter or regular margarine	3 c. sifted flour
1 c. brown sugar, firmly packed	1 tsp. salt
2 eggs	½ c. finely chopped nuts (optional)
1½ tsp. vanilla	

Thoroughly mix together butter, brown sugar, eggs and vanilla. Stir in flour, salt and nuts. Divide dough in thirds. With hands, firmly shape each portion in a roll 1½″ in diameter. The rolls will be about 7″ long. Wrap each roll tightly in waxed paper, lightweight aluminum foil or plastic wrap. Twist ends to make seal. Chill in refrigerator until firm, about 4 hours, or no longer than 2 or 3 days before baking. Or overwrap rolls, if covered with waxed paper, in aluminum foil and freeze. (Frozen dough may be kept up to 6 months before baking.)

To bake, cut roll in slices ¼″ thick. (For crisper wafers, slice them ⅛″ thick.) Be sure slices are the same thickness to insure even baking. Place about 1″ apart on ungreased baking sheet; bake in hot oven (400°) 8 to 10 minutes, until light brown. Remove from baking sheet immediately and spread on wire racks to cool. One roll makes about 28 cookies.

CHAPTER 4

Entertaining at Dinner

. . . *MIDDAY OR EVENING MEALS*

Much of country cooking's fame was earned around the dinner table. "Dinnertime" in the country usually has been synonymous with noon, when it has been customary to serve the day's heartiest meal.

Regardless of the time of day you serve the dinner menus in this chapter to guests, you will find the food lives up to the long-established reputation for superior flavor and eye appeal. Definitely on the hearty side with a wide variety of foods in every menu, these dinners are not difficult if you plan ahead. Our timetables incorporate some make-ahead dishes to relieve the hostess of last-minute pressures.

Serving of predinner appetizers in the living room also pleasantly occupies the host and guests while the hostess returns to the kitchen to put the finishing touches on the meal. Greater use of help-yourself foods, buffet style of service, and other techniques used by country women for easy company dinners are included.

The menus will make you hungry for a good country dinner. Notice that the recipes feature some of the old-time country favorites with up-to-date touches. This is true in the many chicken specials—Sesame Chicken, Summer Chicken with Peas and New Potatoes, Royal Chicken Pie, Southern Stuffed Chicken Breasts and others.

Men's liking for meat and potatoes is considered in country dinners. You'll find directions for cooking to perfection the king of the platter, a standing rib beef roast. And you will get a new concept of how versatile, intriguing and delicious pot roasts can taste. For instance, you can broil them in the oven or grill them over coals. The secret is the marinade in which the beef chills 24 to 48 hours. Ground beef and meat balls show up in delicious variety. Pork Roast Danish Style is elegant. Pork/Sauerkraut Skillet wins praise as do Party Pork Rolls.

It seems unfair to single out a few dishes for honorable mention from a chapter overflowing with them. Special salads include FARM

JOURNAL's famed beauty, Three-Row Garden Salad, and a brand new Green Pea Salad. And farm women are experts with vegetables and at serving potatoes in many ways—many of these recipes came from their kitchens.

Homemade breads are so good . . . Overnight Sourdough Bread, for instance. Desserts include FARM JOURNAL's lovely Strawberry Satin Pie, Orange Meringue Pie, spicy Pumpkin Cake and Orange/ Peanut Cake.

Don't miss the Wild Duck Dinner, Summer Fish Dinner and Iowa Corn Dinner. Sweet corn, of course, rushed from the patch, cooked and served at once with plenty of butter.

Recipes for all dishes starred (*) are in this cookbook.

IMPORTANT CHICKEN DINNER

Chilled Tomato Juice
Sauerkraut Balls*   Crackers
Southern Stuffed Chicken Breasts*
Buffet Cheese Potatoes*
Baby Beet Salad*
Lemon Sherbet
Coconut Pound Cake*

Some occasions challenge the country hostess to serve an elegant chicken dinner. The guest of honor often is the visiting speaker at a community meeting or a returned native who achieved success in faraway places. An exceptional chicken dish frequently is the center of interest in the meal.

In this menu the main dish consists of stuffed chicken breasts pan-fried in butter until golden. The meal starts in the living room with chilled tomato juice (home-canned if available), crisp crackers and intriguing appetizer balls tangy and flavorful with sauerkraut and corned beef.

The dinner continues with potatoes with cheese sauce, a salad of little beets from the garden (or canned midget beets) touched up with a yellow and white country garnish of chopped hard-cooked eggs. By dessert time appetites no longer are ravenous, but a southern-accented meal ending, lemon sherbet with small wedges of homemade coconut pound cake, is just right.

TIMETABLE

Do-Ahead: Bake cake a day, or several days ahead and freeze. Cook beets for salad, or drain canned beets, pour on salad dressing, cover and chill. Prepare potatoes, place in loaf pan, cover and refrigerate; chill sauce separately. Get chicken ready for browning, cover and chill. Make mixture for appetizer balls, shape, roll in crumbs and refrigerate.

On Guest Day: Whenever convenient, set cake on kitchen counter to thaw in its wrap. Unmold potatoes ready for baking; refrigerate. Chop eggs for salad, cover and chill. Put potatoes in oven 1 hour before dinner. Cook and brown chicken the last half hour before mealtime. When guests arrive, remove potatoes from oven and broil appetizer balls just long enough to brown lightly. Carry them and tomato juice to the living room, but before you leave kitchen, put potatoes and chicken, uncovered, in very slow oven (275°) with door open to keep warm. When you return to the kitchen to put the final touches on the food for the main course, enlist a friend or relative to help you. Ask her to assemble the salad. Heat the cheese sauce.

SERVING SUGGESTIONS

Serve the chicken, potatoes and salad buffet style. Put salad in lettuce-lined salad bowl, or if you prefer, spoon it into individual bowls or on individual plates and set in place on the dinner table. Serve hot cheese sauce in gravy boat or bowl. At dessert time, cut the cake at the table and pass it. Serve sherbet in stemmed dessert glasses.

SAUERKRAUT BALLS

Men always single out these appetizers as especially praiseworthy

¼ c. shortening
1 medium onion, minced
2 tblsp. minced parsley
¼ c. flour
1 tsp. dry mustard
½ c. milk

1 (12 oz.) can corned beef, finely
  chopped
1 (1 lb.) can sauerkraut, well
  drained (about 2 c.)
1 egg, well beaten
2 tblsp. cold water
¾ c. fine bread crumbs

Melt shortening in small skillet; add onion and parsley. Cook over low heat, stirring until lightly browned. Stir in flour, mixed with mustard. Gradually add milk, stirring to blend well. Cook until smooth and thick, stirring constantly.

Add corned beef and sauerkraut, blending well. Cool and chill several hours or overnight. Shape in 50 small balls.

Combine beaten egg with water and blend thoroughly. Roll sauerkraut balls in egg mixture, then in bread crumbs. (If made ahead, chill until serving time.) Place on cold broiler grid and broil to brown lightly on all sides, turning as necessary to brown entire surface. Makes about 50 appetizers.

SOUTHERN STUFFED CHICKEN BREASTS

Delicious adaptation of chicken Kiev omits the deep fat frying

4 large chicken breasts, boned and
   cut in halves lengthwise
Salt
½ c. softened butter
½ c. chopped onion
½ c. chopped parsley

Flour
1 egg, well beaten
1 tblsp. water
½ c. fine bread crumbs
¼ c. butter or regular margarine

Remove skin from chicken breasts; pound with wooden mallet or rolling pin to flatten to ¼″ thickness. Sprinkle with salt.

Cream ½ c. softened butter; add onion and parsley. Divide mixture into 8 even portions. Spread butter mixture at the end of each chicken breast. Roll as for jelly roll; tuck in sides of meat. Press to seal; fasten with toothpicks, or tie with string to secure.

Dust each chicken roll with flour; dip into egg beaten with the water, and roll in bread crumbs. Chill at least 1 hour.

Melt ¼ c. butter in a skillet; brown the chicken rolls on all sides. Cover and cook gently 12 minutes; uncover and cook 5 minutes longer, or until crisp, turning the rolls once. Remove toothpicks or string. Serve hot. Makes 6 to 8 servings.

BUFFET CHEESE POTATOES

You can make these in a ring mold but a loaf is easier to unmold

6 c. cubed cooked potatoes (6 or 7)
½ tsp. salt
¼ tsp. pepper
¼ c. butter or regular margarine
¼ c. flour
½ tsp. salt
⅛ tsp. pepper

½ tsp. dry mustard
2 c. milk
½ lb. sharp Cheddar cheese, shredded
2 tblsp. crushed round buttery crackers
½ c. grated Cheddar cheese
1 to 2 tblsp. milk

Combine potatoes, ½ tsp. salt and ¼ tsp. pepper in mixing bowl.

Melt butter in saucepan, blend in flour, ½ tsp. salt, ⅛ tsp. pepper and dry mustard. Add milk and cook over low heat until sauce is thickened. Stir in shredded cheese and continue cooking until cheese melts. Remove sauce from heat.

Mix just enough cheese sauce into potatoes to hold them together. Place in a well-greased 9×5×3″ loaf pan. Cover and refrigerate several hours or overnight.

Refrigerate remaining cheese sauce.

Remove potatoes from refrigerator, run knife carefully around edges of pan. Place ovenproof platter or baking sheet on top of loaf pan. Invert and let stand a few minutes. Tap gently to loosen potatoes. Remove loaf pan. Sprinkle potatoes with cracker crumbs and grated cheese. Bake in hot oven (400°) about 25 minutes, until potatoes are lightly browned and heated through.

Serve with remaining cheese sauce. To heat sauce, add 1 to 2 tblsp. milk to cold sauce and place over medium heat, stirring frequently. Makes 8 servings.

BABY BEET SALAD

Beets the size of ping-pong balls are ideal for this colorful salad

1 c. French dressing
2 drops Tabasco sauce
½ tsp. minced fresh thyme leaves, or ¼ tsp. dried thyme leaves

3 c. cooked baby beets, quartered
Lettuce
2 hard-cooked eggs, chopped

Mix French dressing, Tabasco and thyme in saucepan; simmer 5 minutes. Add beets, cover and refrigerate overnight. Drain.

Arrange beets on lettuce or other crisp greens. Sprinkle with chopped eggs. Makes 6 servings.

COCONUT POUND CAKE

A big cake that's a favorite of a charming Virginia hostess

1 c. butter	1 c. milk
2 c. sugar	1 (3½ oz.) can flaked coconut
5 eggs	(1⅓ c.)
3 c. sifted flour	1 tsp. lemon extract
¼ tsp. salt	½ tsp. vanilla

Using medium speed on mixer, cream together butter and sugar until light and fluffy. Add eggs, one at a time, beating well after each addition (this takes about 10 minutes).

Sift flour with salt; add alternately with milk to creamed mixture, beating after each addition. Add remaining ingredients. Pour into greased and floured 10″ tube pan.

Bake in slow oven (325°) 1 hour and 30 minutes, or until cake tests done. Cool 10 minutes, then remove from pan and complete cooling on rack. Makes 12 servings.

CHICKEN BARBECUE DINNER

Hawaiian Dip*   Sesame Seed Crackers
Rye Crackers   Chilled Fruit Juices
Barbecued Chicken Halves*   Rice Pilaf*
Buttered Asparagus   Fruit Salad
Homemade Vanilla Ice Cream*

The charm of entertaining along palm-fringed Hawaiian shores or island cattle ranches has been copied in country homes on the mainland in this flavorful dinner. Teamwork is the key to getting this meal ready; everyone in the family will feel he's an important part of the party. The menu divides readily into three parts.

The host assumes the responsibility for building the fire and cooking the chicken to perfection. The hostess takes on the cooking in the kitchen. How the children help depends largely on their age. An ideal assignment for them is to turn the ice cream freezer. The reward for them on the completion of this job is to sample the ice cream that clings to the dasher. A teen-age daughter or son will be expert at fixing the dip and fruit juice.

TIMETABLE

On Guest Day: Freeze the ice cream at least 4 hours before dinnertime so it will ripen. Make the barbecue sauce 2 or more hours before you want to use it. Allow a minimum of 1½ hours for getting the coals ready for cooking and grilling the chicken. During that time, fix the dip and chill it; arrange crackers on trays. Break cauliflower into flowerets; place in cold water ready to drain and serve. Combine equal parts of reconstituted frozen lemonade and pineapple juice concentrates (or pineapple and grapefruit concentrates). Cook the frozen asparagus and the rice during the last few minutes before serving.

SERVING SUGGESTIONS

Serve the food from a buffet table set up near the grill, or, if it is warm and the house is air-conditioned, serve and eat indoors. Pour the beverage, icy cold, from a pitcher. Set the bowl of dip on a tray and surround with the crackers. Place drained cauliflowerets in a bowl for dipping.

HAWAIIAN DIP

Ranch hostesses in our newest state excel in informal entertaining; try this Hawaiian-inspired dip and its interesting accompaniments

1 c. mayonnaise, chilled	2 tblsp. finely chopped candied
1 c. dairy sour cream	ginger
¼ c. finely minced onion	1 tblsp. soy sauce
¼ c. minced parsley	1 clove garlic, crushed
½ c. finely chopped canned water	Salt
chestnuts	

Combine mayonnaise and sour cream; add remaining ingredients and mix well. Cover and chill. Serve with sesame seed crackers, rye crackers and cauliflowerets for dunking. Makes about 3 cups.

BARBECUED CHICKEN HALVES

*Lemon barbecue sauce and unhurried cooking give delicious results.
Recipe is for one chicken but you can increase it to fit your crowd*

1 clove garlic, crushed (optional)	2 tblsp. grated onion
½ tsp. salt	¼ tsp. pepper
¼ c. salad oil	Salt
½ c. lemon juice	1 broiler-fryer, split in half
1 tsp. Worchestershire sauce	

Put garlic and ½ tsp. salt in bowl; stir in oil, lemon juice, Worcestershire sauce, onion and pepper. Let this sauce stand 1 to 2 hours to blend flavors.

When the charcoal has a white covering, it is ready for the grilling. (It takes about 30 minutes after igniting to reach this stage.) Spread the coals out about the size of the area the chicken will occupy. Salt chicken halves lightly. Then brush skin side of chicken lightly with barbecue sauce and place this side down on grill, 8 to 10″ above the coals. Grill 15 minutes. Brush top side of chicken generously with sauce while skin side cooks. Turn chicken and cook other side about 15 minutes, brushing top with sauce. Repeat turning and brushing with sauce until chicken has broiled at least 1 hour. The chicken is done when its juices stop dripping. Makes 2 or 4 servings. Most people will eat a half chicken, although others prefer a quarter. If quarters are desired, divide halves after cooking.

RICE PILAF

You can make this skillet version of pilaf with canned chicken broth

1 medium onion, finely chopped	1½ tsp. salt
¾ c. thinly sliced celery	¼ tsp. pepper
1½ c. long grain rice	½ tsp. thyme leaves
¼ c. butter or regular margarine	3½ c. chicken broth

Sauté onion, celery and rice in butter over low heat until vegetables are transparent and rice is golden. Add salt, pepper, thyme and chicken broth.

Cover skillet with a tight-fitting lid and cook over low heat until broth is absorbed, about 20 to 25 minutes. Makes 8 servings.

HOMEMADE VANILLA ICE CREAM

Easy-to-make, velvety ice cream—there's no cooking of ingredients

4 eggs, beaten well	1½ qts. dairy half-and-half
1 c. plus 2 tblsp. sugar	1 qt. milk
1 (14 oz.) can sweetened	2 tblsp. vanilla
condensed milk	Dash of salt

Mix all ingredients in a 1-gal. ice cream freezer can, adding a little milk if necessary to fill can almost three fourths full. Adjust dasher and cover. Pack crushed ice and rock salt around can, using 6 parts ice to 1 part salt.

Turn dasher slowly until the ice melts enough to make a brine. Add more ice and salt, mixed in the proper proportion, to maintain the ice level. Turn the handle fast and steadily until it turns hard. Then remove ice until the level is below the lid of can; take off lid and remove the dasher.

Plug the hole in lid and cover can with several thicknesses of waxed paper or foil to make a tight fit for the lid. Pack more ice-salt mixture, using 4 parts ice to 1 part salt, around can and filling the freezer. Cover with a blanket, canvas or other heavy cloth, or with newspaper. Let the ice cream ripen 4 hours before serving. Or put it in the home freezer for an hour. Makes 1 gallon.

N O T E : If you use an electric ice cream freezer, follow the manufacturer's directions.

SIT-DOWN DINNER

Orange/Cranberry Juice   Corn Chips
Royal Chicken Pie*   Mashed Winter Squash
Lima Beans with Mushrooms   Pickled Beets
Sun Gold Fruit Salad*   Cookie Tray
Milk   Coffee

When the guest list includes children, consider this dinner menu. All the food, from the chilled juice at the beginning to the cookies at the end, appeals to people of all ages. And children can easily manage it. They like chicken pie—this country way with chicken never goes out of style. It changes with the years, but the delicious old-fashioned taste remains.

The salad mold answers both for salad and dessert, but, because youngsters, as well as many grownups, like to end meals on a sweet note, we include a tray of homemade cookies. Be sure to have milk for the children and coffee for adults—plenty of milk because some adults will likely choose it for their beverage too.

TIMETABLE

Do-Ahead: A day before the company dinner make and pour the salad into a mold and chill. Cook the chicken, cool; remove meat from bones, dice and refrigerate meat and broth separately (fat will rise to top of broth for use in sauce). Bake cookies unless you have a supply in the freezer.

On Guest Day: Frost salad; return to refrigerator. Cook squash, drain and mash; season at your convenience to reheat before serving. You will need about 9 c. diced peeled butternut or Hubbard squash for 8 or 9 servings. Prepare chicken filling for pie when you have time, but be sure to reheat it until bubbly hot before putting on the crust to bake. Cook 3 (10 oz.) pkgs. frozen lima beans by package directions, drain; add 1 (6 oz.) can sliced mushrooms, drained, and ¼ c. butter or regular margarine. Reheat. Combine equal parts reconstituted frozen orange juice concentrate and canned cranberry juice cocktail.

SERVING SUGGESTIONS

Pour fruit juice mixture into pitcher over cracked ice, carry with bowl of corn chips on tray to living room and serve in juice glasses. Since the salad is beautiful, it's a good idea to serve it at the dinner table. Sugar cookies and chocolate chip cookies make an attractive tray—children love a chance to make a choice.

ROYAL CHICKEN PIE

Cheese and olives impart special flavor to biscuit crust spirals

¼ c. chopped onion	2½ c. chicken broth
1 branch celery, chopped	½ tsp. soy sauce
¼ c. chicken fat	¼ tsp. pepper
½ c. chopped pimiento	¼ tsp. garlic salt
3 c. diced cooked chicken	Crust
3½ tblsp. flour	

Sauté onion and celery in 2 tblsp. chicken fat until onion is transparent, but not brown; add pimiento. Add chicken and pour into 2-qt. casserole.

Melt remaining 2 tblsp. chicken fat in skillet. Add flour and stir until smooth. Add chicken broth, soy sauce, pepper and garlic salt; cook and stir over medium heat until sauce thickens. Pour over chicken in casserole, cover and place in hot oven (425°) about 20 minutes, or until bubbly hot. Remove from oven.

Arrange slices of crust over top of hot chicken in casserole. Return to oven and bake about 12 minutes more, or until crust is light golden brown. Makes 8 servings.

Crust: Make biscuit dough with 2 c. all-purpose buttermilk biscuit mix following package directions. Roll in 10×9″ rectangle. Sprinkle with ¾ c. shredded Cheddar cheese and ¼ c. finely chopped pimiento-stuffed olives. Roll as for jelly roll; cut in ½″ slices and place on hot chicken mixture. Brush top with 1 tblsp. melted butter or regular margarine.

N O T E : You can substitute chopped green pepper for the pimiento; sauté it with onion and celery.

SUN GOLD FRUIT SALAD

Frosting with shredded cheese trim substitutes for salad dressing

2 (3 oz.) pkgs. orange flavor gelatin
2 c. boiling water
1½ c. cold water
1 (11 oz.) can mandarin oranges
1 (8¾ oz.) can apricot halves
1 c. seedless white grapes, fresh or canned
2 large bananas, sliced
Fluffy Topping
¼ c. grated American cheese

Dissolve gelatin in boiling water; add cold water. Refrigerate until syrupy.

Drain fruit, reserving 1 c. liquid. Fold fruit into gelatin mixture; pour into 9×5×3″ loaf pan or 11½×7⅜×1½″ glass dish. Refrigerate overnight.

Unmold salad and frost with Fluffy Topping. Sprinkle top with cheese. Refrigerate until topping sets, about 1 hour. Makes 12 servings.

Fluffy Topping: Combine 6 tblsp. sugar and 2 tblsp. cornstarch in a heavy saucepan. Blend in 1 egg, slightly beaten, and the 1 c. reserved fruit liquid. Cook, stirring constantly, over low heat until thickened. Remove from heat; stir in 2 tblsp. butter and 1 tblsp. lemon juice. Cool. Whip 1 c. heavy cream, or 1 envelope dessert topping mix; fold into the cooled mixture.

COLORFUL CHICKEN DINNER

Golden Broiled Chicken*   Cranberry/Orange Garnish
Broccoli/Cauliflower Scallop*
Green Pea Salad*
Hot Rolls   Apricot Preserves
Glorified Rice with Green Grapes*

Broiled chicken requires some attention while cooking, but it is ready to serve when you take it from the oven (no carving). It cooks only 45 minutes—tastes great. To the delight of weight-watching guests, it is lower in calories than many other platter favorites.

In this menu two old-time friends, chicken and rice, appear but the rice assumes the dessert role. It's really a glamorized edition of a country rice pudding. Broccoli and cauliflower teamed together in a baking dish make a pretty green and white combination. And the vegetable salad provides a change from the universal tossed greens.

TIMETABLE

Do-Ahead: Make the dessert the evening before the dinner party or, if easier, the next morning. It needs to chill several hours.

On Guest Day: Make the salad at least 2 to 3 hours before you want to serve it; cover and refrigerate. Get the broccoli and cauliflower ready to bake; refrigerate. About 1¾ hours before dinnertime, add the marinade to the chicken. And 45 minutes before you want to serve it, place chicken in preheated broiler oven. When you remove it from oven, set the regulator at 350° and put the Broccoli/Cauliflower Scallop in oven to heat for 15 to 20 minutes. Put the foil-wrapped rolls alongside the last 10 minutes.

SERVING SUGGESTIONS

Serve chicken on a warm platter and garnish with orange slices topped with circles (round slices) of canned jellied cranberry sauce. The scallop requires no trim—it's decorative by itself. Serve the salad in a bowl, or if you prefer, in lettuce cups on individual salad plates. When it's time for dessert, fold in whipped cream and spoon rice into stemmed dessert glasses; garnish each serving with a tiny cluster of green grapes. This is an ideal dinner to serve buffet style.

GOLDEN BROILED CHICKEN

Weight-watchers rejoice! One 3-ounce serving has only 185 calories

1 c. cider vinegar	½ tsp. white pepper
¾ c. salad oil	1 egg, beaten
4½ tsp. salt	½ c. sliced onion
1 tblsp. poultry seasoning	2 (3 lb.) broiler-fryers, quartered

Combine vinegar, oil, salt, poultry seasoning, pepper, egg and onion in a 2-qt. saucepan. Stirring constantly, bring mixture to a boil. Pour over chicken and let stand at room temperature 1 hour.

Place chicken skin side down on broiler pan. Place pan in broiler, 7 to 9″ from heat. Broil 30 minutes, basting frequently with marinade. Turn chicken and baste. Broil another 15 minutes or until chicken is tender and golden. Makes 4 to 8 servings.

BROCCOLI/CAULIFLOWER SCALLOP

Contrast in color gives this vegetable combination a party look

2 (10 oz.) pkgs. frozen broccoli (spears)	1½ c. milk
1 (10 oz.) pkg. frozen cauliflower	1 c. cut-up process American cheese
2 tblsp. flour	⅛ tsp. salt
2 tblsp. melted butter or regular margarine	Dash of pepper
1 (4 oz.) can mushrooms	2 tblsp. butter
	1 c. bread crumbs

Cook broccoli and cauliflower separately by package directions; do not overcook. Drain and cool.

Add flour to 2 tblsp. melted butter and stir over low heat to make a smooth paste, but do not brown.

Drain mushrooms. Mix liquid drained from mushroom with milk; gradually add to flour-butter mixture, and cook, stirring. As mixture thickens, add cheese. Season with salt and pepper. Stir until cheese melts. Remove from heat and add mushrooms.

Arrange broccoli and cauliflower in alternate rows in shallow 11×7×1½″ glass baking dish or shallow casserole. Pour cheese sauce over top.

Melt 2 tblsp. butter in small skillet, add crumbs and cook, stirring until crumbs are golden brown. Spoon crumbs around edge of Broccoli/Cauliflower Scallop to make a border. Heat in moderate oven (350°) 15 to 20 minutes, or until bubbly. Serves 8 to 10.

GREEN PEA SALAD

Avoid overcooking peas or you will lose bright green color. Just heat them well. Perfect escort for lamb roasts and chops

2 (10 oz.) pkgs. frozen peas	1 tsp. sugar
½ c. salad oil	1 tblsp. minced fresh mint leaves
⅓ c. red wine vinegar	½ c. chopped celery
1½ tsp. salt	½ c. redskin peanuts
¼ tsp. pepper	¼ c. dairy sour cream

Cook peas by package directions, only to heat through. Drain.

Combine salad oil, vinegar, salt, pepper, sugar and mint leaves. Pour over peas; cover and chill at least 2 to 3 hours. Just before serving stir in celery, peanuts and sour cream. Makes 6 to 8 servings.

GLORIFIED RICE WITH GREEN GRAPES

No rice pudding ever tasted better than this luscious chilled version

2 c. cooked regular rice	½ c. sugar
1 c. canned crushed pineapple, drained	1 tsp. vanilla
	1 c. seedless green grapes
2 c. miniature marshmallows	1 c. heavy cream, whipped

Combine rice, pineapple, marshmallows, sugar, vanilla and grapes. Cover and chill at least 1 hour, or several hours in refrigerator. Just before serving fold in whipped cream. Makes 6 to 8 servings.

A DINNER TO TOTE

Sesame Chicken*
Scalloped Corn* or Honey-Glazed Sweet Potatoes*
Tomato Salad Ring*   Herb Bread*
Chocolate Cake

Picture the food for this cooperative dinner on your buffet: golden-crusted chicken; casserole of yellow corn with a crunchy, brown top; the scarlet salad ring; homemade bread, and a lovely chocolate cake. Members of the club will feel proud of this cooperative meal to which they contributed.

All the dishes in this menu travel successfully, although if the weather is warm, substitute a fresh tomato-cucumber salad for the molded ring. Wrap the bread in foil and heat it before taking it to the gathering place, where you'll want to put it in a low oven to keep warm until serving time. Do the same with the corn.

This is also a menu which one woman can prepare and serve to guests in her home. The following timetable is for her rather than for the cooperative, share-the-load dinner. If serving more than 6 people, the chicken recipe needs to be doubled and there will not be room for two pans and the corn casserole in the oven at the same time. Fix Honey-Glazed Sweet Potatoes instead of the corn.

TIMETABLE

Do-Ahead: Make the salad ring a day ahead and refrigerate. Bake the bread and cake a day or several days ahead and freeze.

On Guest Day: Put the chicken in the oven about 1¼ hours before serving time. The sweet potatoes are a fast-fix dish, but allow 15 to 20 minutes for them. Heat the foil-wrapped bread 15 to 20 minutes, or 25 to 30 minutes if frozen.

SERVING SUGGESTIONS

This is an excellent dinner to serve buffet style.

SESAME CHICKEN

A sophisticated main dish that's tasty. It will impress your guests

Breasts, thighs and legs of 2 broiler-fryers	⅓ c. Toasted Sesame Seeds
1 tblsp. melted butter	1 pkg. cheese-flavored salad dressing mix
1 tsp. prepared mustard	¾ c. evaporated milk
2 tblsp. lemon juice	1½ c. prepared pancake mix
1 tsp. salt	1 tblsp. paprika
2 tblsp. flour	½ c. shortening

Wash chicken; pat dry with paper towels. Mix butter, mustard, lemon juice, salt, flour, sesame seeds and salad dressing mix to make a paste. Spread on the chicken to coat pieces.

Dip chicken in milk, then in pancake mix combined with paprika. Lightly brown in hot shortening; turn carefully with tongs.

Place in 13×9×2″ baking pan. Cover pan with aluminum foil. Bake in moderate oven (375°) 35 minutes. Then bake uncovered 25 minutes, or until chicken is tender. Makes 6 servings.

Toasted Sesame Seeds: Spread sesame seeds in shallow baking pan; bake in moderate oven (350°) about 20 minutes, until seeds turn a pale brown. Watch them to prevent overbrowning, which destroys the seeds' finest flavor.

SCALLOPED CORN

Corn vies with scalloped potatoes for top honors in country kitchens

½ c. chopped onion	½ tsp. dry mustard
½ c. chopped green pepper	1½ c. milk
¼ c. butter or regular margarine	2 (1 lb.) cans whole kernel corn
¼ c. flour	2 eggs, slightly beaten
1½ tsp. salt	¾ c. cracker crumbs
¼ tsp. pepper	2 tblsp. melted butter

Cook and stir onion and green pepper in ¼ c. melted butter until onion is tender; do not brown. Remove from heat and stir in flour, salt, pepper and mustard. Cook and stir over low heat until mixture is bubbly hot. Remove from heat and gradually stir in milk. Stir and heat to boiling; boil 5 minutes. Stir in corn and eggs.

Pour into greased 2-qt. casserole. Combine cracker crumbs with

2 tblsp. melted butter; sprinkle over top of corn. Bake in moderate oven (350°) 40 to 45 minutes. Makes 8 servings.

HONEY-GLAZED SWEET POTATOES

Take your choice of candying these in oven or on top of range

¼ c. strained honey
2 tblsp. brown sugar
2 tblsp. butter or regular
  margarine
¼ tsp. salt
1 (17 oz.) can vacuum pack sweet
  potatoes, drained

Combine honey, brown sugar, butter, salt and the liquid drained from sweet potatoes in saucepan. Boil until thickened. Add sweet potatoes and heat; spoon glaze over potatoes occasionally. Or put sweet potatoes in an oiled shallow baking dish (if sweet potatoes are large, cut in halves). Pour the syrup over and bake in moderate oven (375°) about 30 minutes. Makes 4 servings.

TOMATO SALAD RING

Set out salad dressing to spoon over colorful salad if desired

4 c. tomato juice
⅓ c. chopped onion
¼ c. chopped celery leaves
2 tblsp. brown sugar
1 tsp. salt
1 small bay leaf
3 whole cloves
2 envelopes unflavored gelatin
3 tblsp. lemon juice
1 c. finely chopped celery
Lettuce

Combine 2 c. tomato juice, onion, celery leaves, brown sugar, salt, bay leaf and cloves. Simmer 5 minutes; strain.

Soften gelatin in 1 c. remaining tomato juice. Add to hot tomato juice mixture and stir until gelatin dissolves. Add remaining 1 c. tomato juice and lemon juice. Chill until mixture is consistency of unbeaten egg white. Fold in celery and pour into a 5-c. ring mold. Chill until firm. Unmold and serve on lettuce. Makes 8 servings.

HERB BREAD

Herb seasoning does something good to the chicken it accompanies

2 pkgs. active dry yeast	1 c. scalded milk
¼ c. warm water (110 to 115°)	2 eggs
⅓ c. shortening	4½ to 5 c. flour
¼ c. sugar	Herb Butter
1 tblsp. salt	

Sprinkle yeast on warm water; stir to dissolve.

In mixing bowl, combine shortening, sugar, salt and hot scalded milk; stir until shortening melts and sugar dissolves. Cool to luke-warm.

Blend unbeaten eggs and yeast into lukewarm mixture. Gradually add flour to make a soft dough that leaves the sides of bowl.

Turn onto lightly floured board and knead until smooth and elastic. Place in lightly greased bowl; turn dough over to grease top. Cover and let rise in warm place until doubled, about 1½ hours.

Roll out half of dough ⅛" thick. Cut in 3 to 3½" rounds. Spread top of each round with Herb Butter. Fold dough in half (buttered side inside) and lay on greased baking sheet. Spread top with Herb Butter. Continue placing buttered and folded rounds on baking sheet, folded side down, overlapping previous folded round three fourths of the way. You will have about 14 folded rolls, which make a loaf. Spread top of this loaf with Herb Butter. Let rise 30 to 40 minutes. Repeat with second half of dough.

Bake in moderate oven (350°) 20 to 25 minutes. Makes 2 loaves.

Herb Butter: Combine ½ c. softened butter or regular margarine, ½ tsp. caraway seeds, ½ tsp. sweet basil leaves, ½ tsp. grated onion, ¼ tsp. orégano leaves and ⅛ tsp. garlic powder. Mix.

GARDEN DINNER

Summer Chicken with Peas and New Potatoes*
Wilted Garden Lettuce
Strawberry Satin Pie*

June, the time of roses, is also the time for the first batch of succulent peas. Berry patches redden with ripe strawberries and new potatoes appear more abundantly in supermarkets. It's the perfect time to ask friends to a dinner of wonderful country foods.

This menu is an easy one to execute. The chicken, potatoes and peas cook together in the same skillet. You can get the meal ready from start to finish, if you bake the pie ahead, in an hour. The pie is something to remember with pleasure—both visually and gastronomically!

TIMETABLE

Do-Ahead: Bake and cool pie shell. Make the cream filling, pour it into the pie shell and chill overnight.

On Guest Day: Arrange berries with precision on top of filling in pie shell, glaze and return to refrigerator. Chill at least 3 hours. Look in Index for recipe for Wilted Garden Lettuce (included in "Supper in Lilac Time" menu). Gather leaf lettuce, wash, place in plastic bags and chill. About 1 hour before dinnertime, start cooking chicken and potatoes. Shell peas. Add them after the chicken has cooked 30 minutes. When chicken and vegetables are cooked, remove from skillet and make the sauce or gravy. Wilt the lettuce.

SERVING SUGGESTIONS

This is a sit-down dinner. Serve chicken, potatoes and peas on one large platter. If peas are not overcooked, they will retain their bright green color to contrast with the red skins of the small potatoes. Pour sauce over chicken or pass it in gravy boat or bowl. Garnish with snipped fresh parsley if you wish.

SUMMER CHICKEN WITH PEAS AND NEW POTATOES

Perfect combination of late spring or early summer country foods

6 tblsp. butter or regular margarine

1 broiler-fryer (about 2½ lbs.) cut in serving pieces

1 lb. small new potatoes, scrubbed, with a strip peeled around the centers

Salt

Freshly ground pepper

2 tblsp. lemon juice

3 green onions with tops, thinly sliced

1 lb. fresh peas, shelled (about 1 c.), or 1 (10 oz.) pkg. frozen peas

¼ c. chopped fresh parsley

1 c. dairy sour cream

1 tsp. thyme leaves, crumbled

½ tsp. salt

¼ tsp. pepper

Parsley (for garnish)

Melt butter in a large skillet. Add chicken and potatoes and brown slowly on all sides; season with salt and pepper. (Be generous with pepper.) Sprinkle chicken with lemon juice; reduce heat, cover pan and simmer 30 minutes.

Add green onions to butter in bottom of skillet; sprinkle peas and parsley over chicken and potatoes; cover again and simmer 10 minutes more, or until chicken and potatoes are tender.

Remove chicken and vegetables to serving platter; keep warm.

Remove skillet from heat. Add sour cream, thyme, ½ tsp. salt and ¼ tsp. pepper; stir to mix well and to loosen pan drippings.

Pour over chicken or pass as sauce. Garnish with additional parsley; serve immediately. Makes 4 servings.

N O T E : You may want to make two skilletfuls for 8 servings.

STRAWBERRY SATIN PIE

The beauty of the pie depends on artistic arrangement of the berries

Baked 9″ pie shell

½ c. sliced toasted almonds

Creamy Satin Filling

1½ c. fresh strawberries

Shiny Glaze

Cover bottom of baked pie shell with almonds.

Cover almonds with Creamy Satin Filling. Chill thoroughly at least 3 hours, or overnight.

Slice strawberries in halves, reserving a few perfect berries for center of pie. Arrange on filling in layers, starting at outer edge.

Place some berries cut side up to make a pattern. Cover with Shiny Glaze. Refrigerate 1 hour, or until serving time. Makes 8 servings.

CREAMY SATIN FILLING

Perfect filling for strawberry pie—so smooth—it deserves its name

½ c. sugar	2 c. milk
3 tblsp. cornstarch	1 egg, slightly beaten
3 tblsp. flour	½ c. heavy cream, whipped
½ tsp. salt	1 tsp. vanilla

Combine sugar, cornstarch, flour and salt in saucepan.

Gradually add milk, stirring until smooth. Cook, stirring constantly, until mixture is thick and bubbling.

Stir a little of this hot mixture into egg, then add to hot mixture and cook until just bubbling hot again.

Cool, then chill thoroughly. This mixture will be very thick. Beat with mixer or rotary beater until smooth.

Fold in whipped cream and vanilla.

Shiny Glaze: Crush ½ c. fresh strawberries. Add ½ c. water and cook 2 minutes; strain through sieve. Combine ¼ c. sugar and 1 tblsp. cornstarch in small saucepan; stir in berry juice. Cook, stirring constantly, until thick and clear. Cool; spoon carefully over strawberries in the pie.

SUMMER CHICKEN DINNER

Chicken Parmesan*	Dilly Potato Salad*
Corn on the Cob	Ripe Tomato Platter
Vanilla Ice Cream	Chocolate Peppermint Sauce*

When plump, juicy tomatoes hang heavy on vines and sweet corn is ready in the garden or field, it's a great time to invite friends to dinner. Team these vegetables with new-potato salad and chicken and you have a feast. A country dinner like this makes everyone wish summer never would end.

TIMETABLE

Do-Ahead: Make the potato salad and chocolate sauce a day ahead and refrigerate.

On Guest Day: Since the chicken needs to cook 1 hour, put it in the oven about 1¼ hours before mealtime. Bring the corn to the kitchen as near the dinner hour as you can. Allow 2 ears per person. If you buy it, select ears with deep green husks. To test it, puncture a kernel with the thumbnail. If a thin, milky liquid spurts out, the corn is in its prime. If the milky juice is thick and the skin on kernels tough, the corn is too old. When it must wait in the kitchen, keep it, unhusked, in the refrigerator. Husk and remove silk just before cooking. Cook briefly at the last minute. One good way is to place the ears in a large kettle, cover with cold, unsalted water and bring quickly to a boil. Lift ears from the hot water with tongs, drain and rush to table. While it cooks, peel, quarter and arrange tomatoes on platter or tray and carry, along with the potato salad, to the table. Move ice cream from freezer to refrigerator when dinner is served. If you like warm sauce on ice cream, set it over low heat while you dish up the ice cream.

SERVING SUGGESTIONS

Sprinkle tomatoes with chopped parsley. For attractive service, center olives and pickle slices on tomato platter. Garnish potato salad with hard-cooked egg slices. Either spoon chocolate sauce on the ice cream or pass it in a pitcher so everyone can help himself. For dessert you can serve chilled watermelon or other melon instead of ice cream.

CHICKEN PARMESAN

The coating on this chicken turns golden—guests like the flavor

1⅓ c. packaged herb-seasoned stuffing	⅛ tsp. pepper
	1¼ tsp. monosodium glutamate
½ c. shredded Parmesan cheese	¾ c. butter
¼ tsp. garlic salt	16 pieces chicken (breasts, thighs
1¼ tsp. salt	and legs)

Roll stuffing to make fine crumbs; put in pie pan. Mix in cheese and seasonings.

Melt ½ c. butter (1 stick) in shallow pan. Dip chicken pieces, one at a time, in butter, then roll in crumbs to coat.

Arrange chicken in large, shallow baking pan lined with foil. Do not overlap pieces. Dot with remaining butter, breaking it in bits.

Bake, uncovered, in moderate oven (350°) 1 hour. Serves 8.

DILLY POTATO SALAD

Chilling enhances the good taste—permits flavors to blend

5 c. cubed cooked potatoes
4 hard-cooked eggs, chopped
¼ c. chopped dill pickle
½ c. chopped onion
¼ c. vinegar
1 tsp. salt

2 tsp. sugar
½ tsp. pepper
1 tsp. chopped fresh dill, or ¾ tsp.
  dried dill weed
½ c. mayonnaise
Paprika

Toss together potatoes, eggs, pickle and onion. Mix vinegar, salt, sugar, pepper, dill and mayonnaise; pour over the potatoes. Toss lightly. Sprinkle with paprika. Cover and chill. Makes 8 servings.

CHOCOLATE PEPPERMINT SAUCE

Most everyone prefers the sauce warm—try it on chocolate ice cream

2 squares unsweetened chocolate
⅓ c. water
½ c. sugar
Dash of salt

2 tblsp. butter or regular
  margarine
½ tsp. peppermint extract
½ c. chopped nuts

Combine chocolate and water in small saucepan. Stir over low heat until smooth. Add sugar and salt. Cook, stirring constantly until sugar dissolves. Add butter, extract and nuts; stir to mix. Serve warm or cold. Makes about 1 cup.

HARVEST FESTIVAL DINNER

Oven-Fried Pecan Chicken*   Potato Roses*
Smoky Green Beans
Ripe Tomato Salad*   Overnight Refrigerator Pan Rolls*
Corn Relish   Peach Pickles   Raspberry Jam
Melon Compote*

When the days are cooler, but before frost strikes, the generous bounty of food in country places inspires many women to ask friends over to dinner. They never underestimate the appeal of fried chicken, mashed potatoes, sliced tomatoes, green beans and piping hot, home-made rolls.

Our menu gives new and easier versions of these old-time favorites. It's a good idea to point up the flavors of food in the main course with relishes. End the dinner with a luscious melon compote as a bow to a departing season; melons soon will be a memory of summer. Or substitute apple pies for them if you have time to bake them. Made with freshly harvested fruit, they are hard to beat.

TIMETABLE

Do-Ahead: Make dough for rolls and cook and shape Potato Roses a day ahead; refrigerate.

On Guest Day: Shape dough for rolls, let rise until doubled, 1 to 1½ hours, and bake 15 to 20 minutes. You can bake them early in the day and reheat at mealtime after you take the potatoes from the oven. Or you can bake them while serving the main course. They will be ready to pass shortly after everyone starts to eat.

Peel melon, cover and refrigerate at any convenient time. Combine honey and lime juice, cover and chill. Cook the chicken 1 or 2 hours, whichever time is best for you (see recipe directions). While it is in the oven, cook the green beans. If you have fresh beans, cook them in a little water, lightly salted, until just tender, 10 to 15 minutes. Drain and season with 6 tblsp. butter or margarine and ¾ tsp. smoky salt. Or cook 3 (10 oz.) pkgs. frozen green beans by package directions and season like the fresh beans.

SERVING SUGGESTIONS

Serve this dinner buffet style if you like. Heap the golden fried chicken on a platter, serve the pretty potatoes on another platter, the green beans and salad in bowls. Display the relishes on a lazy susan if you have one. If you have a sit-down meal, you may wish to serve the plates in the kitchen. Enlisting the help of one of your guests simplifies and speeds up the serving. Serve the melon in compote dishes, or if you have a sit-down dinner, stemmed dessert glasses are a good choice. Use sprigs of fresh mint to garnish the inviting melon.

OVEN-FRIED PECAN CHICKEN

Crisp-coated, golden brown chicken has a rich, pecan taste

1 c. all-purpose buttermilk biscuit mix
½ tsp. salt
2 tsp. paprika
½ tsp. poultry seasoning
½ c. finely chopped pecans

1 (2½ to 4 lb.) broiler-fryer, cut in serving pieces
½ c. evaporated milk
½ c. melted butter or regular margarine

Combine biscuit mix, seasonings and pecans. Dip chicken into evaporated milk; then coat well with the flour mixture. Place in 13×9×2″ baking pan.

Pour melted butter over the chicken, completely covering every piece. Bake in moderate oven (375°) 1 hour or in very slow oven (200°) for 2 hours, or until chicken is fork tender. Makes about 5 servings.

N O T E : To oven-fry chicken for 8 to 10 servings, double the recipe and arrange chicken pieces in two 13×9×2″ baking pans. Bake, uncovered, on 2 racks in a moderate oven (375°) 30 minutes; reverse position of pans on shelves in oven and bake 30 minutes longer, or until chicken is tender.

POTATO ROSES

They sound fancy but are easier to make than you may think

4 lbs. baking potatoes
¼ c. butter
1 tblsp. minced onion
1½ tsp. salt
⅛ tsp. pepper
1 tblsp. minced parsley

2 tblsp. grated Parmesan or Romano cheese
1 egg
Paprika
½ c. melted butter

Peel potatoes; cut in halves and cook in boiling, lightly salted water until tender. Mash slightly.

Place potatoes in large mixer bowl; beat until light and fluffy. Add ¼ c. butter, onion, salt, pepper, parsley, cheese and egg. Whip until well mixed. Cool.

Moisten hands; shape potato mixture into balls, about ¾ c. each. Place on greased baking sheet; flatten slightly on bottom.

To form roses, dip forefinger in water; make an indentation in center of each potato ball. Swirl finger clockwise to make a spiral. If you wish, cover and chill overnight.

Before baking, sprinkle lightly with paprika and drizzle ½ c. melted butter over roses. Bake in very hot oven (450°) 8 minutes. Let set a few minutes. Makes 10 servings.

RIPE TOMATO SALAD

This salad features famous teammates, juicy red tomatoes and basil

4 ripe tomatoes, cut in wedges
Salt
2 tblsp. finely chopped fresh basil
  leaves or ½ tsp. dried basil
  leaves

2 tblsp. salad oil
Juice of ½ lemon

Sprinkle tomatoes with salt to season. Add basil to salad oil (if you use dried basil, crumble it). Sprinkle over tomatoes. Chill at least 1 hour.

Squeeze lemon juice over top just before serving. Serve on large plate or in shallow bowl. Lemon quarters and chopped parsley make an attractive garnish. Makes 6 to 8 servings.

OVERNIGHT REFRIGERATOR PAN ROLLS

Puffy, light, homemade rolls from dough that requires no kneading

2 pkgs. active dry yeast
2½ c. warm water (110 to 115°)
¾ c. soft or melted shortening
¾ c. sugar

2 eggs, well beaten
8 to 8½ c. flour
2½ tsp. salt

Soften yeast in warm water. Add shortening, sugar, eggs, 4 c. flour and salt. Stir to mix and then beat until smooth, about 1 minute.

Stir in remaining flour. (You may want to use your hands to mix in the last 2 cups.) This will be a soft dough.

Place in a greased bowl and lightly grease surface of dough. Cover tightly. Store in the refrigerator overnight or until needed. (Dough will keep about 4 days, but punch it down daily. Count days from time dough is placed in refrigerator.) Make pan rolls according to directions that follow. Dough makes 36 rolls. (This dough also will make two Golden Crown Coffee Cakes, included in Morning Coffee menu—see Index.)

Punch down refrigerated dough and pinch off one third. Cover the remaining dough and put back in the refrigerator.

Shape the one third dough into 12 rolls and place them in a greased 9×9×2″ baking pan. Cover with a clean towel and let rise until doubled, 1 to 1½ hours.

Bake in a hot oven (400°) 15 to 20 minutes. Turn out on wire rack. Serve hot.

MELON COMPOTE

Lime juice and honey complement melons—especially honeydews

8 c. bite-size melon pieces   ¼ c. honey
Juice of 2 limes

Use honeydew melon or a combination of honeydews and cantaloupe. Chill. Combine lime juice and honey; cover and chill. Just before serving, mix gently with melon. Makes 8 servings.

WILD DUCK DINNER

Tomato Juice Starter*   Country Cheese/Bacon Dip*
Carrot Sticks   Celery   Chips
Texas Barbecued Ducks* or California Rare Duck*
Stuffed Baked Sweet Potatoes*   Buttered Broccoli
Hard Rolls   Currant Jelly   Lemon Velvet Pie*

When the duck hunter returns home with his bounty, he'll be eager to share the treat with friends. Chances are good that his wife knows (from experience) how to meet the challenge. She plans a dinner menu that gives the ducks the spotlight, with all food accompaniments taking a secondary role.

Her menu is a blueprint for a delicious country-style duck dinner. You may wish to substitute traditional wild rice for the sweet potatoes, but the strain will be greater on your pocketbook if you do. The potatoes, a special favorite in southern game dinners, taste wonderful and add color to the meal. The appetizers are of course optional.

TIMETABLE

Do-Ahead: Bake and stuff sweet potatoes and make the barbecue sauce for the duck the day before your dinner. Cover and refrigerate.

On Guest Day: Make the pie in the morning and refrigerate. (You may need to bake two pies; it depends on the size of your family and guest list.) Fix the tomato juice drink; cover and chill. Blend the dip any convenient time in the afternoon (for serving in evening); cover and chill.

About 1½ hours before dinner put the ducks in the oven to bake. There are regional preferences for ways to cook wild ducks. You may choose to have California Rare Duck; it spends only 25 to 35 minutes in the oven. Reheat sweet potatoes 30 to 40 minutes alongside ducks if oven space permits. Otherwise increase the oven temperature to 400° and heat them after you remove the ducks from the oven, while you are getting the ducks ready to serve and cooking the frozen broccoli. You will need 3 (10 oz.) pkgs. for 8 to 9 servings; cook by package directions.

SERVING SUGGESTIONS

Serve the tomato juice drink and accompaniments in the living room before dinner. Join the guests there if you can spare time from the kitchen, but make your duck hunter responsible for serving this course and keeping guests happy. Many farmers consider it ideal to serve each person a whole duck, while others believe half a duck is adequate. The size of the birds influences the size of serving portions. Be sure to split birds in half lengthwise.

Display the ducks on a big platter if you have one. Clusters of seedless grapes make an interesting garnish (see photo). Another good way to serve this dinner is to arrange the food on the plates in the kitchen. Assign specific duties to your helper if you have one. How about asking a guest to help? She can serve the sweet potatoes and broccoli and garnish tops of sweet potatoes with half an orange slice.

TOMATO JUICE STARTER

Colorful start for a game dinner; this recipe can be doubled

2 (14 oz.) cans tomato juice	1 tsp. sugar
2 tsp. instant minced onion	1 tsp. salt
3 tblsp. celery seeds	2″ stick cinnamon (optional)
½ tsp. Worcestershire sauce	1 tsp. prepared horse-radish

Combine all ingredients; cover and chill at least 3 hours to blend flavors. Strain and serve over cracked ice in juice glasses (also good heated and served in mugs). Makes 6 servings.

COUNTRY CHEESE/BACON DIP

Good with potato chips and vegetables—an easy recipe to double

1 c. creamed cottage cheese	1 tsp. lemon juice
3 slices crisp-cooked bacon,	1½ tblsp. milk
crumbled	1 clove garlic, cut
½ tsp. onion salt	Paprika
2 tblsp. salad dressing	

Combine cottage cheese, bacon, onion salt, salad dressing, lemon juice and milk; mix well.

Rub a small bowl with cut garlic; fill with cottage cheese mixture. Sprinkle lightly with paprika. Cover and chill. Makes about 1 cup.

TEXAS BARBECUED DUCKS

Roasting in foil is a safe bet—it tenderizes and keeps birds moist

2 wild ducks	Barbecue Sauce
2 tblsp. salad oil	

Rub ducks with oil; brown under broiler. Brush ducks with half the Barbecue Sauce; place 1 tblsp. sauce in cavity. Wrap each bird closely in heavy foil; bake in shallow pan in slow oven (325°) 1 hour, or until tender. Remove foil last 15 minutes, and spoon over remainder of sauce.

To Grill Outdoors: Proceed as above, browning over hot coals and finishing over slow coals.

Barbecue Sauce: Sauté 2 tblsp. chopped onion in ¼ c. butter. Add ½ c. ketchup, ½ c. lemon juice, ¼ tsp. paprika, ½ tsp. salt, ¼ tsp. pepper, ¼ tsp. ground red pepper, 2 tblsp. brown sugar and 2 tblsp. Worcestershire sauce. Simmer 15 minutes.

CALIFORNIA RARE DUCK

Glaze makes skin crisp and shiny—pink flesh tastes like beef

1 wild duck	¼ tsp. garlic salt
1 tsp. salt	Glaze
½ tsp. pepper	

Rub cavity and outside of duck with seasonings. Bake on rack in shallow pan, uncovered, in extremely hot oven (500°) 25 to 35 minutes, brushing with Glaze.

Glaze: Ten to 15 minutes after placing duck in oven, brush several times with mixture of 2 tblsp. light or dark corn syrup and 1 tsp. bottled browning sauce.

STUFFED BAKED SWEET POTATOES

The orange flavor is great with duck—make ahead if time is short

8 medium sweet potatoes	1½ tsp. salt
½ c. butter or regular margarine	Orange juice
2 tblsp. grated orange peel	

Bake sweet potatoes in hot oven (400°) 30 to 40 minutes, until soft. Cut a slice from top of each potato. Scoop out hot pulp (save shells) and mash; add butter, orange peel, salt and enough orange juice to moisten (the way you add milk when mashing white potatoes). Beat with electric mixer until smooth and fluffy. You should have about 8 c. mashed potatoes.

Refill shells, piling the mixture lightly. For a fancy look, put mashed, seasoned sweet potatoes through pastry tube. Makes about 8 servings.

LEMON VELVET PIE

This luscious pie filling has two layers, one like a good lemon meringue, the other like a fine lemon chiffon pie

Baked 9″ pie shell	1 tsp. grated lemon peel
1⅓ c. sugar	1 tsp. vanilla
6 tblsp. cornstarch	1 envelope unflavored gelatin
½ tsp. salt	¼ c. cold water
1½ c. cold water	1 c. light cream
2 egg yolks, slightly beaten	2 egg whites, stiffly beaten
2 tblsp. butter	1 c. heavy cream, whipped
⅓ c. lemon juice	

Combine sugar, cornstarch and salt in saucepan. Gradually stir in 1½ c. water. Cook over medium heat, stirring constantly, until mixture is smooth and thick enough to mound when dropped from a spoon. Stir some of the hot mixture into egg yolks. Slowly stir yolks and butter into remaining hot mixture; cook 2 minutes. Remove from heat and stir in lemon juice, peel and vanilla. Remove 1 c. filling (for top layer) and set it aside to cool.

Soften gelatin in ¼ c. water. Add to remaining hot filling and stir until dissolved. Gradually stir in light cream. Cool.

When mixture begins to thicken, fold in egg whites. Pour into pie shell. Chill 15 minutes. Spread with reserved filling. Chill well. Decorate with whipped cream. Makes 6 to 8 servings.

REGAL BEEF DINNER

Standing Rib Roast*
Special Stuffed Baked Potatoes*
Favorite Green Beans*
Fiesta Relish Tray
Strawberry/Cheese Pie*

This is a splendid menu for your husband's birthday dinner, an impressive selection for many other special occasions. You get off to a good start with the meal because a standing rib roast commands great respect. Country men and women know that in comparison with other cuts, it is not the extravagant luxury for an important dinner party that some people think. With a good piece of meat and plenty of it, the remainder of the meal can be less expensive and simple. And even a new cook can take a perfect roast from the oven if she follows the easy rules.

When there are 8 people at a dinner, the country host and hostess tend to choose a 7- to 8-lb. roast. It's a tradition to have more beef than is absolutely necessary and to be able to give generous servings. (The leftovers are used later in many interesting ways.)

This dinner, in addition to the regal roast, features marvelous stuffed baked potatoes, flavored with sour cream and cumin. You can get them ready ahead to reheat shortly before serving. Green beans, expertly seasoned, ably support the potatoes. A tray of assorted colorful relishes carries the salad role with attractive distinction.

You can skip dessert or have a mini-sweet ending, like small scoops of ice cream, but Strawberry/Cheese Pie is so lovely to look at and delicious to eat that you may wish to end the dinner with it, even if you postpone serving it. By the time forks cut the second bite of this pie, compliments for it circulate round and round the table like gentle breezes.

TIMETABLE

Do-Ahead: Make pie filling and pour into crust; chill overnight. Bake, stuff and cool potatoes a day ahead and refrigerate, or wrap and freeze several days before the dinner party.

On Guest Day: Cook and cool strawberry topping for pie; spread on the pie and return to refrigerator. Early in the day fix the vegetables for the relish tray. Cut carrots, celery and green pepper in strips and break flowerets from the cauliflower head. Wash and chill cherry tomatoes. Put carrots, celery and cauliflower in separate jars, add a little water to each, cover and chill. Place green pepper in a plastic bag and refrigerate.

The time to put the roast in the oven depends on its weight and to what stage of doneness you wish to cook it. Consult the roasting guide that follows. The cardinal rule is to let the meat thermometer tell you when the roast is cooked the way you want it. Place potatoes in an uncovered pan in the oven with the meat for the last 40 to 45 minutes before dinner; increase the time 10 or 15 minutes if potatoes are frozen. Do not thaw frozen potatoes before putting them in the oven. Meanwhile, cook the green beans and arrange an attractive tray with the uncooked vegetables and some of your own homemade bread and butter and mustard pickles.

SERVING SUGGESTIONS

This is a sit-down dinner and carving the roast gets the spotlight. To make carving easier, be sure the meatman separated the backbone from the ribs. Then you can remove the backbone in the kitchen before carrying the platter to the dining table. If the host does not wish to carve the roast at the dining table, he can follow the same directions in the kitchen without spectators. Arrange the slices on the platter, overlapping them.

To carve a standing rib roast the easiest way, place the largest side down. If the roast wobbles, cut a wedge-shaped slice from the large end so the roast will stand firm.

Insert fork below the first rib. Slice from the outside of the roast to the rib side. Cut several slices in this manner. Then cut along the inner side of the rib to release a slice. Slide knife under slice and lift to serving plate. Repeat until everyone is served.

Pass the potatoes, green beans and relishes. Either serve the dessert at dinner's end, or later in the evening.

STANDING RIB ROAST

Place the roast, fat side up, in a shallow roasting pan. The ribs form a natural rack that holds the meat out of the drippings. Season with salt and pepper if you like; salt penetrates the meat no more than ½" at the most.

Insert the meat thermometer into the thickest part of the meat so that it neither touches a bone nor rests in fat. Do not cover, add water or baste meat while cooking.

Roast meat in a slow oven (325°) to the desired stage of doneness—rare, medium or well done. Let the meat thermometer tell you when the beef is cooked the way you want to serve it. Timing by the clock is approximate at best. Since meat carves easier if allowed to stand or "set" 15 to 20 minutes after removed from the oven, take it out when the thermometer registers 5 to 10° lower than the temperature for the desired degree of doneness. It will continue to cook out of the oven and reach the desired temperature.

Guide for Cooking a 6- to 8-lb.
Standing Rib Roast in 325° Oven

Temperature	Total Cooking Time
140° (rare)	2¾ to 3 hours
160° (medium)	3 to 3½ hours
170° (well done)	3¾ to 4 hours

SPECIAL STUFFED BAKED POTATOES

Cumin, a seasoning used since biblical times and an ingredient in chili powder, gives potatoes a subtle new flavor

8 medium baking potatoes	1½ c. milk
2 (1½ oz.) envelopes sour cream sauce mix	¼ c. butter or regular margarine
1 tsp. ground cumin	6 tblsp. grated process American cheese
1 tsp. salt	
Dash of pepper	4 slices bacon

Bake potatoes in hot oven (425°), 50 to 60 minutes until tender.

Meanwhile, combine sauce mix, cumin, salt, pepper and milk. Let stand 10 minutes to blend flavors.

Cut a slice from top of potatoes and discard. Scoop out potatoes, saving shells. Place in large electric mixer bowl and beat, adding the sauce mixture and butter. Beat until light and fluffy, adding more milk if necessary. The amount needed varies with the potatoes.

Fill potato shells with fluffy potatoes, sprinkle with grated cheese and heat in slow oven (325°) 40 to 45 minutes, or until thoroughly heated. Cook bacon until crisp; drain and crumble. Sprinkle over tops of potatoes. Makes 8 servings.

FAVORITE GREEN BEANS

Seasonings from Italian-American kitchens make this special

2 (10 oz.) pkgs. frozen green
  beans
1 tblsp. salad oil
1 tblsp. wine vinegar
1 tsp. chopped shallots or green
  onion

¼ tsp. garlic salt
¾ c. croutons
2 to 3 tblsp. grated Parmesan
  cheese

Cook beans by package directions; drain if necessary.

Combine oil, vinegar, shallots and garlic salt. Pour over beans. Add croutons; heat and stir until well heated. Pour into serving dish and sprinkle with cheese. Makes 6 to 8 servings.

STRAWBERRY/CHEESE PIE

Tastes like elegant cheese cake . . . it's topped with strawberry glaze

1¾ c. graham cracker crumbs
¼ c. sugar
½ c. melted butter or regular
  margarine
2 (8 oz.) pkgs. cream cheese at
  room temperature
3 eggs

⅔ c. sugar
⅛ tsp. vanilla
1 (10 oz.) pkg. frozen
  strawberries, thawed
1 tblsp. cornstarch
Few drops red food color

To make crust, combine crumbs with ¼ c. sugar; stir in melted butter. Press into 10″ pie pan to make shell.

For filling, beat cheese until light and fluffy. Add eggs, one at a time, beating well after each addition. Beat in ⅔ c. sugar and vanilla. Pour into pie shell. Bake in slow oven (325°) 50 minutes. Cool and chill.

For glaze, in small saucepan blend together a little of the strawberry liquid and cornstarch. Add remaining strawberries. Cook over medium heat, stirring constantly until thickened and clear. Remove from heat; stir in red food color. Cool. Spread over pie and chill. Makes 8 servings.

DISTINCTIVE POT ROAST DINNER

California Pot Roast*
Fluffy Rice   Buttered Broccoli
Tossed Green Salad
Fruit Dessert Tree*

Almost every hostess at some time faces a situation when she wants to serve guests a distinctive dinner. Frequently it's the pending arrival of a rather sophisticated guest. Try this menu—it's impressive.

TIMETABLE

Do-Ahead: Build the tree for the fruit a day or a few days ahead. Wash, drain, chill and store salad greens in plastic bags a day ahead. Assemble fruits and cheese for the dessert treat and refrigerate.

On Guest Day: Put the pot roast on to cook about 3½ to 4 hours before dinnertime. Cooked in a tightly covered Dutch oven, it will require little watching, except to check occasionally to see if you need to add a little water. During the last half hour before dinner, cook the rice and frozen broccoli; arrange fruit on tree. Toss salad and make coffee.

SERVING SUGGESTIONS

This is a sit-down dinner with the dessert served in the living room. Carve the meat in the kitchen or at the table. Arrange salad in individual bowls or on plates. If you wish, have it on the table when guests are seated. Served this way, it becomes an appetizer-salad and separate first course. For the main course, pass the bowls of rice and broccoli and the gravy in bowl or gravy boat. Suggest that everyone move to the living room to "pick" fruit from the tree for dessert. Serve coffee.

CALIFORNIA POT ROAST

Tender, brown pot roast carries a delightful oriental flavor

2 tblsp. flour	¼ c. water
1½ tsp. salt	¼ c. honey
⅛ tsp. pepper	¼ c. soy sauce
½ tsp. curry powder	2 tblsp. chopped candied ginger,
1 (3½ to 4 lb.) blade or arm pot	or ¼ tsp. ground ginger
roast	Water
3 tblsp. fat or drippings	¼ c. flour

Combine 2 tblsp. flour, salt, pepper and curry powder. Dredge meat in mixture.

Melt fat in heavy pan or Dutch oven; brown meat well on all sides. Pour off excess fat. Add ¼ c. water, honey, soy sauce and ginger. Cover tightly and cook slowly 3 to 3½ hours, or until meat is tender.

Remove meat from pan. Add enough water to cooking liquid to make 2 cups. Thicken with ¼ c. flour to make gravy. Makes about 8 servings.

FRUIT DESSERT TREE

One perfect way to end a guest dinner is with a fruit and cheese

Place your fruit tree on a low coffee table or buffet where you can see it from the dining table.

To build your tree, assemble trays, cake stands and footed dishes, graduated in size; place the heaviest pieces on the bottom. Roll florist's clay (available from a florist) into long thin strips. Use clay to anchor each dish firmly to the one below it. If your trays and dishes don't match in color and material, cover glass or metal pieces with contact paper and spray with copper or gold paint.

Begin at the bottom to stack fruits and work up (we used five layers). Intersperse fruits with green leaves from your yard—ivy, holly, laurel, or whatever you have or can get.

Supplement your own homegrown fruits with an assortment from the food store. Add color with a few out-of-season strawberries or cherry tomatoes. Quarter fresh pineapple by cutting right through the crown (leaves). Remove the core with a sharp knife, loosen fruit from rind, then cut in bite-size pieces to spear with toothpicks.

Serve at least three cheeses. We recommend pineapple cheese, blue or Roquefort, Liederkranz and an aged Cheddar. Set a basket of interesting crackers nearby. Some of your guests may prefer to eat them instead of fruit with the cheese.

Keep your tree to replenish throughout the holiday season. Refrigerate perishable fruits and most cheeses until just before guests arrive.

GRILLED OR BROILED POT ROAST DINNER

Grilled or Broiled Pot Roast*
Texas Gumbo Rice*
Country Coleslaw*
Strawberry Ice Cream
Brownies
Coffee   Iced Tea

Your friends will think you're a magician when you serve them broiled or grilled pot roast that's tender like steak and tastes like it. The secret is the marinade in which the beef chills at least 24 hours, but better 48 hours. The pot roast is 2½ to 3″ thick so you need to cook it a little longer than 2″ steaks, or about 1 hour. And to produce a topnotch "steak," baste the meat about every 5 minutes while it broils in the kitchen or over charcoal in the yard.

The host, if he takes over the grilling, will have a real opportunity to demonstrate his expertise. For cooking meat 1 hour, he will want to use a thicker bed of coals than for quick-cooking fish and meats.

As accompaniment, the rice dish, which simmers in a skillet, scores high. With broiled pot roast, it is best to serve a companion dish that cooks on top of the range. Coleslaws vary greatly, but the true country-kitchen type with sour cream dressing surpasses other kinds, we think.

TIMETABLE

Do-Ahead: Make barbecue sauce, pour over beef, cover and chill 2 days, turning meat occasionally.

On Guest Day: Have the coals at the proper stage for grilling a good hour before dinnertime. When the beef starts to cook, fix the rice dish, allowing 30 minutes for it from start to finish. Shred fresh, crisp cabbage with a sharp knife; a blunt or dull-edged knife bruises it. Add the dressing just before serving.

SERVING SUGGESTIONS

Eat indoors or out, whichever is more convenient. Regardless of where you dine, be sure to slice the grilled or broiled meat diagonally across the grain.

GRILLED OR BROILED POT ROAST

Truly delicious cooked over coals or in the range broiling oven

1 (about 4 lb.) boneless round chuck or rump pot roast, cut 2½ to 3″ thick
2 cloves garlic, minced
2 tblsp. salad oil
¼ tsp. dry mustard
1 tblsp. soy sauce
½ tsp. crushed rosemary leaves
6 tblsp. wine vinegar
2 tblsp. ketchup
1 tblsp. Worcestershire sauce
1 tblsp. bottled steak sauce

Place beef in shallow baking dish.

Sauté garlic in oil until golden. Blend in mustard, soy sauce, rosemary and vinegar. Pour sauce over meat. Cover and refrigerate 24 to 48 hours, turning meat occasionally.

Place roast on cold broiler grid about 4 to 5″ from heat.

To the sauce remaining from marinating meat, add ketchup, Worcestershire sauce and bottled steak sauce. Use to baste meat during cooking.

Broil meat on one side about 10 minutes; baste with sauce and turn. Broil on other side about 7 minutes, basting with sauce. Reduce heat (or spread out coals) and continue broiling, turning and basting roast with sauce every 5 minutes for 35 to 45 minutes more, depending on size of roast. Slice meat diagonally to serve. Makes about 8 servings.

TEXAS GUMBO RICE

Rice cooks with tomatoes, green pepper, onion, okra and corn. Bacon and chili powder contribute a taste of Texas

4 slices bacon
1 large onion, minced
6 medium tomatoes, cut up
1 green pepper, chopped
1 c. sliced okra

1 (16 oz.) can whole kernel corn
  (undrained)
2 tsp. salt
¼ tsp. pepper
½ tsp. chili powder
½ c. long grain rice

Cook bacon in large skillet until crisp. Remove from pan and drain.

Measure 3 tblsp. bacon fat into skillet; add onion and sauté until tender. Add remaining ingredients. Cover and simmer 20 minutes, or until rice is tender. Place in serving dish; crumble bacon over top. Makes 6 servings.

COUNTRY COLESLAW

Use cabbage shredded fine, tossed with dressing just before serving

6 c. finely shredded cabbage
⅓ c. finely chopped onion
¾ c. dairy sour cream
6 tblsp. mayonnaise or salad
  dressing

¾ tsp. salt
½ tsp. dry mustard
Dash of pepper
Paprika

Combine cabbage and onion. Place in large salad bowl.

Blend together sour cream, mayonnaise, salt, mustard and pepper. Pour over cabbage. Toss to distribute dressing. Sprinkle lightly with paprika. Makes 8 servings.

COUNTRY STEAK DINNER

Charcoal Grilled or Broiled Beef Steaks*
Grated au Gratin Potatoes*
Buttered Peas with Almonds
Fresh Mushroom Salad* or Tossed Salad with Creamy Dressing*
Orange/Peanut Cake*
Coffee

People acquainted with country steak dinners take an invitation to one enthusiastically. It's a great American feast. If you look in the freezer in farm homes, you'll know the reason why—among the packages of beef, a few are labeled to reserve to share with friends. These are the exceptionally good steaks, cut 2″ thick.

Now that Americans appreciate that cooking over coals is an excellent way to handle a fine steak, part of the kitchen occasionally moves outdoors and the chef who takes over there is often the host. The hostess, with the help of the older children, assumes responsibility for the remainder of the dinner.

This menu gives you a choice of cooking steak over charcoal or broiling it in the kitchen. Grilling steaks outdoors divides the work and delivers beef to the table with superb flavors. And it frees the oven in the kitchen for cooking other foods, such as big baked potatoes.

Baked potatoes appeal whenever they appear in the steak dinner, but timing the cooking often creates trouble. These favorites need to reach the table promptly when done. To help avoid a timing problem, this menu suggests grated potatoes teamed with cream and cheese. They wait more successfully if the steak is not ready. And they are out-of-this-world in taste. You can prepare the potatoes for baking and freeze them—a good make-ahead.

A currently popular addition to the meal is the Fresh Mushroom Salad favored especially by young people. Because the mushrooms are not always available in many localities, we suggest a good tossed salad as an alternate. Both salads have a creamy dressing.

The dessert, a generous orange-flavored cake made with a mix is decorated with peanut brittle trim. Men like the crunchy sweet.

TIMETABLE

Do-Ahead: Bake the cake a day ahead. Fix the potatoes and chill them overnight, or freeze them for a few days. Frozen steaks cut 2" thick are best thawed (or at least partially thawed) before grilling or broiling. Thaw them in the refrigerator for 24 to 36 hours before cooking.

On Guest Day: Frost the cake with whipped cream and decorate with peanut brittle about 3 hours before dinner. Keep it in the refrigerator until time to cut and serve it. Work out your timetable— His Timetable for grilling beef steak over coals or Her Timetable for broiling the steak in the oven. Allow plenty of time to have the steak ready at dinnertime. Put the potatoes in the oven about 1 hour before you want to serve them. Meanwhile, cook the peas by package directions. Make the coffee; then fix the salad during the last few minutes before dinner.

SERVING SUGGESTIONS

Serve the steak on a *warm* platter. Garnish it with a few very thin lemon slices and dot with butter or margarine. Arrange a parsley bouquet on the platter if you wish. Sprinkle buttered, hot peas with toasted slivered almonds just before serving, or heat them briefly in the melted butter before adding them to the peas. Serve the dessert at dinner's end, or postpone its appearance until later in the evening.

CHARCOAL GRILLED OR BROILED BEEF STEAKS

Trim off excess fat from high-quality sirloin, porterhouse or T-bone steaks. Allow about 1 lb. per person for bone-in steaks, ½ to ¾ lb. for boneless.

Brown meat on one side before turning; it should be about half done. Use timetable for a guide even though the timing is approximate. Grilling and broiling are mainly an art rather than a science. Season with salt and pepper after browning. Salt penetrates the meat no more than ½" at the most and it draws out juices that interfere with browning. To check for doneness, cut into the meat—near the bone if there is one.

Season the cooked meat with salt and pepper and serve at once on a warm platter.

Timetable for Charcoal-Grilling Beef Steaks on One Side

Rare	Medium	Well
12 to 13 minutes	15 to 17 minutes	22 to 25 minutes

Timetable for Broiling 2" Beef Steaks on One Side

Cut	Rare	Medium
Sirloin	16 to 20 minutes	23 minutes
Porterhouse and T-bone	20 minutes	23 minutes
Club	17 minutes	18 to 23 minutes

To Charcoal-Grill Steaks: Cut remaining fat on edges at 2" intervals to prevent curling. Be careful not to cut into lean meat. Rub heated grill with suet to grease lightly. Lay steak on grill about 4" from coals (gray embers) and use the timetable as a guide.

To Broil Steaks: Set oven control at broil (550°), or follow range manufacturer's broiling guide. Cut remaining fat around edges at 1" intervals to prevent curling. Rub heated broiler rack with suet to grease lightly. Broil meat 3 to 5" from source of heat. Use timetable as a guide to cooking time.

GRATED AU GRATIN POTATOES

You partially cook the potatoes, shred them, combine with other ingredients and bake. They require no last-minute attention

6 to 8 medium red potatoes	Salt
6 to 8 oz. mild Cheddar cheese or process American cheese	Pepper
	1 c. heavy cream

Cook potatoes in jackets until almost tender; do not cook completely. Cool and remove skins. With coarse grater, grate a layer of potatoes into a buttered 9" square shallow baking dish. Grate a thin layer of cheese evenly over them. Season with salt and pepper as desired. Repeat until baking dish is full. Pour cream over. Bake, uncovered, in moderate oven (350°) 50 to 55 minutes, until a golden brown. Makes 8 servings.

NOTE: To freeze the potatoes, bake 40 to 45 minutes. Cool, wrap and freeze. To serve, partially thaw and pour over from ¼ to ⅓ c. additional cream. Place in slow oven (325°) 35 to 40 minutes. If a deep casserole is used, increase the baking time a few minutes.

FRESH MUSHROOM SALAD

Mushrooms, a faithful partner to steak, appear in a new way

2 c. water
2 tblsp. lemon juice
1 lb. fresh mushrooms, cut in ⅛″ slices
½ c. heavy cream

1½ tsp. grated onion
⅛ tsp. white pepper
1 tsp. salt
Lettuce
Chopped fresh chives

Bring water and lemon juice to a boil in saucepan. Add mushrooms, cover pan and reduce heat. Simmer gently 2 to 3 minutes. Remove from heat, drain and pat mushrooms dry with paper towels. In a 2-qt. bowl combine cream, onion, pepper and salt. Add mushrooms and toss lightly in creamy mixture until well coated. Serve on lettuce and garnish with chopped chives. Makes 4 to 6 servings.

TOSSED SALAD WITH CREAMY DRESSING

It's the special dressing that makes this salad taste so good

¾ c. mayonnaise
¼ c. milk
½ tsp. salt
½ tsp. lemon-pepper seasoning

1 large head iceberg lettuce, shredded
2 medium tomatoes, peeled and quartered
1 medium green pepper, diced

In a small bowl combine mayonnaise, milk, salt and lemon-pepper; mix well. Cover and refrigerate at least 1 hour.

At serving time place lettuce, tomatoes and green pepper in big salad bowl, pour over dressing and toss gently. Serve at once. Makes 8 servings.

ORANGE/PEANUT CAKE

Even steak-and-potatoes men find this cake irresistible

1 (1 lb. 2.5 oz.) pkg. orange chiffon cake mix
1½ c. heavy cream

3 tblsp. confectioners sugar
½ tsp. almond extract
½ lb. peanut brittle

Prepare batter and bake cake by package directions. Cool and store as package directs.

About 3 hours before serving cake, whip cream with sugar in a chilled bowl until stiff, adding almond extract during the last minute or two of beating. Spread on top and sides of cake.

Crush peanut brittle with rolling pin and sprinkle over the cake. Place in refrigerator at once. Makes 10 servings.

SUNDOWN BARBECUE

Grilled Flank Steak*
Potato Salad*
Vegetable Salad Tray
Mayonnaise Dip   Creamy Cheese Dip*
Garlic Bread
Lattice Apple Pie with Cream*

You will recognize this menu as a men's special. Not that it does not please women and children, for it does. But, starting with grilled beef and ending with apple pie, it's bound to appeal to the masculine members of the party.

As the timetable shows, you prepare most of the food for the meal on barbecue day. This creates no hardship because you can get all the cooking out of the way before noon. The steak, of course, must be grilled during the last 15 minutes before eating, but this is the host's chore. While he cooks the beef, the hostess and children can take the salad, vegetable tray, bread and the dips to the table and pour the beverages—milk for the youngsters, coffee for the adults.

TIMETABLE

Do-Ahead: Make marinade a day before you want to use it, cover and chill. It's a good idea to pour it over the steak, cover and let it chill overnight, although you can leave this until the following day. Fix the blue cheese dip and chill overnight.

On Guest Day: Bake pies in the morning—two of them for 8 to 12 servings. Make the potato salad and chill several hours. Turn the steak in the marinade several times during the day. Prepare the vegetables for the tray sometime during the afternoon; put celery sticks, cauliflowerets and peeled thick cucumber slices in ice water. Add peeled tomatoes, quartered, or cherry tomatoes when assembling vegetables on tray at serving time. Stir a little lemon juice into mayonnaise and chill for a raw vegetable dip children especially like. Stir it before serving. Let the host take charge of lighting the charcoal and getting the coals to the right stage for cooking the steaks at the proper time. It takes from 8 to 15 minutes for total cooking, depending on degree of doneness desired.

SERVING SUGGESTIONS

Eat indoors or out, whichever you prefer. The weather may make the decision for you. Near the vegetable tray, designed secretly by the menu planner to include uncooked vegetables in the meal, set the bowls containing the dips. Warm the pie in a preheated slow oven (300°) 5 to 8 minutes just before sitting down to eat the main course. Turn the heat off and leave pie in oven until time to cut and serve it. Faintly warm, this apple pie is at its best.

GRILLED FLANK STEAK

Steak is best broiled very rare and cut across grain to serve

2 unscored flank steaks, about 1½ lbs. each
3 c. Special Marinade

At least 2 hours before barbecue time, place the steaks in Special Marinade. (Two hours is the minimum time.) It should cover the steaks. Turn steaks at least two or three times while in the marinade.

Set grill about 6″ above hot coals. (Hold your hand, palm down, over the grill near the cooking level. If you can keep it there only about 2 seconds, it is hot enough for the steaks.)

Grease grill lightly, place steaks on grill and cook to desired doneness. For total cooking time, allow about 8 minutes for rare to medium (4 minutes for each side); 10 to 15 minutes for medium to well done (5 to 8 minutes on each side). Turn once during grilling. Serve hot, cut diagonally across the grain. Makes 8 servings.

N O T E : You can cook the steak in the broiling oven. Broil it 2 or 3″ from heat, about 5 minutes on each side. When cooked this way it is called London Broil.

SPECIAL MARINADE

Give sauce a share of credit for steak's wonderful flavor

1½ c. salad oil	2 tsp. coarse black pepper
¾ c. soy sauce	½ c. wine vinegar
¼ c. Worcestershire sauce	2 tsp. parsley flakes
2 tblsp. dry mustard	2 cloves garlic, crushed
2 tsp. salt	⅓ c. lemon juice

Combine all ingredients; stir to blend. Make this sauce the day before using if possible. Makes 3 cups.

POTATO SALAD

Add the salad dressing to the warm potatoes for superior flavors

6 to 8 potatoes	¼ c. chopped onion
⅔ c. salad dressing	½ c. diced celery
2 tblsp. vinegar	2 tblsp. chopped green pepper
1½ tsp. salt	2 tblsp. diced sweet pickle
⅛ tsp. ground red pepper (more if you like it)	3 hard-cooked eggs, sliced

Cook potatoes in jackets; let cool 15 to 30 minutes, until you can handle them.

Meanwhile, mix together salad dressing, vinegar, salt and red pepper.

Peel and cube warm potatoes (should have about 6 c.); combine with remaining ingredients. Add salad dressing carefully, stirring in lightly. Let chill in refrigerator 2 to 4 hours before serving. Sprinkle lightly with paprika, if desired. Makes 6 to 8 servings.

N O T E : You can double this recipe for 12 to 16 servings.

CREAMY CHEESE DIP

For a great eating experience, dunk raw vegetables in tangy dip

¼ lb. blue or Roquefort cheese	¼ tsp. coarsely ground black pepper
1 c. mayonnaise	
½ c. dairy sour cream	¼ tsp. garlic salt
2 tblsp. lemon juice	Salt to taste
2 tblsp. chopped parsley	Dash of ground red pepper
1 tsp. grated onion	

Place cheese in bowl and mash with a fork; gradually blend in mayonnaise and sour cream, creaming until smooth.

Add remaining ingredients and mix thoroughly. Chill several hours or overnight. Makes 2 cups.

LATTICE APPLE PIE WITH CREAM

Try the old-time custom of pouring cream on pie, or the new way of spreading on sour cream and sprinkling with brown sugar

Pastry for 2-crust 9″ pie
4 large quick-cooking apples,
  peeled and cut in eighths
1 c. sugar
½ tsp. ground cinnamon

½ tsp. ground allspice
3 tblsp. butter or regular
  margarine
Brown sugar
Dairy sour or sweet cream

Arrange apples in pastry-lined pan. Sprinkle with ½ c. sugar mixed with cinnamon.

Sift together remaining ½ c. sugar and allspice. Cut in butter with pastry blender or fork until mixture is crumbly. Sprinkle over apples and top with pastry lattice; flute edges.

Bake in hot oven (425°) 40 minutes. Turn off heat and leave pie in oven another 10 minutes. Serve pie at table and pass a bowl of brown sugar that pours and a bowl of dairy sour cream, or a pitcher of sweet cream to pour over pie.

HAWAIIAN-STYLE DINNER

Teriyaki Steak*
Fluffy Rice   Orange-Glazed Carrots*
Spinach/Sesame Salad*
Bread Sticks
Poppyseed Cake*   Pineapple

You can treat your guests to this Hawaiian-style dinner even though you live far from the islands. Teriyaki Steak has the spotlight in this meal. In the beginning it is a pot roast, but you convert it into tender steak slices. Marinating the beef in a sauce has much to do with the transformation.

This dinner contains colorful foods, such as orange carrots and crisp, dark green leaves of young spinach. Even the Poppyseed Cake looks different. The fluted tube pan takes the responsibility for this change. Fresh pineapple, if available, accompanies the cake, but in case it is unavailable, serve chilled canned pineapple chunks or slices packed in juice with no sugar added.

TIMETABLE

Do-Ahead: Bake cake a day ahead. Put beef in glass or ceramic baking dish or bowl, cover with the marinade and refrigerate 12 to 24 hours, turning several times. Wash and drain spinach; place in a plastic bag and chill. Make salad dressing. If serving fresh pineapple, cut it up, and sugar lightly. Cover and chill.

On Guest Day: Put beef in preheated broiler at least 30 minutes before dinnertime. Meanwhile, cook rice, toast sesame seeds by spreading in small shallow pan and heating in a moderate oven (350°) until light brown. Cook carrots. Toss salad at the last minute.

SERVING SUGGESTIONS

Carve meat in kitchen or at the table, as desired. Serve it on a warm platter. Pass rice and carrots in bowls. Dust the cooled cake with confectioners sugar.

TERIYAKI STEAK

Be sure to carve steak diagonally across grain in thin slices

½ c. soy sauce	1 clove garlic, minced
⅓ c. water	1 (3 to 4 lb.) boneless bottom
1 tblsp. brown sugar	round, chuck or rump pot
½ tsp. ground ginger	roast, cut 2 to 2½″ thick

Combine soy sauce, water, brown sugar, ginger and garlic. Pour over pot roast in glass or ceramic dish; cover and refrigerate 12 to 24 hours, turning roast occasionally.

Remove meat from marinade, place on broiler rack and broil 5 to 6″ from source of heat about 15 minutes, or until very crusty. Turn and broil on other side until inside is desired doneness (usually rather rare). To serve, cut meat across grain at slanted angle into thin slices. Serve with drippings and, if desired, additional teriyaki sauce, made as for marinade. Makes 8 servings.

ORANGE-GLAZED CARROTS

The orange flavor enhances the taste of orange-colored carrots

10 medium carrots, peeled and sliced	½ tsp. salt
2 tblsp. sugar	½ tsp. ground ginger
2 tsp. cornstarch	½ c. orange juice
	¼ c. butter

Slice carrots crosswise on the bias about ½" thick. Cook, covered, in a little boiling salted water (½ tsp. salt to 1 c. water) until just tender, about 20 minutes. Drain.

Meanwhile, combine sugar, cornstarch, salt and ginger in a small saucepan. Add orange juice; cook, stirring constantly, until mixture thickens and bubbles. Boil 1 minute. Stir in butter. Pour over hot carrots and toss to coat with orange sauce. Makes 8 servings.

SPINACH/SESAME SALAD

Add sesame seeds at the last minute so they'll retain crispness

1 lb. young spinach (2 qts.)	¼ tsp. paprika
½ c. sugar	1 tblsp. finely grated onion
¼ c. vinegar	1 tblsp. Toasted Sesame Seeds
¼ c. salad oil	(see Index)
½ tsp. salt	

Wash spinach; drain, dry, place in plastic bag and chill.

In a small saucepan combine sugar and vinegar; bring to a boil. Remove from heat. Pour into a small jar; add oil, salt, paprika and onion; mix well. Cover and chill.

Tear spinach into bite-size pieces. Add enough of the dressing (shake before using) to coat leaves. Add sesame seeds, toss and serve immediately. Makes 6 servings.

POPPYSEED CAKE

Salad oil gives cake a rich flavor, it's baked in an interesting shape

4 eggs, well beaten	1½ tsp. baking soda
2 c. sugar	⅔ c. evaporated milk
1½ c. salad oil	3 tblsp. poppyseeds
3 c. sifted flour	Confectioners sugar (optional)
½ tsp. salt	

Combine eggs and sugar and beat well; add oil and blend.

Sift together flour, salt and soda; add alternately with milk to beaten mixture. Stir in poppyseeds. Spoon into well-greased and floured 10″ fluted tube pan. Bake in moderate oven (375°) 40 to 45 minutes, or until cake tests done. Cool on rack 10 minutes, then remove from pan. Dust with sifted confectioners sugar, if desired.

FONDUE FOURSOME

CowBelles' Beef Fondue*   Dipping Sauces*
Tossed Green Salad
Sliced Hard Rolls
Fruit

When entertaining a couple at an evening meal, whether dinner or supper, give beef fondue a try. This main dish responds to many names, but in farm and ranch country it's called CowBelles' Beef Fondue. CowBelles, the wives of cattlemen, say a menu featuring cook-your-own steak is an easy-on-the-hostess choice that produces a meal their husbands really like. These people know good beef when they see it. Only the very tender cuts enter their fondue pots.

If you have more than one fondue pot with a metal cooker, or can borrow one, you can increase your guest list. More than four fondue forks dipping into the same pot often tangle. And it's easier to keep the cooking oil at the proper temperature with a foursome participating.

Serve several sauces in bowls. Let everyone spoon his selections for dunking onto his plate, or if you have enough small bowls or Chinese teacups without handles, give everyone his own sauces. We give you recipes for some delicious ones; you may also set out ketchup, chili sauce, prepared mustard, prepared horse-radish and some bottled meat sauces, however. Some men prefer to dunk their beef in these old favorites. And remember to put salt and pepper shakers on the table.

Make the remainder of the meal simple . . . a tossed green salad or lettuce wedges with a choice of bottled dressings. Sliced hard rolls or French bread will be enjoyed. Wind up with fruit, such as a cup of orange and grapefruit sections with sliced bananas, or with some frozen sliced peaches, partially thawed. Keep the coffeepot filled.

TIMETABLE

On Guest Day: Make the sauces and chill. Cut the trimmed beef in bite-size cubes. Wash, drain and chill salad greens in a plastic bag. Make the fruit cup an hour before mealtime and refrigerate, or put the frozen peaches in the refrigerator to partially thaw. Set the table, slice the rolls, make the coffee and toss the salad. Heat the cooking oil in the metal fondue cooker on the kitchen range. Carry it to the table and place over fondue burner. (If using an electric fondue pot, heat the oil on its unit.) Start cooking at once.

SERVING SUGGESTIONS

Provide everyone with a plate, fondue fork, dinner fork and teaspoon. Have plenty of paper napkins handy.

COWBELLES' BEEF FONDUE

Have beef cubes at room temperature when you dip them into hot oil

Salad oil   Dipping Sauces
Salt
1½ lbs. trimmed beef tenderloin,
  rib-eye or sirloin, cut in ¾"
  cubes

Pour oil into metal fondue cooker to the depth of 2". Never fill it to more than half its capacity. Heat on range to 425° on fat thermometer. Add 1 tsp. salt. Carry to the table. (Or follow manufacturer's directions with electric fondue pot.) Start cooking at once. If the oil cools during the cooking, reheat it.

Spear meat with fondue fork and dip it into the hot oil. It cooks quickly, or in 10 to 20 seconds for rare beef, about 50 seconds for well done. Transfer beef to dinner fork and dip it in your choice of sauces. Makes 4 servings.

NOTE: You can cook 1" cubes of raw pork like the beef, but give them 2 to 3 minutes in the hot oil to make sure they are well done. You also can cook ¾" cubes of chicken or turkey meat and lamb, or fully cooked ham, like the beef. It takes 2 to 3 minutes for the chicken and turkey, ¾ to 1 minute for lamb and 1 minute for the ham to cook.

DIPPING SAUCES FOR MEAT AND CHICKEN FONDUES

Garlic Butter: Cream ½ c. butter until fluffy. Stir in 1 small clove garlic, crushed. Cover and let stand at room temperature ½ to 1 hour, in refrigerator for longer storage. Makes about ½ cup.

Countryman's Choice: Combine 6 tblsp. ketchup, 6 tblsp. chili sauce, 2 tblsp. prepared horse-radish, 2 tsp. lemon juice and, if you like, a dash of hot pepper sauce. Makes about 1 cup.

Dill Sauce: Combine 1 c. dairy sour cream, 1 tblsp. chopped chives, 1 tsp. vinegar, ½ tsp. grated onion, ½ tsp. dill weed and salt to season, about ¼ tsp. Mix well. Makes about 1 cup.

Swiss Cheese Sauce: Blend ½ c. mayonnaise and ¼ c. grated Swiss cheese. Makes about ⅔ cup.

Green Goddess Dip: Blend 2 tblsp. milk into 2 (3 oz.) pkgs. cream cheese; beat well. Stir in ½ c. chopped cucumber, 1 tsp. finely chopped onion, ½ tsp. salt and ¼ tsp. ground cumin. Makes about 1⅓ cups.

Wine Sauce: Combine ¾ c. sauterne and ¼ c. ketchup in saucepan. Stir and bring to a boil. Reduce heat and simmer uncovered about 5 minutes. (The wine's alcohol evaporates and leaves the characteristic grape flavor in the sauce.) Meanwhile, make a paste with 4 tsp. cornstarch and 2 tblsp. cold water. Stir into wine mixture. Add 1 tblsp. butter or regular margarine and cook 1 minute. Makes about ¾ cup.

Brown Mushroom Sauce: Melt 2 tblsp. butter or regular margarine in saucepan; blend in 2 tblsp. flour. Remove from heat and stir in ⅔ c. beef broth (canned or homemade). Return to heat and cook and stir until mixture thickens. Remove from heat. Stir in 1 (3 oz.) can chopped mushrooms, drained and chopped more finely, 1 tsp. Worcestershire sauce and ½ c. dairy sour cream. Heat, but do not let come to a boil. Serve hot. (Reheat at serving time if made ahead.) Makes about 1⅓ cups.

Horse-radish Sauce: Whip ½ c. chilled heavy cream; fold in 3 tblsp. prepared horse-radish, well drained. Season with salt, about ½ tsp. Makes about 1 cup.

IOWA CORN DINNER

Broiled Ground Beef*	Potatoes Basque Style*
Corn on the Cob	Sliced Tomato Platter
Onion/Mustard Buns*	Peach Melba Parfait*

Summer is the delightful time when corn feasts bring families together in many communities around the country to enjoy two of America's food gifts to the world, sweet corn and tomatoes. When you puncture a few kernels of sweet corn with your thumbnail and a milky juice squirts out, it's time to have a corn cookout or dinner. Chances are good that at the same time dead-ripe tomatoes will hang red and heavy on the vines.

This menu gives the two garden specialties the spotlight and teams them with complementary foods. Ground beef, seasoned and shaped like a porterhouse steak (as many steaks as you need) broils to perfection. Cook it kindly and it will taste almost as good as a porterhouse—better, hamburger fans say. Serve the Onion/Mustard Buns with it for a happy surprise.

Be generous with tomatoes, provide plenty of potatoes and at the end of the feast bring out Peach Melba Parfait featuring fresh peaches.

TIMETABLE

Do-Ahead: You can bake the rolls a day or several days ahead, cool, wrap and freeze.

On Guest Day: Peel chilled tomatoes, cut in thick slices and place on platter. Drizzle on a little salad oil if you wish and sprinkle with fresh chopped basil leaves.

Make Peach Melba Parfait and put it in refrigerator just before you prepare the potatoes. Put potatoes on to cook about 30 minutes before mealtime. Preheat the broiler so it will be ready for the meat 15 minutes before dinner. Gather, husk and remove silks from corn and put it on to cook in cold unsalted water to cover when you put the meat in the broiler. Bring water to a full rolling boil, lift out the corn with tongs, drain and serve.

SERVING SUGGESTIONS

Since the meat and corn are at their best when piping hot, this is not a meal that waits successfully. Carry these foods to the table last and start the butter dish and salt shaker, so important to corn lovers, on their rounds immediately.

BROILED GROUND BEEF

Some people call this pennywise steak—everyone calls it good

1½ lbs. ground round steak	3 tblsp. grated onion
1 tsp. salt	1 egg
¼ tsp. pepper	⅓ c. milk
2 tsp. Worcestershire sauce	Melted shortening

Combine all ingredients except shortening; mix until blended. Form entire mixture into the shape of a porterhouse steak about ¾" thick. Place on cold broiler grid. Brush with melted shortening.

Broil 4 to 5" from heat about 8 minutes on each side until well browned. Use two spatulas for easy turning. Makes 6 servings.

POTATOES BASQUE STYLE

Potatoes and other vegetables cook quickly in chicken broth

½ c. finely chopped onion	Water
½ c. chopped celery	2 lbs. potatoes, peeled and cut in
½ c. shredded carrot	1" cubes (about 4 c.)
1 clove garlic, minced	½ tsp. salt
2 tblsp. butter	⅛ tsp. pepper
1 (10½ oz.) can chicken broth	Chopped fresh parsley

Sauté onion, celery, carrot and garlic in melted butter in a 10" skillet until tender.

Combine chicken broth with enough water to make 2 cups. Add chicken broth, potatoes, salt and pepper to sautéed vegetables. Cover; simmer for 10 minutes. Remove cover. Simmer, stirring occasionally, 20 minutes or until broth is thickened. Sprinkle with parsley. Makes 4 to 6 servings.

ONION/MUSTARD BUNS

Tired of plain buns? Try these seasoned specials—you'll love them

1 pkg. active dry yeast	2 c. scalded milk
¼ c. warm water (110 to 115°)	6 c. sifted flour
2 tblsp. sugar	1 egg, slightly beaten
1 tblsp. prepared mustard	2 tblsp. instant minced onion
1½ tsp. salt	¼ c. water
½ tsp. pepper	1 egg, beaten
2 tblsp. instant minced onion	2 tblsp. water
2 tblsp. salad oil	

Dissolve yeast in warm water.

Combine sugar, mustard, salt, pepper, 2 tblsp. instant onion and oil in large bowl. Stir in milk. Cool until lukewarm.

Add 2 c. flour to milk mixture, beating until smooth. Add yeast and slightly beaten egg. Stir in enough remaining flour to make a soft dough.

Turn onto floured surface; knead until smooth, about 5 to 8 minutes. Place in greased bowl; invert to grease top. Cover; let rise until doubled, about 1½ hours. Punch down. Divide dough in half. Let rest 10 minutes. Pat each portion of dough into a 9″ square. Cut each square into 9 portions. Tuck corners under to form buns. Flatten with palm of hand. Let rise until doubled, about 30 minutes.

Meanwhile, combine 2 tblsp. minced onion and ¼ c. water; allow to stand 5 minutes.

Combine beaten egg and 2 tblsp. water; brush rolls with mixture. Sprinkle with onion. Bake in moderate oven (375°) 20 minutes, or until golden brown. Makes 18 buns.

PEACH MELBA PARFAIT

New version of Peaches Melba—mold this beauty in glass dishes

1 (3 oz.) pkg. raspberry flavor gelatin	1 (3 oz.) pkg. peach flavor gelatin
2 c. hot water	½ c. cold water
1 (10 oz.) pkg. frozen raspberries (1¼ c.)	1 pt. vanilla ice cream
	1½ c. diced fresh peaches

Dissolve raspberry gelatin in 1 c. hot water in bowl. Add unthawed raspberries. Stir occasionally to separate berries. Let thaw (it will begin to set).

Pour 1 c. hot water over peach gelatin in another bowl; stir to dissolve. Add ½ c. cold water. Add ice cream in eight chunks; stir to melt. Refrigerate until thick enough to mound up.

Spoon slightly thickened raspberry mixture into 8 dessert dishes.

When ice cream mixture has thickened, fold in peaches and spoon over raspberry mixture. Chill at least 30 minutes before serving. Makes 8 servings.

COUNTRY FAMILY DINNER

Meat Balls in Sour Cream*
Fluffy Rice or Mashed Potatoes
Calico Green Salad*
Dill Pickle Slices
Hot Rolls   Crab Apple Jelly
Cherry Torte*

Swedish meat balls go American in this dinner. Corn chips replace the traditional bread crumbs and provide a subtle flavor difference. Because the food appeals to and is suitable for both children and adults, this is an excellent menu to follow when you entertain a family.

While you do all the cooking on the day company comes, getting this dinner is neither time-consuming nor difficult. The meat balls in gravy taste great spooned over rice, but, if little children are present, you may wish to serve mashed potatoes instead. Packaged instant potatoes make quick work out of fixing them. The rolls and jelly also are favorites with youngsters.

TIMETABLE

Do-Ahead: Make sure you have the necessary ingredients on hand, especially those used less frequently, such as corn chips, dairy sour cream, olives for salad and canned cherry pie filling. Wash and drain the salad greens a day ahead. Chill them in plastic bags. Make the salad dressing and put the bottle of olives in the refrigerator.

On Guest Day: Make the Cherry Torte. Brown bread cubes for salad. About 45 minutes before dinnertime, mix, shape and put meat balls in oven to brown. Put rice on to cook; heat and season the canned or frozen green beans. Place all the salad ingredients, except bread cubes and dressing, in the salad bowl. Make sauce and add the meat balls to it.

SERVING SUGGESTIONS

This is a sit-down dinner. It is a good idea to serve the plates in the kitchen to adjust size of servings for people of different ages. Smaller ones, for young children, larger ones for teen-age boys. If you are serving mashed potatoes, arrange mounds of them on plate. Make a depression in each one with the back of a spoon. Fill with melted butter and sprinkle the yellow pools with chopped chives (or parsley for children). Spoon the meat balls alongside.

MEAT BALLS IN SOUR CREAM

Ground beef plays many roles in meals—this is a tasty one

1 c. crushed corn chips	1 c. finely chopped onion
1 c. milk	2 tblsp. flour
1 clove garlic, minced	1 can condensed beef broth
1 tblsp. parsley flakes	½ c. water
1 tsp. salt	1 tsp. Worcestershire sauce
Dash of pepper	1 c. dairy sour cream
2 lbs. lean ground beef	Paprika
3 tblsp. butter or regular margarine	Hot cooked rice

Combine corn chips, milk, garlic, parsley, salt and pepper. Add beef and mix well. Shape in small balls and place in large, shallow pan. Bake in moderate oven (375°) 20 minutes, shaking pan several times to turn balls.

Melt butter in a 3-qt. saucepan; add onion and cook until tender, but do not brown. Blend in flour. Add beef broth, water and Worcestershire sauce all at once. Cook, stirring until mixture comes to a boil. Reduce heat and blend in sour cream. Heat, but do not boil. Add meat balls and stir gently to avoid breaking them. Sprinkle with paprika. Serve over cooked rice, or with mashed potatoes. Makes 8 servings.

CALICO GREEN SALAD

Homemade or other firm-textured bread makes the best cubes

4 slices white bread

¼ c. butter or regular margarine

2 cloves garlic, minced

½ head romaine, torn in bite-size pieces

1 medium head iceberg lettuce, torn in bite-size pieces

¾ c. sliced pimiento-stuffed olives

¾ c. thinly sliced carrots

¼ c. minced green onion

Vinegar/Oil Dressing

Trim crusts from bread; cut bread in ½" cubes.

Melt butter in skillet; add garlic and cook 1 minute without browning, stirring constantly. Add bread cubes and cook, tossing to prevent burning, until golden brown. Drain on paper toweling until cool.

Place romaine, head lettuce, olives, carrots and onion in salad bowl. Just before serving, toss with Vinegar/Oil Dressing (shake well before using). Add bread cubes and toss again. Makes 8 servings.

Vinegar/Oil Dressing: Combine ⅔ c. salad oil, 2 tblsp. red wine vinegar, ½ tsp. salt, ⅛ tsp. orégano leaves, crushed, and a dash of pepper. Chill. Shake before using.

CHERRY TORTE

Big dessert has a crumb crust, cherry filling and meringue on top

Crust:

2 c. sifted flour

½ tsp. salt

¼ c. confectioners sugar

¾ c. butter or regular margarine

1 tsp. grated lemon peel

½ c. finely chopped walnuts

Filling:

1 (1 lb. 8 oz. or 1 lb. 5 oz.) jar cherry pie filling

1½ tsp. cornstarch, dissolved in 1 tblsp. water

1 tblsp. butter or regular margarine

Meringue:

4 egg whites

⅛ tsp. salt

⅛ tsp. cream of tartar

½ tsp. vanilla

8 tblsp. sugar

Sift together dry ingredients for crust; cut in butter to make a mixture the consistency of coarse cornmeal. Toss with lemon peel and nuts. Press into shallow 2-qt. glass baking dish. Bake in moderate oven (375°) 20 minutes, or until lightly browned.

Combine pie filling and cornstarch mixture; cook over medium heat, stirring constantly, until thickened. Remove from heat; stir in butter. Pour hot filling into hot crust; top with meringue.

To make meringue, combine egg whites, salt, cream of tartar and vanilla; beat until foamy. Beat in sugar, 1 tblsp. at a time, beating thoroughly after each addition. Swirl on pie filling. Brown in moderate oven (350°) about 15 minutes. Makes 10 to 12 servings.

FOUR-SEASON DINNER

Glazed Beef Balls*   Indiana Succotash*
Lettuce   Red Clover Salad Dressing*
Hard Rolls
Applesauce Meringue Pie*

This menu is good for any month on the calendar; it's adaptable to seasonal changes. You needn't tinker with the beef, however—it's right for meals the year around.

To make succotash in the good old summertime you can gather green beans fresh from the vines and cut sweet corn from the cob. But when it's snowing, try canned or frozen beans and corn (easier and quicker).

You can fill the baked pie shell with that wonderful tart-sweet applesauce made with early-summer fruit. If you do, you can cut in half the amount of lemon juice and grated peel which point up the flavor of sauce from bland, sweet apples.

Tailoring meals and recipes to fit the season, or to the foods most available and to the weather, is a well-established pattern in farm kitchens. The country woman always has had to be a flexible cook!

TIMETABLE

Do-Ahead: You can make the salad dressing and applesauce a day ahead; refrigerate. You also can bake the pie shell.

On Guest Day: Mix and shape meat balls a couple of hours before you plan to serve them. They need to chill at least an hour. Make the glaze while the meat balls bake. Cut the green beans for the succotash some time while meat balls are chilling. Cook them so they'll be ready to season and heat with the corn. (Cutting beans is somewhat tedious; you *can* use larger pieces, but the fine ones look and taste better.) The recipe is a big one, but appetites are also big when succotash appears.

Bake the pie at any time during the day. Be sure to cool it away from drafts so the meringue will stay tall.

SERVING SUGGESTIONS

This is an excellent dinner to serve buffet style. To serve more than 6 people, you will need to fix 2 recipes of beef balls and make 2 pies. Serve beef balls on a big platter and sprinkle with fresh parsley snipped with scissors.

GLAZED BEEF BALLS

Fine, tasty way to glamorize ground beef for special occasions

½ c. fine bread crumbs	1 egg, beaten
1 tsp. salt	½ c. tomato juice
¼ tsp. pepper	2 tblsp. salad oil
1 tblsp. grated onion	1 lb. lean ground beef
½ tsp. prepared horse-radish	Glaze
1 tblsp. Worcestershire sauce	

Blend together all ingredients, except beef and Glaze. Add to beef, mixing well. Chill at least 1 hour.

Shape meat mixture in balls about the size of walnuts. Place in shallow baking pan; bake in extremely hot oven (500°) 10 to 12 minutes, or until browned. Add to Glaze and heat. Makes about 24 balls.

Glaze: Combine in saucepan, ¼ c. brown sugar, firmly packed, 2 tblsp. flour, 1 tsp. dry mustard, ¼ c. chili sauce, ¼ c. dark corn syrup, ½ tsp. salt, dash of Tabasco sauce and ¼ c. orange juice. Cook and stir until slightly thickened.

INDIANA SUCCOTASH

Expert seasonings explain the popularity of this vegetable duo

1½ lbs. green beans	2 (1 lb. 1 oz.) cans whole kernel corn, drained
1½ tsp. salt	¾ tsp. paprika
1½ c. green onions with tops	¾ tsp. celery salt
6 tblsp. butter	1 tsp. sugar

Cut beans in rounds about the size of the yellow corn kernels; cook with ½ tsp. salt in water to cover about 15 minutes, or just until tender. Drain.

Sauté green onions in butter until transparent (do not brown); add corn, 1 tsp. salt, paprika, celery salt and sugar, then beans.

Simmer, covered, about 10 minutes to blend seasonings and heat thoroughly. Makes 12 servings.

N O T E : Fresh corn, cut from the top, may be used when available instead of canned corn.

RED CLOVER SALAD DRESSING

Men especially like this ketchup-flavored, bright red dressing

1 c. honey	½ c. ketchup
1½ tblsp. salt	½ c. lemon juice
1 tblsp. dry mustard	1 c. vinegar
1½ tblsp. paprika	2 c. salad oil

Mix all ingredients, except salad oil, with electric mixer until well blended.

Gradually add salad oil, beating constantly, to blend well and to obtain the consistency of mayonnaise.

Use to serve with greens or fruits. Makes about 5 cups.

APPLESAUCE MERINGUE PIE

Few apple pies equal this one in beauty, and it's delicious. The makings for it usually are on hand—pie shell in freezer, eggs in refrigerator, applesauce in cupboard. Making pie is an easy and fast assembly job—it bakes only to brown the meringue

Baked 9″ pie shell	1 tblsp. cornstarch
2 c. sweetened applesauce	3 eggs, separated
Juice of 1 lemon	¼ tsp. cream of tartar
2 tsp. grated lemon peel	¼ tsp. salt
¼ tsp. salt	6 tblsp. sugar
¼ tsp. ground cinnamon	½ tsp. vanilla

Combine applesauce, lemon juice, peel, ¼ tsp. salt, cinnamon, cornstarch and slightly beaten egg yolks in saucepan; cook until thick and smooth. Cool slightly. Pour into baked pie shell. Spread filling to level.

Cover warm filling with meringue made of beaten egg whites, cream of tartar, ¼ tsp. salt, sugar and vanilla. Spread to cover entire filling; seal to pastry.

Bake in hot oven (425°) 10 to 12 minutes, until meringue is nicely browned. Makes 8 servings.

COMBINATION
FAMILY-FRIENDS DINNER

Meat Ball Stew*
Green Bean Salad
French Cheese Bread*
Vanilla Ice Cream
Choco/Apple Cupcakes*   Caramel Frosting*

This is the kind of family meal you're proud to share with an unexpected last-minute guest. If your son calls and wants to bring a friend home from school for dinner before they take off for the football game or other athletic event, you can be confident the boys will like what they eat. And if you and your husband, shortly before mealtime, decide to invite a neighboring couple for dinner and the evening, you will feel equally comfortable about the food you prepared.

The main dish, a stew, contains vegetables and ground beef shaped in expertly seasoned balls. Sliced French bread, spread with a cheese mixture and toasted, supplies flavorful crispness. The salad is the one food you may wish to dress up a little. One way to do this is to garnish the individual servings with half of a deviled egg.

Caramel-frosted cupcakes, served with a scoop of ice cream, glasses of cold milk and a hot beverage for the grownups sends people from the table satisfied and ready to enjoy the evening.

TIMETABLE

Do-Ahead: Bake and frost the cupcakes a day (or several days) ahead and freeze them. You also can make the salad a day ahead, cover and chill.

On Guest Day: See Index for Green Bean Salad recipe (included in "Make-Ahead Dinner" menu). Cook bacon for garnishing salad at any time convenient, but add it just before serving. An hour before dinnertime, start preparing meat balls and vegetables. Put them on to cook about 35 minutes before you want to serve them. Meanwhile, slice the French bread, spread with cheese mixture. Toast just before you dish up the stew. If cupcakes are frozen, set them out on the kitchen counter to thaw just before you sit down to eat dinner.

SERVING SUGGESTIONS

Serve the stew in a bowl, the salad on individual plates and the bread in a basket or roll warmer. Pass the food around the table family style, letting everyone help himself. Serve the dessert from the kitchen, a cupcake on each dessert plate accompanied with a scoop of ice cream from the freezer.

MEAT BALL STEW

Three reasons men praise this stew: the meat, potatoes and gravy

1½ lbs. ground beef	1 (10½ oz.) can condensed beef
1 c. soft bread crumbs	broth
¼ c. finely chopped onion	4 medium potatoes, peeled and
1 egg, beaten	quartered
1 tsp. salt	4 carrots, scraped and cut in 1″
½ tsp. marjoram leaves	chunks
¼ tsp. thyme leaves	8 small white onions, peeled
2 tblsp. salad oil	2 tblsp. chopped fresh parsley
1 can condensed tomato soup	

Combine ground beef, bread crumbs, chopped onion, egg, salt, marjoram and thyme. Shape into 24 meat balls. Brown in oil in 4-qt. Dutch oven. Remove meat balls as they brown.

Combine soup and broth in Dutch oven. Add meat balls, potatoes, carrots and white onions. Bring to a boil; cover and simmer 30 minutes, or until vegetables are tender. Add parsley. Makes 6 to 8 servings.

FRENCH CHEESE BREAD

Serve this crunchy cheese-topped French bread hot from the oven

¾ stick butter	¼ c. grated process American
¾ stick regular margarine	cheese
½ tsp. garlic salt	1 loaf French bread, cut in ¾″
⅓ c. grated Parmesan cheese	slices

Melt butter and margarine; add garlic salt. Stir in cheeses. With pastry brush, spread butter mixture evenly on one side of bread slices. Broil buttered side until light golden and bubbling hot. Makes about 21 slices.

CHOCO/APPLE CUPCAKES

Next time you bake these cupcakes spread with your favorite fudge frosting instead of caramel. Both are good; so are unfrosted cakes

½ c. shortening	1 tsp. ground cinnamon
1 c. sugar	½ tsp. ground allspice
1 egg	1½ squares unsweetened
1¾ c. sifted flour	chocolate, grated
1 tsp. baking soda	1¼ c. unsweetened applesauce
½ tsp. salt	Caramel Frosting (optional)

Cream shortening and sugar until light and fluffy. Add egg; beat well.

Sift together dry ingredients. Stir in grated chocolate. Add to creamed mixture alternately with applesauce; mix after each addition.

Fill greased muffin-pan cups two thirds full. Bake in moderate oven (375°) 20 minutes. Cool, then frost with Caramel Frosting, if desired. Makes 18.

CARAMEL FROSTING

Press a pecan or walnut half on each frosted cupcake for a quick trim

½ c. butter	¼ tsp. salt
1 c. dark brown sugar, firmly	¼ c. milk
packed	2 c. sifted confectioners sugar

Melt butter in a saucepan over low heat, but do not let it brown. Stir in brown sugar and salt. Bring to a boil over medium heat and boil hard 2 minutes, stirring all the time. Remove from heat.

Add milk and stir vigorously. Return pan to heat and bring mixture to a full boil again. Remove from heat at once and set aside to cool to lukewarm; it will take about 20 minutes.

Stir confectioners sugar into the lukewarm mixture and beat until smooth. If frosting hardens too much to spread, beat in a few drops of milk. Makes enough to frost about 18 cupcakes or two 8 or 9″ cake layers.

DIFFERENT COUNTRY DINNER

Tuna-Stuffed Tomatoes*
Crackers   Hot Chicken Broth
Beef/Vegetables Californian*
Hot Steamed Rice*
Buttered Peas   Hot Rolls
Apricot Custard Ice Cream*
Chocolate Cake

For an imaginative, up-to-date country dinner, follow this menu. Your friends who have traveled, young people who have worked or been in military service overseas, and those who like to experiment with international dishes in their own kitchens will like this menu particularly. (Avoid inviting people who are only ardent meat-and-potato fans.)

This dinner is not Chinese although it shows a couple of Far Eastern influences—in the method of cooking rice in which the Chinese excel, for instance, and in the fast-cook beef-vegetable main dish.

The menu begins with an appetizer course featuring farm favorites —cherry tomatoes, tuna and hot chicken broth—served in a distinctive way. Dinner ends with a velvety homemade custard ice cream flavored with tart-sweet dried apricots. Three foods listed in the menu are optional—peas, hot rolls and chocolate cake.

TIMETABLE

Do-Ahead: Bake the cake a day ahead if you like, or use a packaged mix and bake it on party day. You can freeze the ice cream, pack it in freezer containers and put in the freezer a day or several days ahead. If you prefer to serve it after it has ripened in the can of the crank freezer, put the dried apricots in a bowl the night before, add water, cover and let them stand overnight to soften and absorb the liquid. It's permissible to scoop out the tomatoes, invert them on a plate (to drain) and refrigerate.

On Guest Day: If you did not freeze the ice cream the previous day, freeze it at your convenience in the afternoon and let it ripen. Stuff the tomatoes and chill. Assemble ingredients for the main dish and cut meat in thin strips. Put the rice on to cook about 45 minutes before dinner. Heat the chicken broth. Assemble the tomatoes and crackers and place mugs for broth on tray. Ask your husband or the older children to carry them to the living room and serve the guests while you cook the remainder of the dinner. Heat the peas (you can use the frozen peas in butter sauce that require only heating). Put rolls wrapped in heavy-duty foil in moderate oven (350°) 10 to 12 minutes. Then cook the main dish. You'll have it ready to serve in less than 15 minutes.

SERVING SUGGESTIONS

Arrange stuffed tomatoes on a large plate, the crackers on another plate. Pour the heated chicken broth (homemade or canned) into a pitcher for easy pouring into mugs. Serve the plates in the kitchen. Serve the ice cream the traditional farm way in dessert bowls set on individual plates, the cake slices on the same plates.

TUNA-STUFFED TOMATOES

Colorful and satisfying finger food to enjoy as prelude to dinner

24 to 30 cherry tomatoes	2 tblsp. chopped ripe olives
1 (7 oz.) can tuna, drained	¾ tsp. seasoned salt
1 green onion, finely chopped	Parsley

Wash and drain tomatoes. Cut a thin slice off the top of each and scoop out the pulp. Invert to drain.

Combine tuna, onion, olives and salt; mix well. Stuff into tomato shells and top each stuffed tomato with a tiny sprig of parsley. Refrigerate until serving time. Makes 24 to 30 stuffed tomatoes.

N O T E : These also are pretty—and nice—filled with your favorite avocado dip.

BEEF/VEGETABLES CALIFORNIAN

Celery and onions should cook only until they are barely tender

2 tblsp. salad oil

1½ lbs. flank steak, cut in thin strips

1 tsp. sugar

2 tblsp. soy sauce

2 c. cut celery (cut diagonally in 1″ pieces)

1 sweet onion, thinly sliced

1 (5 oz.) can water chestnuts, drained and chopped

½ (10 oz.) pkg. frozen French-style green beans

¼ lb. fresh mushrooms

1 chicken or beef bouillon cube

½ c. hot water

1 tblsp. cornstarch

¼ c. cold water

1 (10 oz.) pkg. frozen, chopped spinach, or ½ lb. spinach, cleaned and cut-up

Hot Steamed Rice

Heat oil in large skillet. Add meat, sprinkling with sugar and soy sauce. Cook and stir until meat loses red color. Push it to one side of skillet and add celery, onion, water chestnuts, green beans and mushrooms.

Fry, tossing lightly while cooking. Cook only until celery and onions are tender-crisp.

Dissolve bouillon cube in hot water; add to mixture in skillet.

Add cornstarch to cold water. Add to skillet and heat. Add spinach and cook, tossing while heating. Serve at once over Hot Steamed Rice. Makes 4 to 6 servings.

N O T E : For more servings, cook the same ingredients a second time. Do not try to double recipe and cook the double amount.

HOT STEAMED RICE

The Chinese are accomplished rice cooks. This is their method

1⅓ c. regular long grain rice   2⅓ c. cold water

Place rice in sieve and rinse well under running cold water. Drain.

Put rice in a 2-qt. heavy saucepan and add cold water. Bring to the boiling point quickly over high heat (about 5 minutes). Lower heat; cover and simmer (do not let boil) 20 minutes, or until rice is dry. Turn off heat and let stand, tightly covered, 20 minutes longer. Stir with fork to separate grains. Makes 4 cups.

APRICOT CUSTARD ICE CREAM

Rich creamy custard ice cream luscious with the taste of apricots

1 (8 oz.) pkg. dried apricots	1½ c. milk
1½ c. hot water	4 eggs, slightly beaten
1¾ c. sugar	1 qt. heavy cream
¼ c. flour	1 tblsp. vanilla
Dash of salt	

Place apricots in a small bowl, pour on hot water. Cover and let stand overnight. By morning the fruit will be soft and the water will be absorbed. Do not cook. Put apricots through a food mill or whirl in blender to make a purée.

Combine sugar, flour and salt in large saucepan; stir in milk. Cook and stir over medium heat until sauce thickens and bubbles; let it cook 1 minute. Remove from heat. Gradually stir about ¾ c. of hot mixture into eggs; stir constantly. Add eggs to hot milk mixture in saucepan; cook and stir over medium heat about 1 minute. Remove from heat. Pour into a large mixing bowl and cool.

When mixture is cool, stir in cream, vanilla and apricot purée; cover and refrigerate until cold.

Pour cold ice cream mixture into 2-qt. freezer can, filling two thirds to three fourths full. Adjust dasher and cover. Pack crushed ice and rock salt around can, using 6 parts ice to 1 part salt.

Turn dasher slowly until the ice melts enough to make a brine. Add more ice and salt, mixed in the proper proportion to maintain the ice level. Turn the handle fast and steadily until it turns hard. Then remove the ice until the level is below the lid of can; take off lid and remove the dasher.

Plug the hole in lid and cover can with several thicknesses of waxed paper or foil to make a tight fit for the lid. Pack more ice-salt mixture, using 4 parts ice to 1 part salt, around can and filling the freezer. Cover with a blanket, canvas or other heavy cloth, or with newspaper. Let the ice cream ripen 4 hours before serving. Or put it in the home freezer to ripen. Makes about 2 quarts.

DINNER ON FRIDAY

Spicy Grape Juice Frost*
Easy Beef Burgundy* or Traditional Beef Burgundy*
Toasted French Bread
Tossed Green Salad
Chocolate/Almond Cheese Cake*

Follow this blueprint for the first dinner when long-absent friends arrive late Friday afternoon to spend the weekend. There's so much talking when such guests appear that it's difficult for a hostess to keep her mind on food preparations. You can forget about them until the last few minutes before mealtime if you use this plan.

With the beef in the oven and the French bread ready to toast, you can put the main dish out of your thoughts knowing it will turn out beautifully. The simple version of Beef Burgundy listed in the menu skips the browning of the meat and it simmers lazily in the oven without watching. Just in case you prefer to make the more traditional dish, we include the recipe also—take your choice.

A tossed green salad fits perfectly into this meal, which ends with a gorgeous dessert. You will have some of the cheese cake left over to put in a welcome appearance on Sunday. With dinner under control, you can enjoy sipping the grape juice appetizer in the living room and take part in the conversation.

TIMETABLE

Do-Ahead: Make Chocolate/Almond Cheese Cake the day before you serve it. Keep in refrigerator. Wash, drain and chill salad greens in a plastic bag.

On Guest Day: Fix grape juice whenever convenient and chill. Cut the beef in cubes early in the day; refrigerate. Slice bread ready for toasting. Three hours before dinnertime put the main dish in the oven to cook slowly. Frost the cake, decorate and return to refrigerator. All you will have to do just before serving is toss the salad and toast the bread.

SERVING SUGGESTIONS

This is a good meal to serve buffet style; most people enjoy helping themselves. Float thin lemon slices in glasses of grape juice. Serve Easy Beef Burgundy in the casserole, the toast in a bread basket or roll warmer and the salad in a big bowl. At dessert time, cut the cake, place on individual plates and carry from kitchen to the table.

SPICY GRAPE JUICE FROST

If you prefer the juice without spices, add sugar and mix with an equal part of orange juice; omit lemon juice

1 (6 oz.) can frozen grape juice concentrate	1 allspice berry
1 stick cinnamon	2 tblsp. sugar
3 whole cloves	Lemon juice

Reconstitute grape juice by label directions. Add cinnamon, cloves, allspice and sugar. Simmer in covered saucepan 5 minutes. Strain and discard spices.

Refrigerate until cool. Add lemon juice to taste. Cover and chill until serving time. Pour in glasses half filled with crushed ice. Makes 6 to 8 servings.

EASY BEEF BURGUNDY

Once you cube the beef this dish is exceptionally quick to fix

3 medium onions, sliced	½ tsp. thyme leaves, crushed
2½ lbs. round steak, cut in 1" cubes	¼ tsp. pepper
	3 tblsp. flour
2 (4 oz.) cans mushrooms (stems and pieces)	2 beef bouillon cubes
	2 c. red Burgundy wine
1½ tsp. garlic salt	Toasted French bread slices
½ tsp. marjoram leaves, crushed	

Arrange onion slices on bottom of 3-qt. casserole; top with meat cubes.

Drain mushrooms, reserving liquid. Place mushroom pieces on top of meat. Sprinkle with garlic salt, marjoram, thyme and pepper.

In saucepan gradually blend reserved mushroom liquid into flour to make a smooth paste. Add bouillon cubes and Burgundy and cook, stirring constantly until mixture comes to a boil. The bouillon cubes should be dissolved. If not, remove saucepan from heat and stir mixture until they are dissolved. Pour over meat mixture in casserole.

Cover and bake in moderate oven (350°) 2½ to 3 hours, or until meat is tender. Serve over slices of toasted French bread. Makes 8 servings.

TRADITIONAL BEEF BURGUNDY

This Americanized version of the French stew uses more ingredients and different seasonings, requires more work in preparation and more watching while cooking than Easy Beef Burgundy . . . try both

6 bacon slices	1 c. beef consommé
2 lbs. boneless chuck beef roast	1 tblsp. beef-seasoned stock base
2 tblsp. flour	or 1 beef bouillon cube
Salt	2 bay leaves
Pepper	Dash of thyme leaves, crushed
2 cloves garlic, crushed	6 whole cloves
1 medium onion, chopped	12 white boiling onions
1 c. red Burgundy wine	½ c. fresh mushrooms

Pan-fry bacon until crisp; remove from skillet and set aside.

Cut beef in bite-size pieces, dredge in flour seasoned with salt and pepper. Brown lightly in skillet. Add garlic and chopped onion and brown slightly. Add wine, consommé, stock base, bay leaves and thyme. Stick cloves into one of the boiling onions and add to skillet. Cover and simmer gently 1½ to 2 hours, or until beef is tender.

Thirty minutes before beef is cooked add boiling onions. Fifteen minutes later add the mushrooms. Remove clove-studded onion and bay leaves. Crumble bacon and sprinkle over top; keep warm in chafing dish on the buffet if you wish. Serve with rice or noodles. Makes 6 servings.

CHOCOLATE/ALMOND CHEESE CAKE

A jackpot of good flavors—chocolate, cheese and almonds—in this dessert

1¼ c. graham cracker crumbs (18 crackers)	1 c. sugar
¾ c. very finely chopped unblanched almonds (about 3½ oz.)	3 (8 oz.) pkgs. cream cheese
	2 squares unsweetened chocolate
	2 tsp. vanilla
½ c. melted butter or regular margarine	1 c. dairy sour cream
	1 tblsp. sugar
2 tblsp. sugar	Glacé fruit mix
4 eggs	Toasted slivered almonds

Combine crumbs, chopped almonds, butter and 2 tblsp. sugar; mix well. Line sides and bottom of 9″ spring-form pan with mixture, pressing firmly against pan with back of spoon.

Beat eggs well; gradually add 1 c. sugar, beating until mixture is lemon-colored. Add cheese in small amounts, beating until smooth after each addition.

Melt chocolate over hot water; blend into beaten mixture along with vanilla.

Pour into crumb-lined pan. Bake in moderate oven (350°) 35 to 40 minutes, or until cake is set in center. Remove from oven and cool thoroughly. Loosen up ring and remove side of pan.

Blend sour cream with 1 tblsp. sugar. Spread over torte, making wreath around the edge and a medallion in the center. Garnish with glacé fruit and slivered almonds. Makes 16 servings.

MAKE-AHEAD DINNER

Chilled Tomato Juice	Sesame Melba Toast
Beef/Noodle Bake*	Green Bean Salad*
Peppermint Tapioca*	Chocolate Sauce

The main-dish casserole is a country hostess favorite because it cooks with little or no attention and is easily served. You usually can get it ready for baking hours ahead and refrigerate. All you have to do when getting dinner is tuck it in the oven. There was a time when casseroles meant a mixture of leftovers, but such tasty combinations as this beef-noodle special are company fare. The recipe, shared by a Tennessee homemaker, makes a hearty treat of superior flavors.

This dinner menu is the ideal choice for the woman who returns home from work or other activities about an hour before guests arrive. It is a meal that permits the hostess to be with her guests instead of in the kitchen. And it's a perfect menu for a cooperative meal. All the foods carry successfully.

TIMETABLE

Do-Ahead: You can get the casserole ready to bake a day ahead and refrigerate. The salad and the tapioca dessert are at their best chilled several hours or overnight. You can slice the bread, and spread on the butter-cheese mixture so it will be ready for baking.

On Guest Day: Put the casserole in the oven an hour before dinner time. Make the toast just before the guests arrive. Slice day-old bread ¼″ thick. Spread with equal parts butter or margarine and grated Parmesan cheese creamed together. Sprinkle with sesame seeds; place on baking sheet and bake in slow oven (325°) until lightly browned.

SERVING SUGGESTIONS

Serve the tomato juice and toast in the living room. Pass the toast hot from the oven. If you chill the tapioca in dessert glasses it will be ready to serve. Garnish with a little of the crushed red-and-white peppermint candy; pass the chocolate sauce. Serve the bean salad on crisp lettuce.

BEEF/NOODLE BAKE

You can use sour cream with chives for plain cream and onions

1 lb. ground beef	1 (15 oz.) can tomato sauce
1 (2 oz.) can mushrooms, drained	4 oz. noodles, uncooked
1 clove garlic, crushed	4 green onions, finely chopped
1 tsp. salt	1 (8 oz.) pkg. cream cheese
½ tsp. pepper	1 c. dairy sour cream
2 tsp. sugar	½ c. grated Cheddar cheese

Cook and stir ground beef in 10″ skillet until lightly browned. Add mushrooms, garlic, salt, pepper, sugar and tomato sauce. Cover and simmer 15 minutes.

Cook noodles by package directions and drain.

Combine onions, using some of the green tops, with cream cheese and sour cream. Blend well.

In a greased 2-qt. casserole, evenly spread about a fourth of the noodles; top with a fourth of ground beef mixture. Spread about a fourth of the cream cheese mixture over top. Repeat three times; top with Cheddar cheese. Bake in moderate oven (350°) until bubbling hot in center, about 50 minutes if chilled, 30 to 35 minutes if not chilled. Makes 6 to 8 servings.

GREEN BEAN SALAD

To give salad a touch of bright color add 2 tblsp. chopped pimiento

½ c. vinegar	4 c. cooked green beans
¼ c. salad oil	1 medium onion, finely chopped
1 tsp. salt	Lettuce
¼ tsp. pepper	3 slices fried bacon, crumbled
1 tsp. sugar	

Blend together vinegar, oil, salt, pepper and sugar; pour over beans and onion. Chill well. Serve on lettuce; sprinkle on bacon just before serving. Makes 6 to 8 servings.

PEPPERMINT TAPIOCA

New version of the old-time favorite pudding. The blending of peppermint and chocolate flavors makes this a taste delight

1 qt. milk	2 eggs, separated
⅓ c. quick-cooking tapioca	3 tblsp. finely crushed peppermint
⅓ c. finely crushed peppermint	stick candy
stick candy	½ tsp. vanilla
¼ tsp. salt	Chocolate sauce

Scald milk in double boiler. Combine tapioca, ⅓ c. peppermint candy and salt. Gradually add to hot milk, stirring constantly to prevent lumping. Heat and stir over water until pudding thickens and tapioca is clear.

Beat egg yolks until lemon-colored. Stir in a little of the hot pudding, then add yolks slowly to pudding in double boiler, stirring constantly. Remove from heat.

The surprise in Party Pork Rolls (recipe, **page 192**) is the blended flavors of both fresh and smoked ham. Spread fresh ham steak with ground smoked ham and bread stuffing; roll like a jelly roll, bake, glaze with marmalade.

Wild ducks are fine country eating when you follow our recipe for Texas Barbecued Ducks (page 137). For a company dinner, garnish platter with spiced pineapple or other fruit, and green grapes. You can cook ducks over coals.

Put our big 9-quart Frozen Fruit Salad/Dessert (recipe, page 219) into your freezer and you'll have a tasty salad or dessert always ready for company. Slice it on lettuce for salad; serve with whipped cream topping for dessert.

When peaches are ripe, mold and serve this luscious, make-ahead Peach Melba Parfait (page 163) in dessert glasses to display its rich color and sparkling beauty. Vary the gelatin flavors for a change of pace.

Beat egg whites until stiff, but not dry; fold into pudding. Add 3 tblsp. peppermint candy and vanilla. Chill. Serve with your favorite chocolate sauce from the supermarket. Makes 6 to 8 servings.

ROYAL PORK DINNER

Pork Roast Danish Style*
Sweet Potato Bonbons*
Gala Baby Limas*
Cabbage Salad Bowl*
Rosy Peaches à la Mode

Some evening when the winter wind howls, seat guests in the warmth and comfort of your home and serve this dinner. It's a country meal long to be remembered. The pork loin with an irresistible brown crust, pecan-decorated sweet potato nuggets, tiny lima beans, country cabbage salad brightened with red radish slices, thin green pepper rings and shredded carrots, and rosy peaches with creamy ice cream topping—with friends to enjoy the food, who could wish for more?

You may want to invite guests who enjoy an adventure in good eating, for the pork roast is different and distinctive. When you use this menu, you may think it requires more effort and time than a regular roast pork dinner, but it's not difficult.

TIMETABLE

Do-Ahead: Rub seasonings on pork roast and refrigerate overnight. Cook sweet potatoes; mash, season, shape, roll in butter and crumbs, top with pecans and refrigerate. Drain canned peach halves well, place in baking dish, melt red raspberry jelly over low heat and pour over them. Cover and chill.

On Guest Day: About 4 hours before dinner, cut pocket in the pork and stuff with fruits, close and sew to keep opening closed. Put it in the preheated oven 2¾ hours before dinnertime. Make the cabbage salad, cover and chill. About 20 minutes before serving time, fix the lima beans. Take the roast from the oven to stand 15 minutes before carving. Then increase oven heat to 450° and bake the sweet potatoes 8 to 10 minutes if they were not chilled, a few minutes longer if refrigerated. Dessert will need attention only at serving time.

SERVING SUGGESTIONS

Garnish the meat platter with a bouquet of parsley or celery leaves and several cherry tomatoes, but do not crowd the roast on the platter (makes carving easier). Line the salad bowl with reserved green cabbage leaves.

PORK ROAST DANISH STYLE

Succulent fruit-stuffed roast, wrapped in buttery crumbs—a beauty

½ tsp. salt	2 medium apples, peeled, cored
½ tsp. ground cinnamon	and cut in sixths
½ tsp. ground allspice	2 tblsp. raisins
½ tsp. pepper	¼ tsp. ground cinnamon
¼ tsp. ground cloves	¼ c. brandy or apple juice
¼ tsp. ground mace	1½ tblsp. currant jelly, melted
3 to 3½ lbs. boned pork loin roast	1 c. fresh bread crumbs
12 pitted prunes	¼ c. melted butter

Mix salt, ½ tsp. cinnamon, allspice, pepper, cloves and mace; rub into surface of pork. Refrigerate overnight.

Combine prunes, apples, raisins, ¼ tsp. cinnamon and brandy. Refrigerate overnight.

Drain fruit, reserving liquid. Cut a long, deep pocket the length of the roast. Stuff with fruit. Sew closed with large needle; tie with kitchen twine. Brush roast with liquid drained from fruit.

Roast on rack in slow oven (325°) 1 hour. Remove from oven, and brush with jelly. Coat with bread crumbs. Baste with butter. Return meat to oven and roast 1½ hours longer. Let stand 15 minutes before carving. Makes 6 servings.

SWEET POTATO BONBONS

Marshmallow centers, buttery corn flake coating make these special

3 lbs. sweet potatoes, peeled and cooked	½ tsp. grated orange peel
	6 marshmallows, halved
¼ c. butter	⅓ c. melted butter
½ c. brown sugar, firmly packed	4 c. corn flakes, crushed
1 tsp. salt	12 pecan halves

Mash sweet potatoes until light and fluffy. Beat in ¼ c. butter, brown sugar, salt and orange peel. Let cool.

Divide potatoes into 12 equal portions. Center each portion with a marshmallow half, covering it with potatoes; shape in ovals. Coat each with melted butter; roll in corn flakes and top with a pecan half. Place on lightly greased baking sheet.

Bake in very hot oven (450°) 7 to 8 minutes. Serves 6 to 8.

GALA BABY LIMAS

Sour cream and seasoned stuffing mix give the bean flavor a lift

2 (10 oz.) pkgs. frozen baby lima beans

¼ c. butter

1 c. herb-seasoned stuffing mix

2 c. dairy sour cream

2 tsp. onion salt

1 c. grated process American cheese

Cook beans by package directions in a heavy 10″ skillet; remove from heat and drain. Cool slightly.

Melt butter over low heat in small saucepan. Add stuffing mix; heat and stir to coat crumbs with butter and brown.

Add sour cream, onion salt and cheese to beans. Cook over low heat, stirring constantly, just long enough to heat, but do not let come to a boil. Turn into a warm 1½-qt. bowl or casserole and sprinkle hot crumbs over top. Serve at once. Makes 6 servings.

CABBAGE SALAD BOWL

Color-bright vegetables make this a favorite with extra appeal

1 medium head cabbage

1 small green pepper, cut in thin rings

1 c. diced celery

⅔ c. finely shredded carrots

⅓ c. thin radish slices

2 tblsp. minced onion

1 c. salad dressing or mayonnaise

2 tblsp. milk

2 tsp. sugar

2 tblsp. lemon juice or vinegar

¼ tsp. paprika

¾ tsp. salt

Remove outer cabbage leaves and set aside to line salad bowl (if they are not green and pretty, use lettuce leaves). Shred remaining cabbage. Gently toss with green pepper rings, celery, carrots, radishes and onion.

In a small bowl mix salad dressing, milk, sugar, lemon juice, paprika and salt. Add to vegetables and toss lightly. Line salad bowl with reserved cabbage leaves and spoon in the salad. Cover and refrigerate at least 30 minutes, or for several hours. Makes 8 servings.

FAMILY-STYLE COMPANY DINNER

Baked Pork Chops*   Western Carrots*
Buttered Peas   Red Cabbage Salad Mold*
Hot Rolls   Frozen Pumpkin Pie*

This family-style dinner is a happy selection for the host who dislikes to carve meat at the table (or in the kitchen), and for friends who appreciate food set before them that looks and tastes wonderful.

The menu includes four somewhat different foods—beautifully browned pork chops baked with colorful vegetables and chicken soup, fine red cabbage congealed in a gelatin mold, carrots teamed with light raisins and honey-glazed, and pumpkin pie filling on a butter pecan ice cream base held in a crumb or pastry crust and frozen.

Another good feature of the pork chops, at least for the hostess, is that they require practically no attention while baking. They need no basting, but do lift off the cover during the last 15 minutes.

TIMETABLE

Do-Ahead: Make the pie a day ahead and freeze. You can fix the salad then, or the morning of company day, whichever is more convenient.

On Guest Day: Get the pork chops in the preheated oven an hour before you wish to serve dinner. Meanwhile, cook the carrots and just before mealtime, the frozen peas.

SERVING SUGGESTIONS

Place the meat on a warm platter, the vegetables in serving bowls and pass at the table. Serve the salad on lettuce-lined plates and top each serving with a spoonful of salad dressing. Or, if you have attractive green cabbage leaves, substitute them for the lettuce base. Remove the pie from the freezer a few minutes before serving (while you clear the table and refill coffee cups) to make cutting easier.

BAKED PORK CHOPS

These pork chops are fork tender and moist . . . vegetables add color

6 lean loin or rib pork chops, 1"
  thick
Salt (about ¾ tsp.)
Pepper
6 slices tomato (2 medium)

6 slices green pepper (1 large)
6 tblsp. chopped onion
6 tblsp. condensed cream of
  chicken soup

Brown pork chops on both sides in heavy skillet. Place in 13×9×2" pan. Sprinkle lightly with salt and pepper. (If skillet has ovenproof handle bake chops in it.) Lay a slice of tomato on top of each chop; arrange a ring of green pepper on top of tomato slice and fill with chopped onion. Top each chop with undiluted cream of chicken soup.

Cover pan tightly with foil and bake in slow oven (325°) 45 minutes. Remove cover and bake 15 minutes longer. Makes 6 servings.

N O T E : It is easy to double the recipe and bake 2 pans or skillets of chops if you are entertaining more people.

WESTERN CARROTS

An extra-delicious companion for ham, pork roasts and chicken

1 lb. carrots
1 c. light raisins
¼ to ½ c. water
1 tsp. salt
3 tblsp. brown sugar

2 tblsp. honey
3 tblsp. butter or regular
  margarine
2 tblsp. lemon juice

Peel carrots and cut diagonally in thin slices. Combine with raisins, water and salt (use smaller amount of water if you can watch while cooking to prevent scorching). Cook until tender, about 20 minutes. Drain if necessary.

Sprinkle with brown sugar; add honey, butter and lemon juice. Heat over low heat, stirring often, to glaze carrots, about 10 minutes. Makes 6 to 8 servings.

RED CABBAGE SALAD MOLD

Pickles and pickle juice flavor this attractive, tasty cabbage salad

2 tblsp. lemon juice	1 c. finely shredded red cabbage
⅔ c. sweet pickle juice	⅓ c. finely chopped sweet pickles
2 envelopes unflavored gelatin	Lettuce
3 c. water	Salad dressing (optional)
¼ tsp. salt	

Combine lemon and pickle juices in small bowl; sprinkle on gelatin.

Heat water with salt added to the boiling point. Remove from heat and stir in the gelatin mixture. Stir until gelatin dissolves. Cool; refrigerate until mixture mounds slightly when dropped from a spoon. (It will be the consistency of unbeaten egg whites.)

Fold in cabbage and pickles. Pour into a 1½-qt. mold. Cover and chill until firm. Serve on lettuce with salad dressing, if desired. Makes 8 servings.

FROZEN PUMPKIN PIE

New way with an old favorite . . . substitute whipped topping for cream if you wish. A delicious make-ahead dessert

Baked 9" Crumb Crust	½ tsp. ground cinnamon
1 pt. butter pecan ice cream, softened	¼ tsp. ground ginger
	¼ tsp. ground nutmeg
1 c. canned or cooked mashed pumpkin	½ tsp. vanilla
	1½ c. miniature marshmallows
1 c. sugar	1 c. heavy cream, whipped
½ tsp. salt	

Spoon ice cream into cool pie shell; spread in even layer. Freeze.

Mix pumpkin, sugar, salt, spices and vanilla. Fold in marshmallows and whipped cream.

Pour into Crumb Crust on top of ice cream. Cover with foil and freeze several hours or overnight. Let thaw at room temperature 5 minutes before cutting. Makes 6 to 8 servings.

Crumb Crust: Mix 1½ c. graham cracker crumbs, 3 tblsp. sugar and ⅓ c. melted butter or regular margarine. Press mixture firmly and evenly into a 9″ pie pan. Bake in moderate oven (350°) 10 minutes. Cool before filling.

PORK DINNER

Pork/Sauerkraut Skillet*
Boiled Potatoes with Parsley Butter
Mixed Fruit Salad*
Hot Rolls   Grape Jelly
Pumpkin Cake*
Coffee

Do you have a husband who may tell you around noon that he has invited a business guest "for dinner tonight"? This menu will help you with such an occasion. And if the guest doesn't ask for the pork-sauerkraut recipe to take home to his wife, it will be surprising. It's delicious plus—and easy and quick.

The potatoes are man-pleasing and using a little imagination with the ever-popular Waldorf produces a delightful salad. Dessert is unforgettable. This menu will prove you're a great cook!

TIMETABLE

Do-Ahead: There's no time for advance preparations, but you'll probably have the convenience foods on hand to make the cake.

On Guest Day: Bake the cake. It's easier than its appearance and taste lead one to believe. If you don't have the sour cream called for in the main dish, this is one ingredient someone in the family may have to pick up. Start cooking the pork about 45 minutes before dinner; you add the cream just before serving. Cook potatoes and fix the salad. Last of all, make the coffee.

SERVING SUGGESTIONS

This is a sit-down country dinner composed of dishes your husband will be proud to pass. No garnishes other than parsley for the potatoes. If you have no parsley, sprinkle buttered potatoes with a little paprika.

PORK/SAUERKRAUT SKILLET

You can add a few caraway seeds if you like the flavor

2½ lbs. pork shoulder, cut in 1" cubes	2 tsp. paprika
2 tblsp. salad oil	1 tsp. salt
2 c. chopped onion	½ c. water
2 (1 lb.) cans sauerkraut, drained and rinsed	2 c. dairy sour cream

In a 10" skillet brown pork cubes in hot oil. Remove meat from skillet. Add onion to drippings in skillet and cook until tender, but do not brown. Stir frequently.

Return pork to skillet; add sauerkraut, paprika, salt and water. Cover and bring to a boil; reduce heat to low and simmer 35 to 40 minutes, until pork is tender. Remove from heat and stir in sour cream. Heat, but do not let boil. Makes 8 servings.

MIXED FRUIT SALAD

Add cut-up dates to Waldorf salad and you give it a new taste

1 orange	½ c. chopped walnuts (black walnuts can be used)
3 c. diced unpeeled red apples (about 3)	¼ c. salad dressing or mayonnaise
⅔ c. cut-up pitted dates	1 tblsp. sugar
⅔ c. chopped celery	¾ c. heavy cream, whipped
	Lettuce

Peel orange and divide in sections over bowl to catch juices. Cut sections in halves and save juices.

In a medium bowl combine apples, dates, celery, walnuts and orange pieces.

Blend together salad dressing, sugar and reserved orange juice. Fold in whipped cream. Combine with fruit mixture. Serve in lettuce-lined bowl or on individual salad plates. Makes 8 servings.

PUMPKIN CAKE

Filled and frosted, this spice layer cake looks glamorous

1 pkg. spice cake mix (for 2-layer cake)	1 (4½ to 5 oz.) pkg. vanilla pudding and pie filling
1 (1 lb.) can pumpkin	2½ c. milk
2 tsp. baking soda	½ c. chopped pecans
2 eggs	2 envelopes dessert topping mix
⅓ c. water	

In a large bowl combine cake mix, pumpkin, baking soda, eggs and water. Beat according to directions on cake mix package. Pour into two greased and lightly floured 9″ round cake pans. Bake in moderate oven (350°) 25 to 30 minutes. Cool 10 minutes; remove from pans. Cool completely on racks.

Meanwhile, prepare pudding as directed on package, but use only 2½ c. milk. Cool; stir in pecans.

Carefully split each cake layer in half crosswise to make four layers. Put layers together with pudding.

Whip dessert topping by package directions. Spread over top and sides of cake. Garnish with extra pecans, if you like. Makes 10 to 12 servings.

DISTINCTIVE HAM DINNER

Party Pork Rolls*

Oven-Creamed Potatoes*

Three-Row Garden Salad*

Orange Sherbet

Holiday Cranberry Cake*

Use this menu when you entertain a group of varying age levels . . . young and old alike enjoy these dishes.

The pork rolls feature two kinds of ham, fresh and smoked. You wrap the meat around an expertly seasoned stuffing. Then you add an orange-cherry glaze to step up flavors and glamorize the platter specialty.

With this typical country main dish, serve creamed potatoes; they bake in the oven with the pork. The gorgeous salad loaf contributes three vegetables to the dinner—cabbage, beets and carrots. The cake turns any meal into a special occasion. Escorted by orange sherbet, it's a dessert you'll want to serve again and again. Its reception always is that good.

TIMETABLE

Do-Ahead: Bake cake a day or several days ahead and freeze. Make the salad to chill overnight. Also fix salad dressing. Cook, cool and chill potatoes so they'll be ready to cream next day.

On Guest Day: About 1½ hours before dinnertime, prepare stuffing and meat rolls. Put in oven. Meanwhile, prepare potato casserole and bake it the last 30 minutes the meat rolls are in the oven. If cake is frozen, bring it from the freezer. Let it thaw in its wrap.

SERVING SUGGESTIONS

This is an excellent meal to serve buffet style. Slice meat and place on platter. You may want to double the recipe, depending on how many guests you are having. Place bubbling potato casserole beside platter.

The whole salad loaf is attractive, but slices on greens also are picture-pretty. You can arrange the individual servings in the kitchen and put them at place settings. For dessert, spoon the orange sherbet into stemmed dessert glasses and pass the cake.

PARTY PORK ROLLS

Doubly delicious with ham, fresh and smoked. See photo in this book

Ham Stuffing:

2 c. ground cooked smoked ham	1 tsp. poultry seasoning
⅛ tsp. pepper	¼ tsp. pepper
½ c. dry bread or cracker crumbs	1 c. dry bread crumbs
1 egg, slightly beaten	¼ c. hot water

Bread Stuffing:

	3 slices fresh ham steak, ½″ thick
¼ c. finely chopped onion	2 tblsp. butter
⅓ c. butter or regular margarine	½ c. orange marmalade
½ c. finely chopped celery	2 tsp. maraschino cherry juice
2 tsp. salt	

Mix together thoroughly all ingredients for ham stuffing.

To make bread stuffing, cook onion in butter until golden. Add remaining ingredients for bread stuffing and mix.

Bone steaks; pound to flatten. Brown lightly in 2 tblsp. butter.

Spread steaks with ham stuffing. Cover evenly with a layer of bread stuffing. Roll as for jelly roll and tie securely with string.

Bake in covered pan in moderate oven (350°) 30 minutes. Remove from oven.

Combine orange marmalade and cherry juice for glaze; spread over pork rolls. Bake, uncovered, 15 to 20 minutes longer. Remove strings; slice each roll into 2″ slices. Makes 6 servings.

NOTE: You can double this recipe to make 12 servings.

OVEN-CREAMED POTATOES

The easiest way to cream potatoes—no pot watching or turning

2 c. chopped onions	2 tsp. salt
⅔ c. chopped green pepper	¼ tsp. pepper
½ c. chopped celery	6 c. cubed cooked potatoes (about
½ c. butter or regular margarine	6 medium)
6 tblsp. flour	1 c. shredded Cheddar cheese
4 c. milk	

Cook onions, green pepper and celery in butter until soft (do not brown). Stir in flour. Add milk and cook, stirring constantly, until mixture comes to a boil and is thickened. Stir in salt and pepper.

Place potatoes in a greased 3-qt. casserole. Pour sauce over. Top with cheese. Bake in moderate oven (350°) about 30 minutes, until hot and bubbly. Makes 10 to 12 servings.

THREE-ROW GARDEN SALAD

Color-bright, refreshing salad resembles striped ribbon when served

Orange Layer:
1 (3 oz.) pkg. orange flavor gelatin
1 c. boiling water
¾ c. pineapple juice
2 tblsp. lemon juice
1½ c. finely shredded carrots

Green Layer:
1 (3 oz.) pkg. lime flavor gelatin
1 c. boiling water
¾ c. pineapple juice
2 tblsp. lemon juice
1½ c. grated cabbage

Red Layer:
2 tsp. unflavored gelatin
½ c. cold water
1 (3 oz.) pkg. lemon flavor gelatin
½ tsp. salt
1 c. boiling water
2 tblsp. beet juice
2 tblsp. vinegar
1 c. finely diced cooked beets, well
drained
1 tblsp. prepared horse-radish
Cheese/Horse-radish Dressing

Prepare layers separately, allowing about 15 minutes between each so that gelatins set at intervals.

To make orange layer, dissolve orange flavor gelatin in boiling water. Add pineapple and lemon juices; chill until syrupy. Fold in carrots.

To prepare green layer, dissolve lime flavor gelatin in boiling water. Add pineapple and lemon juices; chill until syrupy. Fold in cabbage.

To make red layer, soften unflavored gelatin in cold water. Dissolve lemon flavor gelatin and salt in boiling water; immediately stir in unflavored gelatin mixture. Add beet juice and vinegar; chill until syrupy. Fold in beets and horse-radish.

Layer gelatins—orange, green, then red—in 9×5×3" loaf pan. Allow each layer to set before adding second or third layer. Chill until firm.

To unmold set pan in warm (not hot) water about 5 seconds; loosen around beet layer and turn out on platter. Garnish with green fresh carrot tops, young beet leaves or lettuce. Slice, then serve each person individual salad. Pass Cheese/Horse-radish Dressing. Makes 10 servings.

Cheese/Horse-radish Dressing: Soften 1 (3 oz.) pkg. cream cheese; beat until creamy. Blend in ¼ c. mayonnaise, 2 tblsp. light cream or milk, ½ tsp. celery salt and 2 tsp. horse-radish. Fold in 2 tsp. chopped fresh or dried chives (optional). Makes ¾ cup.

HOLIDAY CRANBERRY CAKE

Serve cake the year around . . . too good to limit to holidays

1 pkg. lemon cake mix (for 2-layer cake)	1¼ c. ground cranberries
	½ c. ground walnuts
1 (3 oz.) pkg. cream cheese, softened	¼ c. sugar
	1 tsp. ground mace (optional)
¾ c. milk	Confectioners sugar (optional)
4 eggs	

Blend cake mix, cream cheese and milk; beat with mixer 2 minutes at medium speed. Add eggs; blend and beat 2 more minutes.

Thoroughly combine cranberries, walnuts, sugar and mace; fold into cake batter. Pour into well-greased and floured 10" tube or fluted tube pan. Bake in moderate oven (350°) 1 hour, or until done. Cool 5 minutes, then remove from pan. Complete cooling on rack. Dust with confectioners sugar, if you wish. Serves 10 to 12.

COUNTRY DINNER SPECIAL

Ham/Vegetable Scallop*	Buttered Broccoli
Tossed Green Bean Salad*	Hot Corn Sticks*
Apple/Peanut Sundae*	Molasses Cookies

Put ham and potatoes in a casserole, add onions, carrot slices, a bit of cheese and mushroom sauce. Bake slowly. You will come up with a homespun, farm-style dish that will win praise. It's a great choice when a family with children comes to dinner. Serve this meal on a day when you'll be at home with time to prepare it. There's little make-ahead food in the menu.

TIMETABLE

Do-Ahead: Put cans of green beans and applesauce in refrigerator a day ahead. If you wish to serve cookies, bake them a day ahead, or several days ahead and freeze. Molasses, raisin or oatmeal cookies are a fine selection.

On Guest Day: The main dish needs to bake at least 1½ hours and to stand 15 to 20 minutes after coming from oven before you serve it. It takes about ½ hour to prepare the ingredients for the casserole so they'll be ready to bake. So start getting dinner about 2¼ hours before you want to serve it. Crush the peanut brittle for the sundae at your convenience. During the last half hour before dinner, cook frozen broccoli by package directions and season with butter or margarine. Assemble salad in bowl ready to toss at the last minute. When you take the casserole from the oven turn heat up to 450°, stir up batter for corn sticks and bake. Pass the corn sticks after casserole, salad and broccoli are served. Fix dessert between courses.

SERVING SUGGESTIONS

Serve this dinner buffet style or as a sit-down meal.

HAM/VEGETABLE SCALLOP

New way to scallop ham and potatoes—a tasty company casserole

1½ lbs. center-cut fresh ham steak
1½ tblsp. flour
2 cans condensed cream of
  mushroom soup
2 c. milk
¾ c. shredded sharp process
  cheese

6 c. thinly sliced peeled potatoes
2 c. thinly sliced carrots
½ c. finely chopped onion
1½ tsp. salt
¼ tsp. pepper

Brown ham lightly on both sides in skillet. Remove and set aside.

Stir flour into drippings in skillet until smooth; add the soup. Slowly stir in milk, mixing well. Heat to a boil, stirring constantly. Remove from heat; add cheese and stir until it is melted.

Cut ham in serving-size pieces. Arrange alternate layers of ham, potatoes, carrots and onion in greased 4-qt. carrerole (or two 2-qt. casseroles). Sprinkle vegetable layers lightly with salt and pepper. Cover with hot soup mixture.

Bake, covered, in slow oven (325°) 1 hour; uncover and bake 30 minutes more, or until potatoes and carrots are tender. Let stand 15 to 20 minutes before serving. Makes 8 servings.

TOSSED GREEN BEAN SALAD

All salad ingredients except greens come from the cupboard shelf

1 qt. bite-size pieces salad greens
1 (1 lb.) can cut green beans,
  chilled
6 tblsp. salad oil
2 tblsp. tarragon vinegar

1 tblsp. cider vinegar
Salt
Pepper
Pimiento

Place lettuce or other salad greens in bowl. Top with drained beans (French-cut beans are a good choice). Sprinkle on oil and toss. Sprinkle on vinegars and toss again. Check for salt and pepper. Serve garnished with strips of pimiento or sliced pimiento-stuffed olives. Makes 6 servings.

N O T E : For serving more than 6, double the recipe.

HOT CORN STICKS

Easy to make—rush them hot from the oven to table or buffet

1½ c. cornmeal	½ tsp. baking soda
⅓ c. flour	¼ c. shortening
3 tsp. baking powder	1½ c. buttermilk
2 tsp. sugar	1 egg
1 tsp. salt	

Preheat oven to very hot (450°). Grease corn stick pans and place in oven to heat.

Meanwhile, stir all ingredients in a bowl and beat just to mix, about 30 seconds. Fill warm corn stick pans two thirds full. Bake about 12 to 15 minutes, until golden brown. Makes 17 or 18 corn sticks.

APPLE/PEANUT SUNDAE

This is a tasty way to add glamor with homemade applesauce

3 pts. vanilla ice cream	¼ lb. peanut brittle, crushed
2 c. chilled, sweetened applesauce	

Scoop ice cream into chilled serving dishes. Spoon applesauce on top; sprinkle with peanut brittle. Makes about 9 servings.

PIG ROAST FOR A CROWD

Whole Pit-Roasted Pig*
Sweet Corn   Roasted Apples
Buttered Buns
Barbecue Sauce
Frozen Pineapple Torte*

Visitors to that paradise of the Pacific, Hawaii, return home wearing leis and treasuring fond memories of the pig roast or luau they enjoyed. And as they give a similar party for the members of their couples club, or any group of friends, they often provide as background music the lilting songs of the islands, recorded.

Farm families have—or can get—what it takes to give a mainland version of a luau—a moonlight summer night, plenty of space in the yard, corn on the cob, corn leaves, rocks from a stream and, some farms can provide the pig.

You don't have to fly across the Pacific Ocean to Hawaii and back to learn how to put on a luau. Our tested directions came from two Illinois farmers and their wives who gave successfully such a party for 80 guests. One of our food editors was present for that pig roast and she learned all the secrets.

We add a few foods to the menu that you do not meet in Hawaiian pig roasts. The buns, for instance, and the barbecue sauce, both gestures to sandwich fans. And we add the delectable frozen pineapple dessert, appropriate for a Hawaiian party.

TIMETABLE

Do-Ahead: Dig the pit of the right size and line with rocks. Measurements depend on the size of the pig. Allow 1 lb. dressed meat per person. Make torte for dessert a day or several days ahead.

On Guest Day: Build fire. When stones are hot, place pig in pit. The time for cooking depends on the size of the pig, but it varies from 2 to 4 hours. (See directions that follow.) About an hour before the pig is done, open the pit, add apples and corn on the cob wrapped in heavy-duty foil, cover and continue cooking until pork is tender.

SERVING SUGGESTIONS

Serve picnic style. Provide barbecue sauce and buns for the sandwich makers. Have pitchers of iced tea and a pot of hot coffee available. You may wish to wait until late in the evening to serve the lovely torte and coffee.

WHOLE PIT-ROASTED PIG

You will need:

Whole young pig, dressed and shaved

Rock-lined pit dug ahead of time

Several rounded rocks from a stream, in 1 to 4 lb. weights (Sun dry them for a week)

3 bushels or more of dry hard wood

Green corn stalks and leaves

Big tongs for handling hot rocks

Chicken wire or fencing—enough to encircle pig

2 baling hooks to carry roasted pig

12 clean burlap sacks

Canvas large enough to cover pit

Dig hole about 2½' deep at center, with diameter of 5½ to 8' depending on size of pig. Line with rocks.

Stack wood on rocks, Indian-tepee style. Light fire. Place round rocks in fire where they will get most heat.

While fire burns down, wet the burlap, and prepare pig. Rub inside of pig with salt and pepper, and garlic if desired. Place pig on chicken wire. Under legs, make slits big enough to insert round rocks. When fire has burned down and rocks are very hot, use tongs to fill abdominal cavity and slits in legs with hot rocks. Tie front legs together, then back legs. Wrap pig in wire, fastening well (so it can be lifted).

Completely cover ashes and rocks with corn stalks and leaves. Lower pig right onto leaves. Cover it generously on top and sides with more leaves.

Place wet burlap over leaves (this will hold heat and steam).

Cover with large canvas; shovel gravel over canvas to keep steam in.

Cooking time starts now. For 25 lb. pig, allow about 2 hours; for 50 lb. pig, 2½ hours; anything heavier, figure on at least 4 hours. If in doubt about doneness, leave pig in longer (because of steam, it won't burn).

To uncover, remove gravel, canvas, burlap and covering leaves. Lift and carry wire-wrapped pig with hooks. Remove wire to serve.

In Hawaii, the servers dip their hands frequently in cold water as they pull pork apart for individual servings.

What to Cook with the Pig:

About 1 hour before the pig is cooked, partly uncover pit and add apples, wrapped in foil, and corn on the cob. Either wrap corn ears individually in foil or peel back husks, remove silks, replace husks and soak in cold water about 15 minutes before adding to pit. (In Hawaii, whole sweet potatoes are roasted with the pig.) Cover the pit at once after adding apples and corn.

FROZEN PINEAPPLE TORTE

Refreshing light dessert to make the day before you entertain

3 egg yolks	3 egg whites
⅛ tsp. salt	2 tblsp. sugar
½ c. sugar	1 tsp. grated lemon peel
1 (8½ oz.) can crushed pineapple (save juice)	1 c. heavy cream, whipped
	1 c. vanilla wafer crumbs
2 tblsp. lemon juice	

Beat egg yolks slightly; add salt and ½ c. sugar and beat a little more. Add pineapple juice (drained from crushed pineapple) and lemon juice. Cook over hot, not boiling, water until custard coats a spoon; stir constantly while cooking. Add pineapple and cool.

Make a meringue with egg whites and 2 tblsp. sugar. Fold in pineapple custard, lemon peel and whipped cream.

Coat sides of a greased 13×9×2″ baking pan with ½ c. vanilla wafer crumbs. Pour custard into pan; sprinkle remaining crumbs over the top. Cover and freeze.

Place dessert in refrigerator about 30 minutes before serving. It then will cut easily. Makes 8 to 10 servings.

FARMHOUSE DINNER

Tomato Juice   Corn Chips
Meat-and-Potato Balls*
Missouri Green Beans
Fresh Cucumber/Onion Relish*
Cloud Biscuits*
Orange Meringue Pie*

The motto of many busy women is: Give your guests the feeling that you just put extra plates on the dinner table for them. These hostesses hold that people like to sense they are welcome and that they made little extra work. As a result of this philosophy, the meal often represents country cooking at its best. The food, although it's free of fancy frills, tastes wonderfully good, there's plenty of it and usually one or two "from scratch" baked foods come to the table. Cloud Biscuits and Orange Meringue Pie, for instance.

Who could miss on Meat-and-Potato Balls made by a recipe from an Iowa farm woman? They really are beef, pork, potatoes and rich gravy combined into one platter specialty. The tomato juice appetizer is optional, but it's refreshing and gives the host and guests something to sip in the living room while the hostess in the kitchen rounds up the remainder of the dinner. Season the juice with a little lemon juice, salt and Worcestershire sauce and serve it hot or cold, depending on the weather.

If you are one of the thousands of farm women who believe frozen green beans lack desirable texture, try them cooked by package directions, drained if necessary and seasoned with cream cheese and celery seeds. Toss the hot beans to melt the cheese so it coats them. You will have performed a cooking miracle. The cucumbers are a cross between the fresh vegetable and pickles. If you serve this dinner when cucumber vines are not bearing, you can substitute dill pickles for them.

TIMETABLE

Do-Ahead: You can shape and brown the Meat-and-Potato Balls a day ahead; cool, place in casserole, cover and refrigerate. And if you like, bake the pie shell.

On Guest Day: When convenient, make pie filling, turn it into the pie shell, top with meringue and brown lightly. You can make, roll and cut biscuits, place them on a baking sheet 1 or 2 hours before time to bake them. Keep them in the refrigerator. Make the Cucumber Relish, cool and chill. Put Meat-and-Potato Balls in the oven 1¼ hours before dinnertime. Meanwhile, fix the green beans.

When you take the Meat-and-Potato Balls from the oven, increase the temperature to 450°. Bake biscuits 10 to 14 minutes. Meanwhile, add sour cream to Meat-and-Potato Balls and carry food to table, the biscuits on the final trip before sitting down to eat.

SERVING SUGGESTIONS

Serve Meat-and-Potato Balls on a warm platter and garnish with finely snipped parsley. Pass one serving of biscuits in a napkin-lined basket or roll warmer. Keep the remainder warm in oven with door open and heat turned off. Assign getting the second serving of biscuits to one of the older children. If you want to add a true country note to the pie, sprinkle the meringue with a little flaked coconut just before putting it in the oven to brown.

MEAT-AND-POTATO BALLS

Mild seasonings and sour cream convert this into a platter treat

2 large potatoes, cooked	2 tsp. salt
1 c. milk	2 eggs, slightly beaten
½ lb. ground beef	½ c. flour
1½ lbs. ground lean pork	3 tblsp. shortening
1 medium onion, finely chopped	½ c. hot water
(about ⅓ c.)	1 c. dairy sour cream

Mash potatoes, adding ¼ c. milk.

Combine beef, pork and onion with potatoes. Mix in salt, eggs and remaining ¾ c. milk. Shape in 2″ balls. Roll in flour.

Brown balls in shortening, half of them at a time. Brown on all sides. Arrange in greased 3-qt. casserole; add hot water. Bake uncovered in moderate oven (350°) about 1 hour. Remove from oven. Let stand a few minutes. Just before serving gently spread sour cream over top with a spoon. Makes about 21 balls.

FRESH CUCUMBER/ONION RELISH

A cross between fresh sliced cucumbers and cucumber pickle slices

2 medium cucumbers	½ c. sugar
3 medium onions	1 tsp. salt
½ c. vinegar	

If cucumbers are homegrown, wash, but do not peel. (They will not have a wax coating.) Score them lengthwise with a fork to make green and white stripes. Cut in medium slices. Peel onions and separate into rings. Add to cucumbers in bowl.

Combine vinegar, sugar and salt and stir over low heat until sugar dissolves. Bring to a boil and pour over cucumbers and onions. Cool, cover and refrigerate. Makes 8 to 10 servings.

CLOUD BISCUITS

They are light as clouds and have golden brown tops—truly delicious. To drop dough instead of rolling, increase milk to ¾ cup

2 c. sifted flour	½ c. shortening
1 tblsp. sugar	1 egg, beaten
4 tsp. baking powder	⅔ c. milk
½ tsp. salt	

Sift together dry ingredients. Cut in shortening until mixture forms coarse crumbs. Combine egg and milk and add to flour mixture; stir until dough follows fork around bowl. Turn onto lightly floured board and knead lightly about 20 times.

Roll dough ¾" thick, cut with lightly floured 2" cutter, cutting straight down through the dough. Place on ungreased baking sheet.

Bake in very hot oven (450°) 10 to 14 minutes, or until biscuits are golden brown. Makes 2 dozen.

ORANGE MERINGUE PIE

Add 1 tblsp. grated orange peel to filling for stronger orange flavor

Baked 9" pie shell	3 tblsp. butter
3 tblsp. cornstarch	1 tblsp. grated orange peel
1 c. sugar	(optional)
⅛ tsp. salt	3 egg whites
3 egg yolks, slightly beaten	¼ tsp. cream of tartar
1 c. orange juice	6 tblsp. sugar
½ c. water	¼ tsp. vanilla
1 tblsp. lemon juice	

Combine cornstarch, 1 c. sugar and salt in medium saucepan. Gradually blend in egg yolks, orange juice and water. Cook over medium heat, stirring constantly, until mixture thickens and boils. Stir and boil 1 minute. Remove from heat.

Stir in lemon juice and butter (orange peel, too, if you add it). Turn at once into pie shell.

Beat egg whites with cream of tartar until foamy. Beat in 6 tblsp. sugar, 1 tablespoon at a time; continue to beat until stiff and glossy. Beat in vanilla. Heap on hot pie filling and spread over it, carefully sealing meringue to edge of crust.

Bake in moderate oven (350°) 12 to 15 minutes, or until meringue peaks are golden brown. Cool away from drafts.

INDIAN SUMMER DINNER

Cider/Pineapple Special*   Crackers   Cheese
Baked Ham Slice with Cherry Sauce*
Kentucky Potatoes*   Green Beans with Almonds*
Lettuce Wedges with Creamy French Dressing*
Parkerhouse Rolls   Pumpkin/Ginger Squares*

Golden Indian summer days promote a social state of mind. This time between autumn and winter comes two to three weeks before Thanksgiving celebrations demand attention. A haze spreads over the hills, a relaxing lull permeates country homes after the hectic rush of the harvest season is over. Friends are ready for an exchange of news and ideas—for visiting. So kick off your fall social season with this sit-down dinner for 8.

This meal features foods at their seasonal best. The cider comes from presses and the dessert features pumpkins, many of which still decorate the front door. This dinner tastes and looks wonderful and it's easy to prepare—the ham and potatoes bake leisurely and require almost no attention.

TIMETABLE

Do-Ahead: Make the dessert and salad dressing a day ahead; refrigerate.

On Guest Day: Get the potatoes in the oven 3 hours before you want to serve them. After they've baked 1½ hours, put the ham slice in the oven. Cut bite-size cubes of sharp Cheddar and Swiss cheese, insert picks in them and refrigerate. Heat the Cider/Pineapple Special shortly before you want to serve it. Put the green beans on to cook about 15 minutes before dinnertime. While they cook, fix the salad.

SERVING SUGGESTIONS

Take the hot cider/pineapple drink and serving glasses or mugs, cheese and crackers to the living room soon after the guests arrive.

(You can serve this fruit drink from a punch bowl or pitcher.) Arrange the cheese cubes on a tray surrounding a small bowl of chili sauce. The sauce adds a spot of color and some guests will enjoy dunking cheese in it. Let your husband assume responsibility for this course, for you will need to return to the kitchen to make last-minute preparations. Cut the dessert just before you serve it.

CIDER/PINEAPPLE SPECIAL

Crackers, cheese and this hot drink make good beginnings for meals

1 qt. sweet apple cider	½ c. crushed mint leaves
2 c. unsweetened pineapple juice	1 qt. ginger ale, unchilled

Pour fruit juices into a 2-qt. saucepan. Add mint and bring to a boil. Strain. Bring to a boil again. Add ginger ale and serve at once. Makes 8 to 10 servings.

NOTE: You may omit the mint. If you do, heat juices only once. The mint does add an interesting flavor note.

BAKED HAM SLICE WITH CHERRY SAUCE

Expertly seasoned and slowly baked, the meat captures the fine flavor associated with old-time farm-cured ham. Cherries add color

1 center slice ham, cut 2½" thick	2 tblsp. flour
(3 lbs.)	¼ tsp. dry mustard
1 (1 lb.) can tart cherries	½ tsp. grated lemon peel
½ c. sugar	2 drops red food color
⅛ tsp. salt	

Score edges of ham. Place in baking pan and bake uncovered in slow oven (300°) long enough to heat, or about 1 hour.

Meanwhile, drain cherries. You should have ¾ c. juice. Heat it in a small saucepan. Mix together sugar, salt, flour and dry mustard; add to cherry juice. Cook and stir over medium heat until thick. Add lemon peel, food color and cherries.

Remove ham from oven and pour on the hot cherry sauce. Bake 30 minutes longer. Serve ham, cut in serving portions, on platter and pour over the cherry sauce from baking pan. Or, if you prefer, pass the cherry sauce. Makes 8 servings.

NOTE: To flame the ham, heat ¼ c. brandy in a little pan, but do not let it come to a boil. Pour over the hot ham as soon as it is baked and while still in the pan. Ignite immediately, spooning brandy up into flame. This adds a fruity flavor; the alcohol burns and disappears. Cut and serve.

KENTUCKY POTATOES

Shredding and slowly cooking spuds in sauce develops fine flavor

¼ c. butter or regular margarine	Pepper to taste (about ¼ tsp.)
¼ c. flour	6 c. shredded potatoes (about 7
4 c. milk	large)
2 tsp. salt	¼ c. finely chopped onion

Melt butter in a large saucepan over low heat; remove from heat and blend in flour. Add a little milk slowly, blending until smooth; then add rest of milk and boil 1 minute, stirring constantly. Add salt, pepper, shredded potatoes and onion.

Pour into greased 15½ × 10½ × 1″ jelly roll pan, or shallow casserole (jelly roll pan fits neatly on oven shelf below ham). Bake in slow oven (300°) about 3 hours. Makes 10 servings.

GREEN BEANS WITH ALMONDS

Ideal vegetable dish with ham—the nuts add crunchy texture

3 (10 oz.) pkgs. quick-frozen	¾ c. sliced almonds
French-style green beans	6 tblsp. butter
3 tblsp. butter	

Cook beans in boiling salted water by package directions. Add 3 tblsp. butter and toss to mix.

Sauté almonds in 6 tblsp. butter until light brown. Toss into beans. Makes 8 servings.

LETTUCE WEDGES WITH CREAMY FRENCH DRESSING

A change of pace in French dressings; try it on other greens

1 tsp. sugar	⅓ c. wine vinegar
1 tblsp. paprika	1 egg, beaten
1 tsp. salt	1 c. salad oil
Dash of ground red pepper	Lettuce

Combine sugar, paprika, salt and red pepper.

Add vinegar to egg and beat well. Beat in ¼ c. salad oil, 1 tsp.

at a time. Gradually add remaining ¾ c. salad oil, beating well after each addition. Add combined dry ingredients. Chill.

Cut heads of iceberg lettuce into as many wedges as needed and of the size desired. With a knife, slash each wedge crosswise in several places, but not completely through. Shake dressing; spoon on lettuce. Dressing makes about 1⅔ cups.

PUMPKIN/GINGER SQUARES

You can use 1 tsp. each of ground cinnamon and ginger and ½ tsp. nutmeg if you do not have pumpkin pie spice. The ice milk, although solid like ice cream, contains less fat, more protein

1 c. sugar	2 c. cooked or canned pumpkin
1 tsp. salt	½ gal. vanilla ice milk, slightly
2½ tsp. pumpkin pie spice	softened
1 c. chopped walnuts	Gingersnaps (about 36)

Mix sugar, salt, spice and walnuts with pumpkin. Mix in the ice milk, using a beater.

Line bottom of 13×9×2″ pan with gingersnaps. Pour on half the pumpkin mixture. Cover with another layer of gingersnaps. Pour on remaining pumpkin mixture. Freeze.

To serve, cut in squares or rectangles, and if you and your guests are not counting calories too seriously, garnish with walnut halves and little puffs of whipped cream. Makes 8 to 10 servings.

AUTUMN OVEN DINNER

Cranberry/Apricot Cooler*
Miniature Ham Loaves*
Butternut Squash and Apples*
Celery
Overnight Sourdough Bread*
Cherry/Cheese Salad*

Autumn's cool evenings encourage home entertaining—visiting leisurely indoors with friends, exchanging vacation and other news. This color-bright, one-course, oven dinner matches Nature's brilliant glow on nearby hills. Cranberry juice, yellow winter squash with rosy apple rings and individual ham loaves provide good eating. The crusty loaves of sourdough bread, speckled with browned cornmeal, suggest that autumn is time for home baking sprees. Country meals, like country people, keep in tune with the seasons.

TIMETABLE

Do-Ahead: Bake the bread several days ahead. (The starter needs to ferment about 16 hours.) Cool, slice, reassemble loaves, wrap in heavy-duty foil and freeze. Make the salad a day ahead.

On Guest Day: Put the ham loaves and squash side by side in the oven to bake about 1 hour. Mix the appetizer juices in a pitcher any time during the day and chill. Heat the foil-wrapped bread in the oven alongside the ham and squash until hot, or about 25 minutes if frozen.

SERVING SUGGESTIONS

Float thin lemon or orange slices in the glasses of the Cranberry/Apricot Cooler. Serve the dinner plates in the kitchen if you wish. Handle the sliced bread like hot rolls; it should be hot enough to melt butter spread on it. Either pass bread in a napkin-lined basket or a roll warmer. Serve the salad-dessert with the remainder of the meal, but when you pour the last cups of coffee, pass a plate of colorful candy mints.

CRANBERRY/APRICOT COOLER

Pour this appetite sharpener from pitcher in small glasses over ice

2 c. cranberry juice cocktail, chilled	3 tblsp. lemon juice
1 c. apricot nectar, chilled	

Blend all ingredients and chill. Makes about 9 servings.

MINIATURE HAM LOAVES

These little loaves seem to say to guests: "made especially for you"

1 lb. ground lean ham	¼ c. vinegar
½ lb. ground lean pork	¼ c. water
½ c. milk	¼ c. brown sugar, firmly pack
1 egg, beaten	1 tsp. dry mustard
1 c. bread crumbs	

Combine ham, pork, milk, egg and bread crumbs. Shape into 8 loaves of equal size. Place in a 10×6×1½″ baking dish.

Combine vinegar with water, brown sugar and mustard, and heat. Pour over the ham. Bake in moderate oven (350°) 1 hour. Makes 8 loaves.

BUTTERNUT SQUASH AND APPLES ✠

You can use buttercup squash—when available—for the butternut

3 lbs. butternut squash	⅔ c. brown sugar, firmly packed
3 baking apples	1½ tblsp. flour
6 tblsp. butter or regular margarine	1¼ tsp. salt

Cut squash in halves, remove seeds and fiber; peel and cut in slices ½ to ¾″ thick. Arrange in 13×9×2″ baking pan.

Core apples, but do not peel. Cut in ½ to ¾″ slices and lay on top of squash.

Mix butter, brown sugar, flour and salt; sprinkle over top of apples and squash. Cover pan tightly with aluminum foil. Bake in moderate oven (350°) about 1 hour, until squash is tender. Makes about 9 servings.

OVERNIGHT SOURDOUGH BREAD

You use all the starter in one baking. Bread tastes like that our grandmothers made by overnight sponge method, but with cornmeal flavor. It tastes best when warm and is heavenly when toasted

1 pkg. active dry yeast	2 tblsp. salad oil
¼ c. warm water (110 to 115°)	½ c. cornmeal
¾ c. milk	4 to 4½ c. flour
2 tblsp. sugar	1 c. lukewarm water
1½ tsp. salt	Melted butter

Dissolve yeast in ¼ c. water.

Scald milk and pour over sugar, salt and oil in big bowl. Cool until lukewarm. Add cornmeal, 1 c. flour and yeast to lukewarm mixture. Cover and put in a warm place to ferment about 16 hours. This is the starter.

After starter has fermented, stir in 1 c. flour and 1 c. lukewarm water. Cover and let stand in warm place 2 hours.

Add enough remaining flour to make a soft dough that you barely can handle. Knead, adding a little flour as necessary, until smooth and elastic, about 10 minutes.

Divide dough in 6 equal parts; shape each to make a little loaf and place on greased baking sheet about 1" apart. Let rise until almost doubled, about 1 hour.

Bake in moderate oven (375°) 30 to 40 minutes, or until golden. Brush with melted butter and cool on racks. Makes 6 loaves.

CHERRY/CHEESE SALAD

The distinctive feature of this luscious fruit salad is the use of canned cherry pie filling. Topping substitutes for salad dressing. When entertaining women for lunch, serve this salad with hot muffins

1 (3 oz.) pkg. raspberry flavor gelatin	1 (3 oz.) pkg. cream cheese
2 c. boiling water	⅓ c. salad dressing or mayonnaise
1 (1 lb. 5 oz.) can cherry pie filling	1 (8 oz.) can crushed pineapple
1 (3 oz.) pkg. lemon flavor gelatin	½ c. heavy cream, whipped
	1 c. miniature marshmallows
	3 tblsp. chopped pecans

Dissolve raspberry gelatin in 1 c. boiling water; stir in cherry pie filling. Pour into a 9" square pan and chill until partially set.

Dissolve lemon gelatin in 1 c. boiling water.

Beat together cream cheese and salad dressing. Gradually add lemon gelatin. Stir in undrained pineapple. Fold in whipped cream, then marshmallows. Spread evenly over cherry layer; sprinkle top with pecans. Chill. Makes 9 servings.

SUMMER FISH DINNER

Oven-Fried Fish*
New Potatoes with Lemon Butter*
Green Beans with Bacon
Tomato/Cucumber Salad
Farm-Style Peach Ice Cream*
Coconut Cookies

When the family fisherman delivers his catch, dressed and cut in filets, to the kitchen, he sets the stage for a company dinner soon to follow. Suggestions for friends with whom he'd like to share his bounty come easy.

In this menu the fish monopolizes the oven. As with chicken, many farm women prefer to fry fish in the oven instead of in a skillet. This method eliminates turning and careful watching. Smooth, round, new little potatoes are a natural accompaniment. The choice of the second vegetable depends on what the garden offers. Are there tender peas to cook and butter or succulent green beans to toss with butter or bacon drippings and crisp bacon pieces?

With thick slices of juicy, ripe tomatoes and crisp cucumbers available, you can decide on a salad in a few seconds. Serve the vegetable team on lettuce, add a few sliced green onions if you like and use your favorite salad dressing.

Among the worthy dessert candidates for ending this meal are fresh peach ice cream, pie or cobbler, or sugared sliced peaches with a pitcher of light cream. You won't go wrong if you choose coconut cookies to serve with the ice cream or sliced fruit.

TIMETABLE

Do-Ahead: It's to be hoped you have coconut cookies in the freezer. Or you can buy them.

On Guest Day: Using fish the same day it leaves the lake, stream or pond is a farm tradition heeded whenever possible. If home-made ice cream wins the dessert position, freeze it first and let it ripen. About an hour before dinner, get the green beans and potatoes ready to cook and the salad vegetables ready to combine. Start cooking vegetables about a half hour before dinner. At the same time, start heating the oven. Allow the fish 12 to 15 minutes in the very hot oven.

SERVING SUGGESTIONS

Hold the garnishes to the minimum and let the appeal of the top-notch foods tempt appetites. Concentrate on the best temperatures for serving the food—the fish, potatoes and beans piping hot, the salad and dessert frosty cold. Lemon wedges on the fish platter and extra snipped chives on the potatoes are optional, but do let the bacon show in the beans.

OVEN-FRIED FISH

For top results use fresh fish, a very hot oven and avoid overcooking

1½ tblsp. salt
¾ c. milk
3 lbs. fish filets

1½ c. dry bread crumbs
6 tblsp. melted butter or regular
   margarine

Add salt to milk and stir to mix. Dip filets, cut in serving-size pieces, into milk and roll in crumbs to coat. Place in well-greased shallow pan or pans. It is important to use enough pan space to spread the fish in a single layer. Pour butter over fish.

Place in an extremely hot oven (500°) on rack slightly above center of oven. Bake, uncovered, until fish flakes easily with fork, 12 to 15 minutes. Serve on hot platter. Makes about 9 servings.

N O T E : If your fisherman has not fileted fish, here's the way to do it. Cut down back from head to tail close to backbone. Cut flesh free from rib bones. Skin fish if you like, starting at the tail end. If the fish has scales, remove them before fileting.

NEW POTATOES WITH LEMON BUTTER

Peel potatoes if you like, cook and pour on melted butter but red skins with white bands are pretty and lemon points up flavors

3 lbs. new potatoes (20 to 24
   small)
¼ c. melted butter or regular
   margarine
½ tsp. grated lemon peel

2 tblsp. lemon juice
2 tblsp. chopped fresh chives
1 tsp. salt
Dash of pepper

Scrub potatoes and leave whole, but peel a narrow strip around center. Place in saucepan containing 1″ salted water (1 tsp. salt to 1 c. water), cover and cook until tender, 20 to 25 minutes. Drain.

Meanwhile, heat remaining ingredients in saucepan to boiling. Turn potatoes into serving dish. Stir hot lemon mixture to mix and pour over potatoes; serve at once. Makes 8 servings.

FARM-STYLE PEACH ICE CREAM

This is a cooked custard ice cream with ripe fresh peaches added

1 c. sugar	4 c. heavy cream, chilled
¼ tsp. salt	⅔ c. sugar
2 c. milk	4 c. mashed fresh peaches (8 to
6 egg yolks, beaten	10)
1½ tblsp. vanilla	

Mix 1 c. sugar, salt, milk and egg yolks in a saucepan. Cook and stir over medium heat to scald, or until bubbles appear around the edges of saucepan. Remove from heat and cool to room temperature. Stir in vanilla and heavy cream.

Mix ⅔ c. sugar with peaches and stir into the cream mixture. Pour into freezer can; fill about three fourths full. Add dasher and cover. Adjust crank in proper position. Pack freezer tub one third full of crushed ice; then add alternate layers of ice and rock salt to cover can, using 6 parts ice to 1 part salt. Turn crank until it turns very hard, drain off water.

Remove ice until level is below lid of can. Take off lid and remove dasher. Pack ice cream down with spoon. Plug hole in lid and cover can with several thicknesses of waxed paper or foil. Pack again with ice and salt using 4 parts ice to 1 part salt. Cover with a blanket, canvas or other heavy cloth and let ice cream ripen several hours. Makes ½ gallon.

WINTER FISH DINNER

Sole/Shrimp Roll-Ups*
Baked Potato Sticks*   Buttered Asparagus
Cherry Tomato Salad*
Open-Face Cranberry Pie*

If you and your husband want to invite another couple to a fish dinner in winter, try this menu. It has three merits that make it acceptable and praiseworthy even to meat-and-potato men. The main dish contains the highly favored shellfish, shrimp. While each serving includes only 5 small or 1 large shrimp, it's enough to boost the appeal. Cheese adds to the seasoning. And the potato sticks will please your male meat-and-potato fans.

While country fish dinners are likely summer specials that feature the family fisherman's catch, cold weather fish dinners are increasingly popular. Today's hostesses are using more imagination in preparing the fish available in their markets.

Cherry tomatoes, available the year around, brighten this dinner and accent flavors. A fruit compote would make a splendid dessert, but the one-crust pie is pretty, delicious and unusual. Or you can end the dinner with chilled grapefruit halves.

TIMETABLE

Do-Ahead: Bake, cool and chill crumb crust a day ahead. Make pie filling and turn into crust. Chill overnight.

On Guest Day: Add tomatoes to dressing and chill 3 hours or longer. Get the potatoes in the oven 45 minutes before dinnertime. Prepare roll-ups and place them in the oven after potatoes have baked 20 minutes. They require the same oven temperature. Remove potatoes from oven just before you place fish under broiler to brown lightly. Spoon the topping on the pie just before you serve it.

SERVING SUGGESTIONS

Serve the tomatoes on crisp lettuce or other greens. You can garnish the fish platter with lemon wedges or slices. Serve the silvery package of potatoes in a basket if you have one. Sprinkle potato tops with chopped parsley.

SOLE/SHRIMP ROLL-UPS

If you use frozen fish filets thaw them enough that they'll roll

20 small or 4 large cooked shrimp	1 c. milk
4 wide filets of sole, lightly salted on both sides	½ c. dry white wine
	½ c. light cream
2 tblsp. chopped onion	½ c. grated Parmesan cheese
3 tblsp. butter or regular margarine	1 tsp. lemon juice
	1 tsp. salt
3 tblsp. flour	Pepper

Roll 5 small or 1 large shrimp in each filet. Fasten with two toothpicks. Lay in shallow greased baking pan.

Cook onion in butter until golden. Blend in flour, milk and wine. Cook and stir until sauce boils and thickens. Blend in cream and cheese; stir in lemon juice, salt and pepper to taste. Pour over fish roll-ups. Sprinkle lightly with a little additional Parmesan cheese.

Bake in hot oven (425°) about 25 minutes. Place under broiler to brown lightly. Makes 4 servings.

BAKED POTATO STICKS

Potatoes cook to perfection with no attention except turning once

4 medium baking potatoes	½ c. shredded process American
¼ tsp. salt	cheese
1 tblsp. finely chopped parsley	½ c. light cream
3 tblsp. butter or regular margarine	

Peel potatoes and cut in lengthwise strips as for French fries. Place on the center of large sheet of heavy-duty aluminum foil. (Use double thickness of foil if you do not have the heavier kind.) Form foil around potatoes to the shape of a baking dish.

Add salt and parsley to potatoes; dot with butter. Sprinkle with shredded cheese. Pour on cream. Bring foil up over potatoes and seal edges to form a tightly closed package. Do not press package. Carefully lift package to a shallow pan.

Bake in hot oven (425°) 45 minutes, turning once (when you put the Sole/Shrimp Roll-ups in oven). To serve, place foil package in a basket or casserole, or on a platter; fold back foil edges. Makes 4 servings.

CHERRY TOMATO SALAD

The trick is chilling tomatoes in the special salad dressing

¼ c. minced parsley	½ tsp. salt
¼ c. salad oil	Pepper (optional)
3 tblsp. wine vinegar	1 tsp. sugar
½ tsp. basil leaves	1 pt. cherry tomatoes
½ tsp. orégano leaves	Lettuce

To make the dressing, combine all ingredients, except tomatoes and lettuce, in a bowl; mix well.

Wash and remove stems from cherry tomatoes; cut them in halves and add to the dressing in bowl. Cover and chill at least 3 hours, stirring gently a few times.

When ready to serve, lift tomatoes with a slotted spoon onto crisp lettuce liners on individual salad plates. Save leftover dressing for tomorrow's salad. Makes 4 servings.

OPEN-FACE CRANBERRY PIE

Tangy sour cream and cranberry sauce blend deliciously in this pie

Baked 9″ Graham Cracker Crumb Crust
¾ c. sugar
1 envelope unflavored gelatin
½ tsp. salt
1 c. cranberry juice cocktail
1 (1 lb.) can whole cranberry sauce
1 c. dairy sour cream
2 tblsp. confectioners sugar

Blend sugar, gelatin and salt in saucepan. Stir in cranberry juice cocktail and cranberry sauce; cook and stir over medium heat until mixture boils. Remove from heat.

Cool and chill until mixture mounds slightly when you drop a small amount from a spoon. Fold in ½ c. sour cream. Pour into chilled Graham Cracker Crumb Crust and refrigerate overnight.

At serving time, sift confectioners sugar over remaining ½ c. sour cream and fold in; spoon over top of pie. Makes 6 to 8 servings.

Graham Cracker Crumb Crust: Mix together 1¼ c. fine graham cracker crumbs, ¼ c. sugar and 6 tblsp. butter until crumbly. Press firmly into a 9″ pie pan. Bake in moderate oven (375°) 6 to 8 minutes, until edges brown. Cool and chill before adding pie filling.

CHAPTER 5

Afternoon and Evening Refreshments

DESSERT PARTIES . . .
SNACKS . . . OPEN HOUSES

Any time of day is a good time to serve the refreshments in this chapter. The Golden Wedding Reception menu is equally correct for afternoon or evening. The homemade, pretty Flower Wedding Cake and Golden Punch will taste delicious either time. After-skating-party refreshments may be for day or evening. The plump Glazed Potato Doughnuts, Popcorn/Peanut Clusters and Tri-Fruit Cooler *always* taste good. The White Cap Punch is an open-house refresher day or evening, and guests enjoy picking "dippers" from the snack tree at any open house during the holidays. (Just give them the chance!)

Even the Moonlight Hayride Supper menu can be adjusted to other events and times, as can the Men's Winter Evening Sandwich Lunch or the Simple Afternoon Tea. The menus that feature coffee or tea and an accompaniment make delightful refreshments for a women's afternoon club meeting, but are just as appropriate for couples to enjoy during a social evening.

This chapter is a treasury of foods that refresh when friends get together. Late Evening Snacks perk up spirits and promote friendly talk and laughter. Strawberry Pink delights women at afternoon bridge parties, but their husbands will welcome the same dessert tastes after evening couples' bridge. Frozen Buttermint Squares, luscious Black Bottom Cupcakes and rich Black-and-White Date Pie always receive compliments. Most everyone delights in dunking bite-size pieces of cake in Caramel Frosting Fondue.

Recipes for all dishes starred (*) are in this cookbook.

REFRESHMENTS TO KEEP ON HAND

Frozen Fruit Salad/Dessert*
Coffee

With this luscious fruit salad or dessert in the freezer, you're always ready for drop-in guests. Especially is it a good idea to keep a supply on hand during the holidays when drop-in visiting reaches the year's peak in country homes.

You can make the fruit salad/dessert right after Thanksgiving Day and have it ready before the Christmas rush gets hectic. If you wish, you can vary the salad from year to year (make it once and you'll make it a tradition) by substituting 1½ c. ground raw cranberries or 3 (1 lb.) pkgs. frozen whole strawberries for the maraschino cherries. If you use the berries, thaw them, drain and save the juice. Use it for part of the orange or pineapple juice called for in the recipe.

TIMETABLE

Do-Ahead: Make the salad a month or a few days ahead and freeze. Quart containers for it are a good size to use.

On Guest Day: A quart of the frozen fruit mixture thaws enough to slice while you make and serve the coffee.

SERVING SUGGESTIONS

For a salad serve slices of the frozen treat on crackling-crisp lettuce or other greens. For a dessert, place slices on individual small plates and, if desired, crown with small puffs of whipped cream, or topping.

FROZEN FRUIT SALAD/DESSERT

Recipe makes a big quantity of this special with a dual role

4 (1 lb. 4 oz.) cans crushed
    pineapple
2 (1 lb.) cans sliced peaches
2 c. fresh white seedless grapes,
    halved, or 2 (1 lb. 4 oz.) cans
1½ c. maraschino cherries, cut in
    eighths
½ lb. marshmallows, quartered
    (30)
2 tsp. crystallized ginger, finely
    chopped
1 envelope unflavored gelatin
¼ c. cold water

1 c. orange juice
¼ c. lemon juice
2½ c. sugar
½ tsp. salt
2 c. coarsely chopped pecans
2 qts. heavy cream, whipped, or
    10 envelopes dessert topping
    mix, whipped, or 1 qt. heavy
    cream and 5 envelopes dessert
    topping mix, whipped
3 c. mayonnaise
Lettuce
Maraschino cherries (for garnish)

Drain fruit; save 1½ c. pineapple syrup. Cut peaches in ½" cubes. Combine fruit, marshmallows and ginger.

Soften gelatin in cold water.

Heat pineapple syrup to boiling. Add gelatin; stir to dissolve. Add orange and lemon juices, sugar and salt; stir to dissolve. Chill.

When mixture starts to thicken, add fruit mixture and nuts. Fold in whipped cream and mayonnaise.

Spoon into 1-qt. cylinder cartons (paper, plastic or metal). Cover and freeze. Makes 9 quarts.

To serve, remove from freezer and thaw enough to slip out of carton. Cut in 1" slices. Serve salad on lettuce; garnish with cherries. For dessert, top with whipped cream. Each quart serves 6 to 8.

MAKE-AHEAD
AFTERNOON REFRESHMENTS

Frozen Buttermint Squares*
Chocolate Cookies
Salted Nuts
Hot Tea

Most every hostess delights in introducing her friends to a luscious, new dessert. Frozen Buttermint Squares are so unusual that they'll dominate the conversation. The distinctive delicacy carries the blended flavors of butter mints and strawberries in the gelatin, complemented by the chocolate cookies and tea.

TIMETABLE

Do-Ahead: Bake the cookies at least a day ahead and freeze. Start making the dessert the night before you wish to serve it.

On Guest Day: Complete making the dessert and freeze it at least 2 to 3 hours before serving. Let the cookies thaw at room temperature at least 10 minutes in their foil wrap.

SERVING SUGGESTIONS

If you have fresh mint, you can top the dessert servings with tiny sprigs of it. Arrange a tray of tea accompaniments, such as sugar, milk and/or cream and thin lemon slices.

FROZEN BUTTERMINT SQUARES

You do not dissolve the colorful strawberry flavor gelatin in water

1 (13¼ oz.) can crushed pineapple

1 (3 oz.) pkg. strawberry flavor gelatin

1 (10½ oz.) pkg. miniature marshmallows

1 c. heavy cream

4 oz. soft butter mints, crushed

Combine undrained pineapple, dry gelatin powder and marshmallows; mix well. Cover and chill overnight.

Whip cream; add butter mints and combine with chilled pineapple mixture. Pour into a 9″ square pan. Freeze 2 to 3 hours. Makes 9 servings.

WOMEN'S ONE O'CLOCK DESSERT

Strawberry Pink*
Coffee

What to serve for dessert to women friends is often a real problem. "Six out of eight members of my afternoon bridge club," an Oklahoma farm homemaker reports, "are avid calorie counters. Our custom is for the hostess to serve dessert when guests arrive at 1 P.M. At the end of the afternoon, we always are in a hurry to get home before the children arrive from school. We ban all rich desserts including those containing or garnished with the country favorite, whipped cream. And we constantly search for something different, distinctive and delicious to serve."

Our nomination for an ideal dessert for such occasions is Strawberry Pink. It's a lovely pink color, as its name implies, and tastes like strawberries fresh from the patch even though long icicles may hang from the roof.

TIMETABLE

Make-Ahead: Fix the dessert a day ahead and freeze.

On Guest Day: About 20 minutes before serving time, bring the dessert from freezer and place in refrigerator. Make the coffee. When time to serve the dessert, cut it in individual servings.

SERVING SUGGESTIONS

If available, top each serving with a fresh mint leaf and a whole strawberry.

STRAWBERRY PINK

Also perfect to serve at bridal and baby showers and parties

½ c. regular margarine	1 (10 oz.) pkg. frozen strawberries, thawed
½ c. chopped walnuts	
¼ c. brown sugar, firmly packed	1 tblsp. lemon juice
1 c. flour	1 tsp. vanilla
¼ tsp. vanilla	1 c. sugar
2 egg whites	

Put margarine in large baking pan; place in medium oven (350°) until melted. Stir in walnuts, brown sugar, flour and ¼ tsp. vanilla. Return to oven and heat for 8 minutes, stirring frequently, until mixture is lightly browned. Remove from oven and stir; then remove crumbs from pan to cool.

Beat egg whites in large bowl until soft peaks form. Add thawed strawberries, lemon juice and 1 tsp. vanilla. While beating, gradually add the sugar (this should take 20 minutes).

Sprinkle half the cool crumb mixture in bottom of a 13×9×2"

pan. Lightly spread strawberry mixture evenly over the top. Sprinkle remaining half of crumbs over top. Freeze overnight. Makes 9 to 12 servings, depending on size desired.

DESSERT BRIDGE PARTY

Rancho Lemon Custard*   Coffee

The country hostess frequently improvises in preparing food, to "make do" with what she has on hand. And when her experiment is successful, she feels the recipe bears her own trademark. This smooth custard with a rich, unusual lemon-caramel flavor is a good example. An Arizona ranch woman originated this and served it at a dessert bridge party; her neighbor guest was so enthusiastic about the custard that she asked to copy the recipe. She learned that her hostess had baked the dessert in an expensive, imported flan pan, but, undaunted, she decided to try a layer cake pan. It worked. She passed her recipe on to a FARM JOURNAL food editor. We recommend it!

TIMETABLE

Do-Ahead: Bake the custard a day ahead and chill.

On Guest Day: Before guests arrive, invert custard on a large plate. You'll find the top and sides coated with a deep amber caramel.

SERVING SUGGESTIONS

Sprinkle custard, just before serving, with toasted slivered or chopped almonds for delightful flavor and texture contrast. Or flame the dessert at serving time. Heat a little rum (about ¼ c.) in a small pan almost to simmering, but do not let boil. Ignite and slowly pour over top of custard. (The alcohol burns, the rum flavor remains.) Cut like pie and serve at once.

RANCHO LEMON CUSTARD

Velvety, tender custard is quite firm—a treat you'll serve often

1 c. sugar	1 tsp. vanilla
6 eggs	1½ c. light cream
½ tsp. salt	½ c. toasted chopped almonds
1 tblsp. grated lemon peel	(optional)

Place ½ c. sugar in 8″ round layer cake pan. Stir constantly over medium heat until sugar liquefies and turns a *light* golden brown. Remove from heat; protect hands with pot holders and roll pan around to coat sides and bottom with melted sugar. Set aside to cool.

Beat eggs with remaining ½ c. sugar until light and lemon-colored. Beat in salt, lemon peel, vanilla and cream. Pour into cake pan (it will be full).

Set pan of custard in pan containing hot water that reaches almost to top of custard pan. Bake in moderate oven (350°) 40 to 50 minutes, until knife inserted in center of custard comes out clean. Remove from oven, place plastic wrap directly on top of custard to cover and chill overnight.

To serve, turn upside down; sprinkle with nuts and cut in wedges like pie. Makes 8 servings.

SIMPLE AFTERNOON TEA

Company Cinnamon Toast*   Tea

Tea for two, or for several friends who stop by without notice, creates no problem for the country hostess. Staples in her kitchen almost always include, besides tea, the makings for this special cinnamon toast—bread, cream, sugar and cinnamon. Serve this teatime treat hot and fragrant from the oven. Be sure the tea is hot and well made. You'll find that most of your guests will give your homespun refreshments extravagant praise.

TIMETABLE

On Guest Day: With little warning friends were coming, you make the preparations after they arrive. If you do not wish to miss out on conversation, invite guests to the kitchen . . . a country custom. You can listen and talk while you fix the toast. Once it's in the oven, assemble the cups, teapot, sugar bowl, plates or trays and place them on a large tray. When the toast is almost golden, make the tea.

SERVING SUGGESTIONS

If you have a lemon, cut it in thin slices for guests who like to add it to their tea. Carry the tea tray to the most inviting spot in your home. This might be by a window with a view of hazy hills in the distance, or by the fireplace in winter. Pour the tea and serve it and the toast on individual plates; pass the sugar and/or lemon slices. A happy, friendly way to spend an hour or two.

COMPANY CINNAMON TOAST

Cream is the ingredient that makes this baked French Toast special. Add a dusting of confectioners sugar just before serving

6 slices bread, 1" thick	⅔ c. heavy cream
6 tblsp. sugar	¼ c. melted butter or regular
2 tblsp. ground cinnamon	margarine

Cut off crusts and cut each bread slice in 3 strips.

Mix sugar and cinnamon together in a shallow dish. Pour the cream into another shallow dish.

Dip bread strips in cream to coat both sides. Brush strip tops with butter; sprinkle all sides with the sugar-cinnamon mixture to make a thick covering.

Place bread strips on rack in a shallow baking pan. Bake in hot oven (400°) 20 minutes. Serve hot. Makes 18 strips.

COUNTRY EVENING REFRESHMENTS

Black Bottom Cupcakes*   Coffee

Once in a blue moon, as our grandmothers used to describe something exceptionally rare, a recipe comes along that yields such superlative results everyone wants to get a copy of it to use when entertaining. These luscious cupcakes deserve such a reception. We predict that your friends, once they sample them, will ask for the recipe. Be a thoughtful hostess and bake enough cupcakes for seconds.

TIMETABLE

Do-Ahead: You can bake the cupcakes a day or several days ahead and freeze them. (It's easy to bake them the day you entertain.)

On Guest Day: If you froze the cupcakes, sometime in the afternoon transfer them from freezer to refrigerator. Unwrap, but cover loosely with waxed paper. Or thaw them at room temperature in their wrap. This will take about 2 hours.

SERVING SUGGESTIONS

The cakes are so tasty that they need no garnish. Everyone will hope there are more cakes and coffee waiting in the kitchen.

BLACK BOTTOM CUPCAKES

Don't be alarmed by the rather thin cake batter—that's its nature

1 (8 oz.) pkg. cream cheese	1 tsp. baking soda
1 egg	½ tsp. salt
⅓ c. sugar	1 c. water
⅛ tsp. salt	⅓ c. salad oil
1 (6 oz.) pkg. semisweet chocolate pieces	1 tblsp. vinegar
1½ c. flour	1 tsp. vanilla
1 c. sugar	Sugar for sprinkling on top
¼ c. cocoa	½ c. chopped almonds

Combine cheese, egg, ⅓ c. sugar and ⅛ tsp. salt in mixing bowl; beat well. Stir in chocolate pieces, and set aside.

Sift together flour, 1 c. sugar, cocoa, soda and ½ tsp. salt. Add water, oil, vinegar and vanilla. Beat to mix well.

Line muffin-pan cups with paper baking cups; fill one third full with the cocoa batter. Top each with 1 heaping teaspoon reserved cream cheese mixture; sprinkle with sugar and almonds.

Bake in moderate oven (350°) 35 minutes. Makes 20 to 24 cupcakes.

CHOCOLATE EVENING DESSERT

Chocolate Fondue*
Dippers

Give chocolate fondue a chance to be the center of attention. It makes a luscious dessert after an extremely light meal, but for evening refreshments, served with at least three dip candidates and coffee, it takes the prize. There are many recipes for this rich, American dessert. This fondue made with milk chocolate certainly rates as one of the best, and to many people it's *the* best.

Choose the dippers from angel food, pound or sponge cake, maraschino cherries, bananas and marshmallows.

TIMETABLE

Do-Ahead: Bake or buy the cake a day ahead.

On Guest Day: Cut cake in bite-size pieces, place in bowls and cover with napkins to prevent drying. Drain the cherries. Make the fondue just before serving time, and ask the host or a guest to cut the bananas in bite-size chunks. Meanwhile, make the coffee.

SERVING SUGGESTIONS

Provide each guest with a plate, fondue fork and dinner fork. Serve the dippers in bowls within easy reach of everyone. You can use bamboo kabob sticks instead of fondue forks.

CHOCOLATE FONDUE

Chocolate fans of all ages like this dessert. It's a teen-age favorite

1 (12 oz.) milk chocolate bar, cut in pieces	1 tsp. instant coffee
6 tblsp. light cream	Dippers

Heat chocolate and light cream in metal fondue cooker over low heat, stirring frequently until chocolate is melted. Stir in the coffee powder. Place fondue on heating unit; keep warm over low heat while dipping bite-size pieces of angel food or pound cake, maraschino cherries, bite-size chunks of bananas and/or large marshmallows. Spear dippers on fondue forks, dip in chocolate fondue, transfer to dinner forks and eat. Makes 6 to 8 servings.

CAKE-AND-COFFEE EVENING

Pound or Angel Food Cake
Caramel Frosting Fondue*
Coffee

There is more than one good way to frost cake. With do-it-yourself parties popular, the hostess need not hesitate to ask her guests of the evening to frost their own pieces of cake. Most of them will think it's fun.

The first step is to select cake that does not break easily. Angel food or pound cake, for instance. Then make Caramel Frosting Fondue and let everyone dunk cubes of cake in it.

If you'd like to use this menu for refreshments during the Halloween season, you can easily expand it. Chilled cider makes a good choice for sipping on autumn evenings. And bite-size chunks of unpeeled red apples dipped in the dessert fondue, taste as good as those memorable caramel apples your mother used to make for children's parties.

TIMETABLE

Do-Ahead: Bake or buy pound or angel food cake a day ahead. Store it tightly covered in a cool place.

On Guest Day: Cut the cake in bite-size pieces, allowing 8 to 12 of them for each person. That provides extras for second helpings. You can make the fondue the last minute before serving, or before guests arrive, reheating it to 230° before pouring it into the fondue pot and placing over low heat on the fondue burner to keep warm. Ask your husband, son or a friend to cut the apples in bite-size pieces *just* before serving so they won't have time to discolor. Or if you wish to cut them ahead, sprinkle them with lemon juice mixed with a little water.

SERVING SUGGESTIONS

At every place on the table, set a serving plate with about 6 pieces of cake on it. Place apple pieces in a bowl to pass. Provide everyone with a fondue and a dinner fork, or use sturdy bamboo sticks, the kind that serve as skewers in cooking, instead of forks. This is one time you'll think a fork is more helpful than a knife in frosting cake!

CARAMEL FROSTING FONDUE

Rich caramel flavor is easy to attain with a candy thermometer. It helps you avoid scorching and development of an unpleasant taste. If sauce gets too thick, stir in a little water. Be sure to use fondue warm, but not hot. Try dipping pretzels and popcorn in it

2 c. brown sugar, firmly packed
1 c. light corn syrup
2 tblsp. water
½ c. melted butter

1 (15¾ oz.) can sweetened
 condensed milk (1⅓ c.)
1 tsp. vanilla

Stir brown sugar, corn syrup and water into saucepan containing melted butter. Bring to a boil over medium heat. Stir in condensed milk and stir and simmer until candy thermometer registers 230°. Remove from heat and add vanilla.

Pour into fondue pot and set over fondue burner on low heat to keep warm. Or cook, and reheat to 230° at serving time. Makes about 3 cups.

N O T E : You may prefer this fondue to the Caramel Fondue with Boys' Burger Supper (see Index).

EVENING'S END REFRESHMENTS

Walnut Whirl*   Small Grape Clusters
                  Coffee

Country coffee cakes are breads that lead a triple life—they star at morning affairs, such as at breakfast or lunch and coffee parties; in after-dark activities for refreshments following an evening of cards or visiting; sometimes they even assume a dessert role in suppers and dinners, often accompanying a fruit compote. On all occasions coffee, as the name indicates, is the favorite escort.

Some coffee cakes are yeast leavened. Walnut Whirl is an example. It looks good and it tastes even better, especially if it's warm.

TIMETABLE

Do-Ahead: Bake the coffee cake a day or several days ahead, wrap in foil and freeze. Or bake it the day you plan to serve it.

On Guest Day: If the cake is frozen, put it, in foil wrapper, in a moderate oven (350°) 25 to 30 minutes; 12 to 15 minutes if not frozen.

SERVING SUGGESTIONS

A bowl holding small clusters of grapes, whatever kind is available, makes a good accompaniment if you're serving the cake for late evening. The dining room or kitchen table provides a friendly, comfortable setting—gather your family and guests around it.

WALNUT WHIRL

Yeast dough winds around a luscious filling like a jelly roll and then is coiled on baking sheet to rise until doubled and bake slowly to a golden brown. It's work, but well worth the time

¼ c. sugar	1 pkg. active dry yeast
1 tsp. salt	¼ c. warm water (110 to 115°)
¼ c. soft butter or regular margarine	1 egg
¾ c. milk, scalded	3¼ to 3¾ c. flour
	Walnut Filling

Add sugar, salt and butter to milk and cool to lukewarm.

Dissolve yeast in water.

Stir egg and half the flour into milk mixture; stir in yeast and beat until smooth. Work in enough remaining flour to make a dough that is easy to handle.

Turn onto floured surface; knead until smooth. Press ball of dough in greased bowl, turn greased side up. Cover with damp cloth. Let rise in warm place until doubled, about 1½ hours.

Punch down dough; let rise again until almost doubled, about 30 minutes.

Cover worktable with several thicknesses of newspaper, then with large dish towel taped down to hold taut.

Roll out dough on floured towel to approximately 30×20″ rectangle; it will be very thin. With rubber spatula, gently spread Walnut Filling over dough—right to the edges. Starting at wide side, lift cloth and let dough roll up like a jelly roll. Pinch edges to seal.

Coil roll loosely on greased baking sheet; cover and let rise until nearly doubled, about 45 minutes.

Bake in slow oven (325°) 40 to 45 minutes. Remove from baking sheet to rack to cool. Makes about 18 servings.

Walnut Filling: Mix ⅓ c. soft butter or regular margarine, ¾ c. brown sugar, firmly packed, and 1 egg. Stir in ⅓ c. milk, 1 tsp. vanilla, 1 tsp. ground cinnamon and 3 c. walnuts, coarsely ground.

Variation

Short-Cut Walnut Whirl: Make coffee cake with hot roll mix (use 13¾ oz. pkg.). Let dough rise, then roll it out as above.

NEW YEAR'S EVE DESSERT PARTY

Snow-on-the-Mountain*   Coffee

Ring out the old and ring in the new year with delicious Snow-on-the-Mountain, a dessert which delights the guests. Brace yourself for compliments, promises the Iowa woman who serves the dessert at her New Year's Eve watch party.

TIMETABLE

Do-Ahead: Make the dessert a day ahead and place in the refrigerator. The chilling blends flavors and firms the snow mountain for cutting.

On Guest Day: All you have to do is make plenty of coffee and take it and the dessert to the buffet.

SERVING SUGGESTIONS

Let your guests see the spectacular, snowy mountain. Cut and serve it from the buffet or table with everyone gathered around to admire and to anticipate the tempting dessert.

SNOW-ON-THE-MOUNTAIN

Showy, delicious, make-ahead dessert—a real company special

Part 1 (*Cake*):
4 eggs
1 c. sugar
½ c. sifted flour
1 tsp. baking powder
½ tsp. salt
2 tsp. vanilla
1 c. chopped dates

1 c. chopped nuts
Part 2 (*Fruit*):
5 oranges
3 bananas
3 tblsp. sugar
Part 3 (*Snow*):
2 c. heavy cream, whipped
½ c. flaked coconut

To make cake, beat eggs until light; gradually add sugar, beating until it dissolves.

Sift together flour, baking powder and salt; add to egg mixture. Fold in vanilla, dates and nuts. Pour into two greased and floured 8″ round layer cake pans.

Bake in moderate oven (350°) about 30 minutes. Cool about 10 minutes in pans, then turn out and complete cooling on racks.

Meanwhile, prepare fruit. Peel oranges, discard seeds if not using navel oranges, and cut sections in small pieces. (You will have about 3 cups.) Peel bananas and slice. (There will be about 3 cups banana slices.) Toss fruit together to coat bananas with juice from the orange pieces to retard discoloration. Stir in sugar to mix well. Let stand while the cake bakes and cools.

To make mountain, break cooled cake in small pieces. Arrange some of the pieces in a layer about 12″ long and 10″ wide on a large platter, tray or plate. This is the base of the mountain. Put a layer of fruit, then a layer of cake pieces, and repeat, shaping the mountain. It should come to a peak. Frost with whipped cream, and sprinkle with coconut. Chill in refrigerator overnight. Cut and lift to dessert plates with cake server. Makes 20 to 24 servings.

WASHINGTON'S BIRTHDAY DESSERT

Lemon/Cheese Torte*   Tea or Coffee

While this handsome cheese cake with its gleaming red top is ideal for the hostess to feature when entertaining in February, it's equally appropriate and appealing the year round. Cottage and cream cheeses and packaged lemon pudding and pie filling unite in this unusual torte. The dessert is so well liked by the three sons of junior and senior high school age in a Wisconsin farm family that they ask their mother to make it for their birthdays instead of cake. You will find that people of all ages give the torte top rating.

TIMETABLE

Do-Ahead: Bake the cake, glaze and chill in refrigerator overnight.

On Guest Day: Cut the torte at serving time in 8 or 10 wedges.

SERVING SUGGESTIONS

The torte is so attractive and tempting that you may wish to cut and serve it at the table or buffet with your guests watching.

LEMON/CHEESE TORTE

Cheerful red cherry glaze makes this a fine February party dessert

¾ c. finely ground graham cracker crumbs	1 c. light cream
1 tblsp. sugar	2 c. creamed cottage cheese
2 tblsp. melted butter	1 (8 oz.) pkg. cream cheese
1 (3½ oz.) pkg. lemon pudding and pie filling mix	4 egg yolks
⅔ c. sugar	¼ tsp. salt
	4 egg whites, beaten to soft peaks
	Cherry Glaze

Combine crumbs, 1 tblsp. sugar and butter; mix well. (This amount may be doubled for a thicker crust.) Press mixture firmly into bottom of a 9″ spring-form pan (or a 3-qt. casserole, but it's easier to remove in good shape from a spring-form pan).

Combine pudding mix, ⅔ c. sugar and light cream in saucepan. Cook and stir until mixture comes to a full boil and is thickened, about 5 minutes. Mixture may curdle while cooking, but it will be smooth when it boils. Remove from heat.

Combine cottage and cream cheeses (both should be at room temperature). Mix well; add egg yolks, one at a time, mixing well after each addition. Add salt and cooked pudding; blend well. Fold in beaten egg whites and pour over crumb mixture in pan.

Bake in slow oven (300°) 1 hour. Cool to room temperature.

Chill thoroughly. Spread on Cherry Glaze. The cake is best when chilled overnight. Makes 8 to 10 servings.

CHERRY GLAZE

½ (3 oz.) pkg. strawberry flavor gelatin (4 tblsp.)
½ c. boiling water
¼ c. sugar

½ c. juice drained from cherries
1 (16 to 17 oz.) can pitted tart cherries (water pack)

Dissolve gelatin in boiling water; stir in sugar. Add juice drained from cherries. Chill until slightly thickened.

Spread well-drained cherries over top of chilled Lemon/Cheese Torte. Pour gelatin mixture over cherries. Chill until ready to serve.

FEBRUARY DESSERT PARTY

Elegant Chocolate Log*   Coffee

Treat your friends to a log cutting! What could be more appropriate for Lincoln's birthday than this delicate one made with chocolate cake? The Utah homemaker/home economist who shares this recipe makes the cake for very special occasions. When entertaining quite a few guests, she bakes two cakes, fills and rolls them; then she puts them together to make one long log and spreads on the frosting. She serves it on a long antique fish platter and her friends say it makes a stunning dessert. (You can use a tray if your platters are not long enough.)

TIMETABLE

Do-Ahead: A week or several days ahead, bake the cake, roll, fill and frost. Place on baking sheet and freeze. When frozen firm, wrap and return to freezer with seam side of roll down. (Some women prefer to frost the log after freezing and thawing.)

On Guest Day: Take the frozen roll from the freezer, remove wrap, cover loosely and let thaw in refrigerator for several hours. You can bake, roll, fill and frost the roll on guest day. Keep it in refrigerator until serving time. One log makes 8 servings.

SERVING SUGGESTIONS

Set the dessert on buffet or table and slice and serve it with admiring guests watching. They'll have runaway appetites. Ask a co-operative guest to pour the coffee.

ELEGANT CHOCOLATE LOG

A beautiful way to serve chocolate cake—perfect for entertaining

1¼ c. sifted confectioners sugar	1 c. heavy cream, whipped
¼ c. plus 1 tblsp. sifted flour	Sugar (about 2 tblsp.)
½ tsp. salt	8 to 12 marshmallows, cut up
5 tblsp. cocoa	1 square unsweetened chocolate
6 eggs, separated	2 c. confectioners sugar
¼ tsp. cream of tartar	Light cream
1¼ tsp. vanilla	¼ c. finely chopped pecans
1 tblsp. water	

Sift together 1¼ c. confectioners sugar, flour, salt and cocoa three times.

Beat egg whites with cream of tartar until stiff.

Beat egg yolks until thick and lemon-colored; beat in vanilla and water. Add sifted dry ingredients and beat into egg yolks until well blended. Fold in beaten egg whites.

Spread in greased, paper-lined 15½×10½×1″ jelly roll pan. Bake in moderate oven (375°) 15 to 20 minutes. Lightly dust clean dish towel with confectioners sugar; loosen cake around edges with spatula. Invert on towel. Lift off pan and carefully peel off paper. With a sharp knife, cut off cake's crisp edges. Roll up cake gently, from narrow end, by folding edge of cake over and then tucking it in; continue rolling cake, lifting towel higher with one hand as you guide the rolling with the other hand, rolling the towel in the cake (to prevent cake sticking). Let cool on rack (wrap tightly in towel to hold it in shape).

Unroll cake on towel; spread with whipped cream, sweetened to taste with granulated sugar (about 2 tblsp.) and with marshmallows added. Roll like jelly roll.

For frosting, melt chocolate; add 2 c. confectioners sugar with enough light cream to make it spreadable. Spread over cake and immediately sprinkle with chopped nuts. Makes 8 to 10 servings.

ST. PATRICK'S DAY DESSERT PARTY

Lime/Chocolate Fascination*   Hot Tea

If you plan to entertain on St. Patrick's Day, consider serving this make-ahead dessert. It wears its green with distinction and the lime and chocolate flavors blend to perfection. The recipe comes from a Minnesota woman who served it to her afternoon bridge club. Her children nicknamed the dessert "the Green Cake." Their mother calls it Lime/Chocolate Fascination because it never fails to fascinate her friends and family. Call it what you wish, the name will not affect the dessert's beauty or tastiness. Serve it with tea to carry out the Irish menu.

TIMETABLE

Do-Ahead: Put the can of evaporated milk in the refrigerator a day or two before you wish to whip it. Make the dessert a day ahead and refrigerate.

On Guest Day: Chill the dessert plates if refrigerator space permits.

SERVING SUGGESTIONS

To add a touch of glamor to the refreshment, serve a green and a chocolate-coated candy mint on each plate with the dessert. Some women keep candy mints of different colors and flavors in their freezers. It is surprising how frequently they add the right color and sweet note to refreshments. Be sure to wrap the packages of candy in moisture-proof wrap when freezing them. The boxes themselves often are not adequate protection for freezer storage. Let the mints thaw in their wrap at room temperature 4 to 8 hours before you serve them.

LIME/CHOCOLATE FASCINATION

A March special, but good every month—guests of all ages like this

1 (14½ oz.) can evaporated milk	2 tsp. lemon juice
1 (3 oz.) pkg. lime flavor gelatin	About 4 drops green food color
2 c. hot water	2 c. chocolate wafer crumbs (8½
1 c. sugar	oz.)
¼ c. lime juice	½ c. melted butter

Chill milk at least 1 day in refrigerator.

Dissolve gelatin in hot water. Chill until mixture is partly congealed (consistency of unbeaten egg whites). Then whip until fluffy. Stir in sugar, lime and lemon juices and food color to tint a delicate green.

Whip milk until light and fluffy; fold into gelatin mixture.

Combine cookie crumbs and melted butter. Reserve ½ c. crumbs for top. Press remaining crumbs into bottom of a 9″ square pan. Add whipped gelatin-milk mixture. Sprinkle reserved ½ c. crumbs on top. Chill overnight or until firm. Makes 9 servings.

BLACK-AND-WHITE WINTER DESSERT

Black-and-White Date Pie*   Coffee

Take a cold, clear winter night, congenial friends gathered in a comfortable home, a hospitable host and hostess and this date pie and coffee for refreshment. You have the right ingredients for a joyful evening. The dessert is rich in calories, but equally rich in luscious flavors. It gives guests a well-fed feeling and sends them home in a happy frame of mind.

TIMETABLE

Do-Ahead: You can line the pie pan with pastry, bake the pie shell, slip it into a plastic bag and put in a cool place overnight, or freeze it for several days.

On Guest Day: Make the pie. At serving time, whip the cream and spread on pie while your husband or a friend makes the coffee.

SERVING SUGGESTIONS

The Iowa farm woman who contributed this recipe says it is a winter favorite of the bridge club to which she and her husband belong. She serves the dessert from a small table, covered with a black cloth which she embroidered with delicate white snowflake designs. Her dessert plates are white and she uses either black or white napkins. The guests, who have been seated around bridge tables during the evening, enjoy going to the buffet for their own servings.

BLACK-AND-WHITE DATE PIE

Pie is rich enough for 8 servings—just right for two tables of bridge

Baked 9″ pie shell	*Top Layer:*
Bottom Layer:	¾ c. sugar
1 c. chopped fresh dates (8 oz. pkg.)	¼ c. flour
	2 tblsp. cornstarch
½ c. water	¼ tsp. salt
⅛ tsp. salt	2 c. milk
½ c. sugar	3 egg yolks, beaten
1 tsp. cornstarch	½ tsp. lemon juice
1 tsp. butter	½ tsp. vanilla
1 tblsp. lemon juice	¾ c. heavy cream, whipped

To make bottom layer, cook dates with water and salt until they are very soft. Combine sugar and cornstarch; add to dates. Simmer 1 minute. Add butter and lemon juice. Cool; then spread in baked pie shell.

For top layer, combine sugar, flour, cornstarch and salt. Scald milk; gradually add to dry mixture, stirring constantly. Cook over boiling water until mixture thickens. Cool.

Add egg yolks, beaten until foamy. Cook over boiling water 3 minutes. Remove from heat; add lemon juice and vanilla. Partially cool. Spread on top of date mixture in pie shell. Cool thoroughly.

Serve topped with whipped cream. Makes 8 servings.

COLD WEATHER DESSERT BUFFET

Tart Bar with Tart Shells* and Tart Fillings*
Garnishes　　　Coffee

Sharing the work, as well as the joys of entertaining, is a firmly established custom in the country. Potlucks have long been a popular way. Progressive dinners or suppers are another. This Dessert Buffet made its debut when a Minnesota couple was asked to serve the last course of a progressive dinner for members of a neighborhood club. Now it has become a tradition in the neighborhood.

The Tart Bar, as its creator calls it, has many merits. It capitalizes on the great American liking for pies. Also you can prepare the food ahead. The Tart Bar with its choice of tempting fillings usually intrigues guests into offering to take a turn at filling the crisp pastry shells. Men especially relish the opportunity to indicate their preferences. And sampling more than one kind does not mark anyone as being greedy; it compliments the hostess who prepared the food.

Four different fillings are adequate. We give recipes for Lemon, Pumpkin and Chocolate Cream; other suggestions are canned cherry, blueberry or other canned fruit pie filling and sugared strawberries with whipped cream or dessert topping mix.

TIMETABLE

Do-Ahead: Bake tart shells and make the pastes for the cream fillings several days ahead and freeze, or a day ahead and refrigerate.

On Guest Day: If you have the basic pastes in the freezer, thaw at room temperature as many portions as you will need. Each portion yields enough filling for six 3″ tart shells. To them, add the whipped dessert topping and mix to make a light filling that you can spoon easily into the tart shells; refrigerate fillings several hours. At serving time make the coffee.

SERVING SUGGESTIONS

Arrange rows of empty tart shells on a tray and place on a serving cart on a side table. Around them set bowls of fillings and toppings, such as chopped nuts, flaked coconut, sliced strawberries and whipped cream, to garnish the tarts. Invite guests to come to the "bar" and name the kind of filling they prefer for their tarts. Also give them a choice of toppings. Spoon the filling into the tart shell, add the topping, place the dessert on an individual plate and hand it to the guest. Invite a friend to pour the coffee. Warning: Guests often return for seconds!

TART SHELLS

You can fill tart shells with ice cream and top with dessert sauce

2 c. sifted flour	¾ c. shortening, or ⅔ c. lard
1 tsp. salt	4 or 5 tblsp. cold water

Combine flour and salt in mixing bowl. Cut in shortening with pastry blender or with two knives until mixture is the consistency of coarse cornmeal.

Sprinkle on cold water, 1 tblsp. at a time, tossing mixture lightly and stirring with fork. Add water each time to the driest part of mixture. The dough should be just moist enough to hold together when pressed gently with a fork. It should not be sticky.

Divide pastry into 6 parts. Shape into smooth balls and roll out each ball to make 4½ to 5″ circles.

Fit pastry circles over backs of inverted 3½″ muffin-pan cups. Make pleats so pastry will fit snugly. Prick entire surface with 4-tined fork. Or fit pastry over inverted custard cups, prick well and set on baking sheet. Refrigerate 30 minutes before baking.

Preheat oven to very hot (450°). Bake tart shells 10 to 12 minutes, or until golden. Cool on racks. Then carefully remove from pans, or custard cups. Fill as desired. Makes about 6 (3″) tarts, depending on how thin the pastry was rolled.

N O T E : Regardless of the size of your muffin-pan cups, you can bake tart shells on them. With a string, measure one of the inverted cups up one side, across the bottom and down on the other side. Cut the string this length. Find a bowl, saucer or small plate in the kitchen that has the same diameter as the string. Or cut a cardboard this size. Use for a pattern to cut the rolled pastry in circles. Fit pastry rounds on alternate muffin cups—6 on a pan with 12 cups. Pleat pastry to fit snugly.

CHOCOLATE CREAM TART FILLING

Strong chocolate flavor—delightful with a snowy drift of coconut

½ c. Cocoa Paste
1 envelope dessert topping mix

Thaw Cocoa Paste.

Prepare topping mix according to package directions. Add Cocoa Paste; continue beating until creamy and smooth. Chill in refrigerator several hours before serving. Makes filling for 6 (3") tarts.

COCOA PASTE

1⅓ c. cocoa
1 c. sugar
2 c. boiling water

Combine cocoa and sugar in heavy saucepan. Add water slowly, stirring to make a smooth mixture.

Cook and stir over high heat until mixture boils. Reduce heat to low and continue cooking for 15 minutes, stirring occasionally.

Pour into bowl; cool. Package in ½ c. portions; freeze, or store in refrigerator. (May be stored up to 4 weeks in refrigerator or freezer.) Makes 2 cups.

PUMPKIN CREAM TART FILLING

True pumpkin flavor—spicy! Garnish filled tarts with toasted pecans

1⅓ c. Pumpkin Paste
1 envelope dessert topping mix

Thaw Pumpkin Paste.

Prepare topping mix according to package directions. Add Pumpkin Paste; continue beating until creamy and smooth. Chill in refrigerator for several hours before serving. Makes filling for 6 (3") tarts.

PUMPKIN PASTE

1 c. sugar	1½ tsp. ground nutmeg
½ c. brown sugar, firmly packed	¾ tsp. salt
⅓ c. sifted flour	3 c. canned pumpkin
1½ tsp. ground cinnamon	¾ c. water

Combine sugars, flour, spices and salt. Add to pumpkin in heavy saucepan; mix thoroughly. Add water.

Cook 15 minutes over low heat, stirring occasionally.

Pour into bowl; cool. Package in 1⅓ c. portions; freeze. (May be stored up to 4 weeks in freezer.) Makes 4 cups.

LEMON CREAM TART FILLING

Light and lemony—and so good when topped with sliced strawberries

½ c. Lemon Paste
1 envelope dessert topping mix

Thaw Lemon Paste; keep cold.

Prepare topping mix according to package directions. Add Lemon Paste; continue beating until creamy and smooth. Add more milk for thinner mixture, if desired. Add food color to give lemon color.

Chill in refrigerator several hours before serving. Makes filling for 6 (3″) tarts.

LEMON PASTE

½ c. butter	1 c. boiling water
⅓ c. sifted flour	½ c. lemon juice
1 c. sugar	1 tblsp. grated lemon peel

Melt butter in heavy saucepan. Add flour and stir to make smooth paste. Mix in ¼ c. sugar. Add water slowly, stirring to make a smooth mixture. Add remaining sugar, lemon juice and peel.

Cook and stir over high heat until mixture boils. Reduce heat to low and continue cooking for 15 minutes, stirring occasionally.

Pour into bowl; cool. Package in ½ c. portions; freeze, or store in refrigerator. (May be stored up to 4 weeks in refrigerator or freezer.) Makes 2 cups.

PARTNERSHIP REFRESHMENTS

Snack Cookies*
Golden Pitcher Punch*

Whenever girls and boys get together, something to sip and snack on is in order. Members of some 4-H Clubs, after a busy summer with work projects, welcome winter meetings with their social moments. Homemade cookies and punch are the favorite refreshments. The girls bake the cookies, and while the boys do not "preside" over punch bowls, they take responsibility for the beverage and often help make it or pour it from pitchers.

This menu suggests Golden Pitcher Punch, a pretty fruit juice punch with ginger ale added for sparkle, but the beverage you serve can be as simple as lemonade with attention-getting ice cubes. To make the ice cubes, mix 1 (12 oz.) can red Hawaiian punch and 2 c. cold water. Pour into ice cube trays and freeze 24 hours or until firm. Apple coolers also win friends. To make a good one, pour 1 qt. apple juice over cracked ice in a pitcher. Add 1 (7 oz.) bottle ginger ale.

The oatmeal drop cookies never fail to awaken enthusiasm, especially when decorated with candy- and chocolate-coated peanuts. The candy coating is in different colors that brighten the cookie plate or tray.

TIMETABLE

Do-Ahead: Bake the cookies a day ahead, or if easier, several days ahead and freeze.

On Guest Day: Both cookies and punch may need to travel to a meeting or gathering. If you tote the cookies, leave them in their wrap. They will thaw on the way to the party. Pour the punch over ice cubes in vacuum container; add ginger ale at serving time.

SERVING SUGGESTIONS

Garnishes of very thin orange slices add interest to the pitcher of punch. Display the colorful cookies on a large tray or plate.

SNACK COOKIES

Crisp oatmeal cookies go glamorous with bright confection trim

½ c. shortening	1 c. flour
½ c. sugar	½ tsp. baking soda
½ c. brown sugar, firmly packed	½ tsp. salt
½ tsp. vanilla	1 c. quick-cooking rolled oats
1 egg	Candy- and chocolate-coated
1 tblsp. water	peanuts

Cream together shortening, sugars and vanilla to make a fluffy mixture. Beat in egg and water.

Sift together flour, baking soda and salt. Add to creamed mixture and blend well. Stir in rolled oats.

Drop by rounded teaspoonfuls about 2″ apart onto greased baking sheet. Press candy- and chocolate-coated peanut in center of each.

Bake in moderate oven (375°) 8 to 10 minutes. Makes 3 dozen.

GOLDEN PITCHER PUNCH

Cheerful as sunshine—three fruit juices bubbling with ginger ale

4 c. cold water	1 c. pineapple juice
1½ c. sugar	1 c. orange juice
½ c. lemon juice	1 (28 oz.) bottle ginger ale

Heat water and sugar until sugar is dissolved, about 5 minutes. Add fruit juices and chill. Pour into large pitcher and add ginger ale at serving time. Pour over ice cubes in glasses. Makes 8 servings.

SOCIAL EVENING REFRESHMENTS

Wisconsin Trio-Cheese Ball*   Assorted Crackers
Celery   Mulled Cider*   Coffee

You can depend on a Wisconsin hostess to recognize a superior cheese blend when she tastes it. One of them shares a favorite. She serves it as an appetizer in the living room before a meal, but more frequently after an evening of visiting or cards. She molds the three-cheese mixture into different shapes, such as a ball, loaf or cylinder. Guests slice and spread it on crackers. She also shapes the cheese mixture into tiny balls, but less often because it's more work and they soften so quickly at room temperature.

TIMETABLE

Do-Ahead: Make cheese ball a day or several days ahead, wrap in foil and refrigerate.

On Guest Day: Roll the ball in chopped parsley and pecans. Return to refrigerator. Make Mulled Cider when convenient. Reheat at serving time.

SERVING SUGGESTIONS

Place cheese on large plate, platter or tray and surround with crackers. Or cut unpeeled, cored red apples in wedges, sprinkle with lemon juice to prevent discoloration and arrange around cheese; serve crackers on a separate plate. The apples taste wonderful spread with the cheese and they add a pleasing touch of color. Serve the cider in mugs or cups and float a thin orange slice, stuck with a whole clove, in each. You may wish to offer guests this refreshing drink early in the evening, and serve the cheese and coffee later.

WISCONSIN TRIO-CHEESE BALL

Provide knives for spreading; cheese softens at room temperature

1 (8 oz.) pkg. cream cheese
¼ lb. blue cheese, crumbled
1 c. shredded sharp Cheddar
  cheese (¼ lb.)
3 tblsp. minced onion

1 tblsp. Worcestershire sauce
½ tsp. salt
½ c. finely chopped pecans
¼ c. finely chopped parsley
  (about)

Put all ingredients, except pecans and parsley, in bowl. Beat with electric mixer at medium speed until mixture is fluffy. Stir in 3 tblsp. pecans; cover and refrigerate 3 to 4 hours.

Remove cheese from bowl, place on aluminum foil and shape with hands into a large ball (or small 1″ balls). Wrap tightly in foil and return to refrigerator. Cheese is soft unless thoroughly chilled. About 30 minutes before serving, unwrap cheese (reshape in ball if necessary); roll in remaining pecans and parsley. Place on serving plate or tray and keep in refrigerator until serving time. Makes 1 (3″) ball or about 50 (1″) balls. You can also mold into a loaf or other shapes.

MULLED CIDER

Also serve this spicy favorite with doughnuts for Halloween

½ c. brown sugar, firmly packed
⅛ tsp. salt
2 qts. apple cider

¾ tsp. whole allspice
½ tsp. whole cloves
3″ stick cinnamon

Combine brown sugar, salt and cider. Tie spices in clean, thin white cloth and add to cider. Bring slowly to a boil; cover and simmer 20 minutes. Remove spices. Serve hot. Makes 10 servings.

LATE EVENING SNACKS

Crab/Cheese Spread*   Dilled Sour Cream Dip*
Texas Meat Balls* with Red Hot Barbecue Sauce*
Carrot, Cucumber and Zucchini Strips
Hard Tack Cookies*
Coffee

When you go to the basketball game, show, concert or other event with friends, invite the party to stop at your house on the way home. It's an easy way to entertain.

This help-yourself menu can satisfy appetites of varying degrees—and take care of additional guests. The food requires only finishing touches. Make the coffee just before serving time. Let the host help by carrying the snacks to the buffet or table in the living or family room.

A crabmeat spread, meat balls with barbecue sauce and a sour cream dip with plenty of uncooked vegetable dippers plus crackers and, if you like, potato or corn chips offer guests an ample choice. If you wish to end with a sweet touch, bring out a plate of Hard Tack Cookies—they are unusual and always bring compliments.

TIMETABLE

Do-Ahead: You can bake Hard Tack Cookies several days ahead and store them in a covered container.

On Guest Day: Mix and shape meat balls early in the day and re-frigerate. Make barbecue sauce. Peel and cut carrots in strips; place them in a jar, add a little water, cover and chill. Before you leave home place the cream cheese on a platter or plate, top with crab-meat and refrigerate. Add the seafood cocktail sauce just before serving. Mix the sour cream dip, cover and chill. After you return home, broil the meat balls and make the coffee; peel the chilled cucumber and cut it and the unpeeled small zucchini in strips.

SERVING SUGGESTIONS

Serve crab spread with a knife for cutting and spreading. Keep meat balls warm in chafing dish or electric skillet, or serve them on a warm platter with the bowl of barbecue sauce near them. Place vegetable dippers on tray alongside sour cream dip. Arrange an assortment of crackers, including shredded wheats, on tray or large plate.

CRAB/CHEESE SPREAD

Open a can of crabmeat, a bottle of seafood cocktail sauce and a package of cream cheese to make this delicious spread—quick

1 (8 oz.) pkg. cream cheese
1 (7½ oz.) can crabmeat, drained and flaked
¾ c. bottled seafood cocktail sauce

Place cream cheese on serving plate or platter and flatten until ½″ in height. Top with crabmeat, then with bottled seafood cocktail sauce. Serve with crackers. Makes about 25 servings.

DILLED SOUR CREAM DIP

Brings out the best flavors of uncooked vegetable dippers

1 c. dairy sour cream
½ c. mayonnaise or salad dressing
1 tblsp. finely chopped green onion

2 tsp. parsley flakes, crushed
1 tsp. dill weed, crushed
1 tsp. bottled salad seasoning

Combine all ingredients. Cover and chill several hours to blend flavors. Serve with carrot, cucumber and zucchini slices. Makes about 1½ cups.

TEXAS MEAT BALLS

Provide plenty of strong picks to spear meat balls for dunking

1 lb. lean ground beef
1 (6 oz.) can evaporated milk
3 tblsp. onion soup mix

2 tsp. Worcestershire sauce
Red Hot Barbecue Sauce

Combine ground beef, milk, soup mix and Worcestershire sauce. Shape into balls, using 1 level tblsp. meat mixture for each ball. Place on rack and broil without turning about 10 to 12 minutes, or until as done as desired. Serve warm with Red Hot Barbecue Sauce. Use picks to dunk meat balls into sauce. Makes about 30 balls.

RED HOT BARBECUE SAUCE

This lively sauce lives up to its name . . . it's really hot

½ c. finely chopped onion	2 tblsp. brown sugar
¼ c. finely chopped green pepper	2½ tblsp. cider vinegar
2 tblsp. butter or regular margarine	1 tblsp. Worcestershire sauce
1½ c. bottled barbecue sauce	⅛ tsp. hot pepper sauce

Cook onion and green pepper in butter over low heat until onion is tender (do not let it brown). Mix in remaining ingredients. Simmer about 15 minutes, until sauce is heated and seasonings are blended. Serve in a bowl. Makes about 2 cups.

HARD TACK COOKIES

Cookies may get too hard several days after baking. Add a slice of bread to cookie jar; in 24 hours they will soften just right

2 eggs	1 c. flaked coconut
1 c. sugar	1 c. chopped dates or raisins
1 c. sifted flour	1 tblsp. confectioners sugar
½ tsp. baking powder	(optional)

Beat eggs until frothy; add sugar and mix.

Sift together flour and baking powder; add to egg mixture. Fold in coconut and dates.

Spread dough in 11×7×1½″ pan; bake in slow oven (325°) 30 to 35 minutes. Cut in bars of desired size while hot. Sprinkle with confectioners sugar. Makes about 20 bars.

OPEN-HOUSE REFRESHMENTS

Party Punch*

Chicken Nuggets*   Wiener/Cheese Appetizers*

Upside-Down Cheese Biscuits*

Potato Chips   Crackers

Smoky Cottage Cheese Dip*

Popcorn Snack*

If in doubt about how to entertain when former neighbors, whom your friends wish to see, are your house guests, have a punch party.

Set aside an evening for this open house. You'll find people of all ages enjoy nibbling on snacks, sipping punch and visiting with friends. Nice and informal, encouraging conversation and circulating.

You can serve cold snacks only, but warm ones are especially appetizing. It's a good idea to get them ready ahead for fast last-minute broiling or baking. Perhaps you are fortunate and have a daughter or special friend who will take over part of the quick cooking for you.

In this menu the hot appetizers are miniatures of popular foods everybody likes—fried chicken, hot biscuits and wieners and cheese. The chilled cheese dip with crisp vegetable dippers appeals to everyone. And so does the crunchy Popcorn Snack. It's so good your supply may run out too soon unless you make two batches.

TIMETABLE

Do-Ahead: Make the Popcorn Snack several days ahead (before your house guests arrive). Store it in an airtight container and place in a cool spot. Get the Chicken Nuggets and Wiener/Cheese Appetizers ready to heat just before serving. Cover them and store in refrigerator.

On Guest Day: Make the dip at your convenience, place in bowl and refrigerate. Get carrot and celery sticks and cauliflowerets ready, place in ice water until crisp; then chill them in plastic bags. Make punch just before time to serve it. Sometime during the evening, slip out to the kitchen and bake a pan of the tiny biscuits and carry them to friends while piping hot. What a surprise!

SERVING SUGGESTIONS

Serve punch in a big pitcher or a punch bowl, whichever you prefer. Set pitcher or bowl on tray or large plate and place on table or buffet. Arrange the appetizers around it. Since they are finger food, you need not provide silverware or plates, but do have plenty of picks and paper napkins.

PARTY PUNCH

So easy to make, so pretty to look at and so refreshing to sip

2 (6 oz.) cans frozen pink lemonade concentrate	2 c. cold water
1 (6 oz.) can frozen grapefruit juice concentrate	1 qt. ginger ale, chilled
	1 qt. club soda, chilled

Combine concentrates and water in punch bowl; stir until they melt. Add 2 trays of ice cubes and stir. Just before serving, carefully pour ginger ale and club soda down side of bowl. Makes about 25 servings.

CHICKEN NUGGETS

Serve warm or cold—they're tasty both ways, the hit of any party

4 whole chicken breasts (broiler-
 fryers)
½ c. unseasoned fine dry bread
 crumbs
¼ c. grated Parmesan cheese

½ tsp. salt
1 tsp. thyme leaves
1 tsp. basil leaves
½ c. melted butter or regular
 margarine

Bone chicken breasts; remove skin. Cut each breast half into nuggets, about 1¼ to 1½" square.

Combine bread crumbs, cheese, salt, thyme and basil. Dip chicken pieces in melted butter and then in crumb mixture. Place in a single layer on foil-lined baking sheet. Bake in hot oven (400°) until golden, about 10 minutes. Serve with picks. Makes 56 to 60 nuggets.

WIENER/CHEESE APPETIZERS

Watch the youngsters gather round the platter for this tasty snack

2 (5½ oz.) pkgs. fully cooked little wieners
¼ lb. process American cheese (about)

Cut wieners lengthwise in halves but not quite through (about three fourths of the way). Slice cheese in thin 1" slivers. Place a sliver in each wiener. Cover and refrigerate.

At serving time, lay wieners on rack in broiler pan and broil until cheese starts to bubble. Serve at once. Makes about 30 appetizers.

UPSIDE-DOWN CHEESE BISCUITS

Serve these piping hot—they'll be popular so make plenty!

1 (5 oz.) jar pasteurized process
 cheese spread
1 tblsp. butter or regular
 margarine

1 can refrigerated biscuits (10)
Chopped fresh parsley (optional)

In a 9" pie pan put cheese spread and butter; place in very hot oven (450°) until butter melts.

Meanwhile, quarter biscuits with kitchen scissors. Stir cheese-butter mixture to combine (mixture will not completely blend). Cover with biscuits, arranging pieces very close together.

Bake in very hot oven (450°) 10 to 12 minutes, until golden brown. Loosen biscuits with spatula and invert at once onto serving plate. Garnish with chopped parsley, if desired. Makes 40 bite-size biscuits.

SMOKY COTTAGE CHEESE DIP

Serve this with carrot, celery and cucumber sticks and cauliflowerets

1 c. cottage cheese	½ tsp. liquid smoke
1 (3 oz.) pkg. cream cheese	¼ tsp. garlic salt
2 tblsp. light cream or milk	½ c. ripe olives, minced
1 tsp. minced onion	

Beat together cottage cheese, cream cheese and cream. Blend in remaining ingredients. Cover and refrigerate. Makes 1⅔ cups.

POPCORN SNACK

Play safe—use candy thermometer. This is too good to risk failure

2 qts. popped corn	1 c. dark corn syrup
2 c. bite-size shredded wheat	¼ tsp. salt
1 (4 oz.) can blanched whole almonds, toasted	½ c. butter or regular margarine
1½ c. sugar	1 tsp. vanilla

Combine popcorn, shredded wheat and almonds in a greased kettle; place in very slow oven (250°) 20 minutes. Keep warm.

Heat sugar, corn syrup, salt and butter in medium saucepan until boiling, stirring constantly. Wipe down sides of saucepan with pastry brush dipped in water and well drained to remove any sugar crystals. Insert candy thermometer and continue cooking without stirring until mixture reaches 290° on thermometer, or until a small amount of mixture dropped in cold water separates into thin hard, but not brittle threads. Remove from heat; add vanilla at once.

Spread corn mixture on two large greased baking sheets. Pour hot syrup over, a little at a time, stirring constantly to coat mixture. Spread quickly on baking sheets. When cool, break in pieces. Store in airtight container. Makes about 2 pounds.

Toasted Almonds: Spread almonds in a single layer in 15½ × 10½ × 1″ jelly roll pan. Bake in moderate oven (375°) about 10 minutes, until a light brown. Remove from pan.

HOLIDAY OPEN HOUSE

White Cap Punch*

Christmas Snack Tree*

Party Cheese Dip*   Quick Mustard Sauce*

Corn Chips   Crackers

Cashew Drop Cookies*   Holiday Gumdrop Cookies*

Caramel Popcorn Balls*   Peanut Brittle

Coffee

When holly wreaths hang on doors and bright lights twinkle on Christmas trees, a friendly spirit permeates the countryside. Take advantage of the season to extend hospitality to neighbors and friends. Treat them to a few evening hours in your home. Invite them to drop by between designated hours that are right for your family and for them.

A snack tree gets the center of attention in this menu. It is both decorative and functional for it holds snacks to dunk in the dips served in bowls at its base. Notice the diversion in beverages—from frigid fruit juice punch to steaming hot coffee—refreshments for people of all ages.

Young people quickly spy the peanut brittle (or other homemade candy of your choice) and the popcorn balls. We give you recipes for two special cookies. The candy gumdrops in one of them are particularly festive in color, and the unusual cashew cookies may be a new eating experience to some of your guests.

TIMETABLE

Do-Ahead: Make the snack tree base several days ahead so it will be ready to trim with food on open-house day. Also make ahead peanut brittle and popcorn balls. Bake cookies and freeze. You can make the dips the day before you'll serve them if it's easier than making them on party day. Refrigerate.

On Guest Day: Make snack tree dippers; refrigerate meat and cheese dippers. Place vegetable dippers in ice water. Make Tomato Roses last of all and chill. When it's almost time for the first car to turn in the drive, make the coffee and punch.

SERVING SUGGESTIONS

Give the snack tree the place of honor on the buffet or table. Arrange the other foods around it. Heap popcorn balls in a market basket for a country look.

WHITE CAP PUNCH

You can increase the number of servings by increasing all ingredients except sherbet—use your judgment on this

2 (6 oz.) cans frozen lemonade concentrate	2 c. water
	1 qt. pineapple sherbet
1 (6 oz.) can frozen orange juice concentrate	1 qt. ginger ale, chilled
	1 qt. club soda, chilled

Combine frozen concentrates and water in punch bowl; stir until concentrates melt. Add 1 pt. sherbet and let stand about 10 minutes. Stir. Just before serving, spoon in remaining sherbet. Carefully pour ginger ale and club soda down the side of punch bowl. Makes 20 to 30 servings.

CHRISTMAS SNACK TREE

Tree shows off colorful snacks for dipping—vary them as you like

Select a Styrofoam cone, 12" to 18" high, at a variety store or florist shop. Give it a firm base by forcing the center part of an 8 or 10" angel food cake pan two inches into the bottom of cone. Anchor pan base to a heavy plate with florist's clay so the tree is secure.

Cover the cone and the base with green foil. Stick toothpicks into appetizers and "trim the tree." Snacks are easier to remove for eating if you make holes in the covered tree with ice pick or skewer, then insert toothpicks. Use Tomato Roses (instructions follow) and evergreens to decorate the base.

How to make Snack Tree dippers

Meat and cheese dippers: Cut 3×1½" rectangles of thinly sliced, cooked ham; roll lengthwise and fasten with toothpicks. Use small cookie cutters to make salami and bologna cutouts. Cut small cubes of semihard cheeses; insert toothpicks carefully.

Vegetable dippers: Wash and separate cauliflower into small flowerets; chill in ice water. For celery fans, cut celery into 1½" lengths. Slit parallel strips one half the length of each piece; chill in ice water until curled. To make carrot daisies, cut peeled carrot crosswise into three pieces. Cut five or six lengthwise notches around the carrot; slice into ½" rounds. Place green pepper square atop carrot slice and insert toothpick. For radish accordions, wash radishes; cut out root ends. Make crosswise parallel notches the length of the radish; crisp in cold water.

TOMATO ROSES

Red roses to make at Christmastime to decorate base of snack tree

Select a large, bright red tomato. Rose is made from outer shell of tomato. With stem end up, insert knife ¾" from stem and cut a crosswise slice only two thirds of the way through (slice serves as base of rose). From this cut, continue peeling tomato in an unbroken spiral, ¾" wide and ⅛" thick.

To form rose, place stem end on plate, skin side down. Starting at free end, roll up spiral toward stem. Secure with a toothpick.

PARTY CHEESE DIP

Three kinds of cheese contribute flavor to this well-seasoned party dip. One taste and its popularity zooms

¼ c. milk	½ small clove garlic
8 oz. cottage cheese	¼ tsp. salt
3 (1") cubes blue cheese	½ tsp. paprika
2 (3 oz.) pkgs. cream cheese, cut in 1" cubes	2 tsp. Worcestershire sauce

Pour milk into the electric blender container. Add cottage cheese; cover and blend on "low" about 20 seconds, or until smooth.

Add blue cheese, cream cheese, garlic, salt, paprika and Worcestershire sauce. Cover and blend on "high" until smooth, about 20 seconds. Refrigerate until serving time. Makes about 1 pint.

N O T E : You can use the electric mixer to make this dip if you don't have a blender.

QUICK MUSTARD SAUCE

Just right for vegetable and meat dippers—and it's so easy to fix

1 pt. dairy sour cream
3 tblsp. prepared horse-radish

½ c. prepared mustard

Combine ingredients. Serve cold, or heat until mixture simmers and serve warm. Makes 2½ cups.

CASHEW DROP COOKIES

You can omit frosting but it brings out the cookies' wonderful flavor

½ c. butter or regular margarine
1 c. brown sugar, firmly packed
1 egg
½ tsp. vanilla
2 c. sifted flour
¾ tsp. baking powder
¾ tsp. baking soda

½ tsp. ground cinnamon
⅛ tsp. ground nutmeg
¼ tsp. salt
⅓ c. dairy sour cream
1 c. broken cashew nuts
Brown Butter Frosting

Cream butter and brown sugar until fluffy. Add egg and vanilla; beat well.

Sift together flour, baking powder, baking soda, cinnamon, nutmeg and salt; add to creamed mixture alternately with sour cream. Stir in cashews.

Drop by teaspoonfuls 2″ apart onto greased baking sheet. Bake in hot oven (400°) 8 to 10 minutes, until lightly browned. Remove from baking sheet at once and cool on racks. Frost with Brown Butter Frosting. Makes 4 dozen.

Brown Butter Frosting: Cook and stir 3 tblsp. butter or regular margarine until browned (use care not to scorch). Gradually beat in 2 c. sifted confectioners sugar, 2 tblsp. milk and ¾ tsp. vanilla to make a smooth frosting of spreading consistency. Spread on cooled cookies.

HOLIDAY GUMDROP COOKIES

Bright colored candy in cookies adds gaiety to holiday buffets

1 c. shortening	¼ tsp. ground cinnamon
1 c. sugar	1⅓ c. quick-cooking rolled oats
1 c. brown sugar, firmly packed	1 c. chopped nuts
1 tsp. vanilla	1 c. shredded coconut
2 eggs	1 c. chopped gumdrops (do not
2 c. sifted flour	use black licorice-flavored
1 tsp. baking soda	candies)
½ tsp. salt	

Cream together shortening and sugars until fluffy. Stir in vanilla; then add eggs, one at a time, beating well after each addition.

Sift together flour, soda, salt and cinnamon. Add to creamed mixture. Stir in remaining ingredients. (Use scissors to cut gumdrops easily.)

Drop by teaspoonfuls about 2″ apart onto well-greased baking sheet. Bake in moderate oven (350°) 10 to 12 minutes. Cool on racks. Makes about 7 dozen.

CARAMEL POPCORN BALLS

Let the children help make these all-time country holiday favorites

2 qts. popped corn	½ c. water
¾ c. sugar	1 tsp. white vinegar
¾ c. brown sugar, firmly packed	1 tsp. salt
½ c. light corn syrup	¾ c. butter or regular margarine

Put popcorn in large bowl and keep warm in slow oven (300°).

Combine sugars, corn syrup, water, vinegar and salt in a 2-qt. saucepan. Bring to a boil over medium heat, stirring frequently. Cook, stirring constantly, to the hard ball stage, 260° on candy thermometer.

Reduce heat to low and stir in butter. When melted, slowly pour hot syrup in thin stream over popcorn, stirring to coat all kernels. Cool briefly. Butter hands and shape mixture in balls of desired size. Cool on waxed paper. Makes about 16 (3″) popcorn balls.

SKATING PARTY REFRESHMENTS

Glazed Potato Doughnuts*
Popcorn/Peanut Clusters*
Bowl of Apples
Tri-Fruit Cooler*

Youngsters like to return home after skating, a few friends "in tow," to find tempting refreshments waiting in the kitchen. You can make ahead all the foods in this menu; perhaps your daughter can do it, or at least help in the preparations. The rewards for your efforts will be rich even if all you do is watch the excited youngsters when they see a fresh batch of glazed doughnuts displayed on cooling racks.

TIMETABLE

Do-Ahead: Make Popcorn/Peanut Clusters a day ahead, cool and store in airtight containers. Polish the apples until they shine.

On Guest Day: How about making the doughnuts while the skating party is in progress? You will need to be at home for at least 2 hours to make the doughnut dough, let it rise, roll, cut and let rise again. Count on about an hour longer to fry the hot cakes, glaze and let them cool. In the meantime, combine the fruit juices and chill.

SERVING SUGGESTIONS

Pour the fruit juice blend into tall glasses over cracked ice; add a scoop of colorful sherbet. Set out the remainder of the refreshments in generous bowls either in the kitchen or family room. Stay in the background while the youngsters "pitch in."

GLAZED POTATO DOUGHNUTS

Fresh from the fry kettle and glazed, they're an unsurpassed treat

1 pkg. active dry yeast	2 eggs, beaten
¼ c. warm water (110 to 115°)	5 to 6 c. sifted flour
1 c. milk, scalded	1 lb. confectioners sugar
¼ c. shortening	6 tblsp. water
¼ c. sugar	1 tblsp. vanilla
1 tsp. salt	
¾ c. mashed potatoes (instant may be used)	

Dissolve yeast in warm water.

Combine milk, shortening, sugar and salt. Cool until lukewarm. Stir in yeast, potatoes and eggs. Gradually add enough flour to make a soft dough. Turn onto floured surface; knead until smooth and satiny. Place in lightly greased bowl; turn over to grease top. Cover. Let rise in warm place until doubled, 1 to 1½ hours.

Roll to ½" thickness; cut with 3" doughnut cutter. Cover; let rise until doubled, about 30 minutes.

Meanwhile, stir confectioners sugar, water and vanilla together. (Glaze will look like very thick cream.)

Fry doughnuts in deep hot fat (375°). Drain on absorbent paper. Drop hot doughnuts into glaze. Place on cooling rack until glaze is set. Makes about 3½ dozen.

POPCORN/PEANUT CLUSTERS

A country confection for people of all ages; it never goes begging

2½ qts. popped corn	½ c. butter or regular margarine
2¼ c. light brown sugar (1 lb.)	2 tsp. salt
½ c. light corn syrup	1 c. salted peanuts
½ c. water	2 tsp. vanilla

Put popcorn in baking pan and keep warm in slow oven (300°).

Combine brown sugar, corn syrup, water, butter and salt in a large saucepan. Cook over moderate heat, stirring occasionally, until mixture reaches 290° on candy thermometer (soft crack stage).

Meanwhile, put popcorn and peanuts in a large buttered bowl; toss to mix well.

Add vanilla to hot syrup. Pour syrup in a thin stream over the popcorn mixture, tossing to mix well and coat corn and peanuts completely with boiling hot syrup. Work fast.

Spread in a thin layer on buttered baking sheets or platters. Using two buttered spoons, immediately separate into small (bite-size) clusters. Makes about 3 quarts.

TRI-FRUIT COOLER

Fruit juice blend tastes good, is pretty and quickly quenches thirst

1 (6 oz.) can frozen orange juice concentrate, thawed

1 qt. apple juice, chilled

1 pt. strawberry or raspberry sherbet

Combine thawed concentrate and apple juice in a large bowl. Beat until well blended. Pour into tall glasses over cracked ice. Top each serving with a small scoop of sherbet. Makes 6 to 8 servings.

MOONLIGHT HAYRIDE SUPPER

Frankfurters   Coney Buns
Home Baked Beans*
Crisp Lettuce Relish*
Ketchup   Mustard   Cucumber Pickles
Sundae Bar

Consult the calendar to find out when the moon will be full. Then invite friends to supper and a moonlight hayride. Instead of hitching old Dobbin and his partner to the flatbed, today's rides are courtesy of a tractor.

Keep the food simple and serve it picnic style at a table in the yard or on the porch. This can be before or after the ride—or better still, serve the main course when guests arrive, the dessert at the end of the evening.

Frankfurters are important in this meal; allow a minimum of two for each person. (Better have extras if there are boys in the crowd.) You can cook them in the house. Just drop franks in a kettle of boiling water and simmer until hot, 5 to 10 minutes, depending on their size. Or you can grill them outdoors over medium coals for 12 to 15 minutes, or until they are heated through, turning often.

The relish is a vegetable salad cut fine. Home baked beans are a highlight of the meal. A hand-cranked ice cream freezer filled with vanilla ice cream is something to return to at the end of the ride. Especially if you set up a make-your-own-sundae bar.

TIMETABLE

Do-Ahead: Bake the beans several days ahead (at least one day) and freeze before the hayride. They freeze successfully and it's easy to reheat them.

On Guest Day: Make the ice cream and let it ripen in the freezer can a few hours. Or make it several days ahead and put in the freezer. (Use your favorite recipe, if you like, but we give a recipe for Homemade Vanilla Ice Cream in the menu "Chicken Barbecue Dinner"—see Index.) Fix vegetables for relish an hour or two ahead, cover and chill, but toss with dressing shortly before serving so the lettuce will stay crisp.

SERVING SUGGESTIONS

Serve frankfurters on a spacious platter wth ketchup and prepared mustard on one side, a basket of split coney buns (long) on the other side handy for people who want to pop franks in them. Serve the beans in a bean pot if you have one, or in a casserole.

At dessert time, bring out a tray holding an array of sundae toppings, such as chocolate and butterscotch sauces or syrups, maple syrup, sliced or crushed fresh strawberries or sliced peaches (sprinkled with 2 tsp. ascorbic acid powder dissolved in about 3 tblsp. water to 1 qt. fruit to prevent darkening). If fresh berries and peaches are not in season, serve strawberry or peach preserves instead (both are good on ice cream). Relax and watch the enjoyment a help-yourself sundae bar provides.

HOME BAKED BEANS

If you live in New England fix Boston baked beans instead of this midwestern and western kind. Both types have ardent champions

2 lbs. navy or pea beans
1 lb. salt pork, or bacon
1 lb. brown sugar
1 (1 lb. 12 oz.) can tomatoes
2 medium onions, chopped (about ¾ c.)

2 tblsp. prepared mustard
½ tsp. salt
½ tsp. pepper

Wash and pick over beans; cover generously with water and soak overnight. Next morning, simmer beans in salted water until they test done. (An easy test is to bite into a bean to find out if it's tender.) Drain beans and save liquid.

Put salt pork or bacon through food chopper, or chop. (If you use bacon, pour boiling water over and let stand 3 to 5 minutes; drain and grind.) Place it in the bottom of a large bean pot or deep casserole. Alternately layer cooked beans with a mixture of brown sugar, tomatoes, onions, mustard, salt and pepper on top of salt pork. Pour on the water in which beans cooked and add enough hot water to cover beans. Adjust the lid, or cover with aluminum foil.

Bake in slow oven (300°) 6 to 8 hours, stirring occasionally and adding more hot water if necessary.

This recipe makes 15 to 25 generous servings. Put the leftover beans in a freezer container and store in the freezer to reheat for the next barbecue.

CRISP LETTUCE RELISH

Quick, easy way to give familiar mixed vegetable salad a new look

1½ qts. shredded head lettuce (iceberg)
2 medium cucumbers, peeled and finely diced
1⅓ c. diced radishes

¾ c. thinly sliced green onions
1 c. vinegar/oil salad dressing (equal parts oil and vinegar with salt and pepper to season)

Cut head lettuce on board, using a French chef's knife, into ½" slices; then cut crisscross to make of relish consistency (not too fine). Add prepared cucumbers, radishes and onions; chill until ready to serve. At the last minute, toss lightly with salad dressing (you can use bottled French dressing, or see Index for the Vinegar/Oil Dressing recipe used with Calico Green Salad). Makes 8 servings.

MEN'S WINTER EVENING SANDWICH LUNCH

Hot Cheese/Tomato Sandwiches*   Dill Pickles
Buttered Pumpernickel Toast   Tossed Green Salad
Ranch House Raisin Cookies*   Cherry/Chocolate Cookies*
Coffee

This menu features food most men like. It is a top favorite of a Colorado man and three of his neighbors with whom he shared the late lunch one cold night when they met at his mountain ranch home to discuss mutual business interests. The host's wife made the advance preparations. He took over at serving time. It's so easy and so pleasing to everyone who tastes it. If you wish to convert the menu into the main evening meal, add a vegetable such as peas with mushrooms or corn with green pepper or pimiento, and substitute apple pie for the cookies. And double the sandwich recipe.

TIMETABLE

Do-Ahead: Bake the cookies unless you have a supply in the freezer.

On Guest Day: Wash salad greens, drain well and chill in a plastic bag. You can get the open-face sandwiches ready to broil several hours before serving them; put them in the refrigerator. When time for lunch, put sandwiches under broiler to heat, but watch them, for it's easy to overdo the cooking. Toss the salad; make coffee.

SERVING SUGGESTIONS

Set toaster, sliced pumpernickel and butter on table so everyone can make additional toast. Serve the plates in the kitchen. On them place sandwiches and dill pickles. Serve the salad in individual bowls, or on individual plates. Pour the coffee.

HOT CHEESE/TOMATO SANDWICHES

Tomato slices and cheese sauce on pumpernickel toast—really good

4 c. shredded sharp Cheddar cheese (1 lb.)	1 tblsp. butter or regular margarine
3 tblsp. flour	1 egg
½ tsp. dry mustard	4 slices pumpernickel toast
¾ c. beer or milk	Chopped chives (optional)
2 tsp. Worcestershire sauce	8 thick tomato slices

Combine cheese, flour and mustard; toss with fork to coat cheese with flour. Place in 2-qt. saucepan; add beer, Worcestershire sauce and butter. Heat over medium heat, stirring constantly until cheese melts and sauce is smooth.

Beat egg slightly and add a little hot cheese sauce; stir to mix. Add to cheese sauce and stir until blended. Remove from heat.

Place pumpernickel toast on an ovenproof platter or baking dish. Pour on all but ½ c. cheese sauce; sprinkle with chives. Then top each piece of toast with 2 tomato slices. Spoon remaining sauce over tomatoes. (You can cover with foil and refrigerate several hours and broil just before serving.) Run under broiler until hot, lightly browned and bubbly. Serve with extra buttered pumpernickel toast, if desired. Makes 4 servings.

RANCH HOUSE RAISIN COOKIES

You cook the raisins before you stir them into the cookie mixture

½ c. raisins	1¾ c. sifted flour
1 c. water	½ tsp. salt
1 c. brown sugar, firmly packed	½ tsp. baking powder
½ c. shortening	½ tsp. baking soda
1 egg	½ c. chopped nuts
½ tsp. vanilla	

Bring raisins to a boil with water. Cool thoroughly.

Cream sugar and shortening until fluffy. Add egg and vanilla. Beat to mix.

Sift together flour, salt, baking powder and soda. Alternately add to creamed mixture with cooled raisins (there should be ½ c. liquid with raisins; if not, add water to make ½ c.). Stir in nuts.

Drop dough by teaspoonfuls at least 2″ apart onto greased baking sheets.

Bake in moderate oven (350°) 10 to 12 minutes. Remove cookies and cool on racks. Makes 4 dozen.

CHERRY/CHOCOLATE COOKIES

Cherry-chocolate blend tastes good; try making them wth nuts, too

½ c. butter or regular margarine
1 c. sugar
1 egg
2 squares unsweetened chocolate, melted and cooled
⅓ c. buttermilk
1 tsp. vanilla
1¾ c. sifted flour

½ tsp. baking soda
½ tsp. salt
2 c. cut-up maraschino cherries, drained, or cut-up candied cherries
Chocolate Frosting
Maraschino cherry halves, well drained (for garnish)

Thoroughly mix butter, sugar, egg, chocolate, buttermilk and vanilla.

Sift together flour, soda and salt; stir into chocolate mixture. Add cherries and mix to distribute in dough. Cover and chill an hour or longer. (Dough is soft.)

Drop dough 2″ apart onto ungreased baking sheet. Bake in hot oven (400°) 8 to 10 minutes, or until almost no imprint shows when touched with finger. Remove from baking sheet at once; cool on racks. Frost tops with Chocolate Frosting and garnish each cookie with a maraschino cherry half, rounded side up. Makes about 54 cookies.

Chocolate Frosting: Melt 2 squares unsweetened chocolate and 2 tblsp. butter over medium heat. Remove from heat and blend in 2 to 3 tblsp. light cream. Stir in about 2 c. sifted confectioners sugar, or enough to make a frosting of spreading consistency.

NOTE: 1 c. chopped pecans may be substituted for 2 c. cut-up cherries. Decorate frosted cookies with nuts.

GOLDEN WEDDING RECEPTION

Flower Wedding Cake*
Golden Punch*
Yellow and White Candy Mints   Salted Nuts
Coffee

Golden wedding receptions can be as simple as punch and cake, as delicious and beautiful as Golden Punch and Flower Wedding Cake.

You make the lovely cake with a recipe developed by home economists in our Countryside Kitchens. It is the answer to many requests for a wedding cake that tastes as good as it looks.

You make the cake from scratch, baking it in a 1" deep jelly roll pan and an 8" square pan 2" deep. Use of deeper pans destroys top results. The secret to success in making the cake is to organize the production steps. Follow the timetable.

The pastel yellow flowers that decorate the wedding cake are plastic, but you dip them in a glaze for a glossy coating. The pretty punch is refreshing—do have coffee also for guests who prefer it.

TIMETABLE

Do-Ahead: A week before the reception dip the flowers in Dipping Frosting. Lay them in a waxed paper-lined box and store in a dry place. Bake the cake a week ahead, cool and freeze. Or bake it a day ahead, cool and wrap in waxed paper to prevent drying. Build the cake a day before the reception, spreading it with your choice of fillings. Spread surfaces first with Sealing Frosting to avoid crumbing. Decide where to place the flowers so you can arrange them quickly the next day. Chill cans of apricot nectar and pineapple juice and the bottles of carbonated beverage for the punch.

On Guest Day: Frost the cake and place the flowers on it. Fill the punch bowl with a large plastic bag holding ice cubes to chill it. It is easy to lift out the bag at the last minute and to add the punch.

SERVING SUGGESTIONS

Set the cake on a large plate or tray and encircle it and the punch bowl with delicate ferns, or with ivy. Float a few thin orange slices in the punch. Lift off the top tier of the cake and save it for the honored couple. Cut the middle tier in 14 pieces, the bottom tier in 36 pieces. You will have 50 servings of wedding cake that really taste good.

FLOWER WEDDING CAKE

You'll need to make two recipes of this cake to make the 3-tier beauty. Cake serves 50

3⅓ c. sifted cake flour	½ c. shortening
4 tsp. baking powder	1¾ c. sugar
1½ tsp. salt	1 egg yolk
7 egg whites	2 tsp. vanilla
½ c. sugar	1 tsp. almond extract
½ c. butter	1⅓ c. milk

Pans are important. This cake *must* bake in shallow layers. Do not try to bake deeper cakes. Line a 15½ × 10½ × 1″ jelly roll pan and an 8″ square baking pan with plain brown paper. (*Do not* grease and flour pans, since this makes a crust that's too heavy.)

Sift cake flour, baking powder and salt together 3 times.

Beat egg whites until foamy. Add ½ c. sugar gradually; continue beating only until meringue will hold *soft* peaks. Set aside.

Cream butter and shortening together until well blended and smooth. Gradually add 1¾ c. sugar; beat until light and fluffy. Add the egg yolk and beat until well blended.

Add extracts to milk. Add milk alternately with dry ingredients to the creamed mixture, a small amount at a time; beat after each addition until smooth.

Add meringue and beat thoroughly into batter.

Spread batter in the two pans, about ½″ deep in each pan. Spread batter out to corners, leaving a slight depression in center. Tap pans sharply on counter top several times to remove large air bubbles.

Bake in moderate oven (350°) 25 to 30 minutes.

Cool on racks 10 minutes. Remove from pans and finish cooling on racks. To keep from drying, wrap as soon as cool.

ALMOND CREAM FILLING AND SEALING FROSTING

Take your pick of this or Orange/Raisin Filling—both luscious

4 egg yolks, slightly beaten	2 tsp. vanilla
1⅓ c. evaporated milk	2 c. finely chopped toasted
1⅓ c. sugar	almonds
½ c. butter or regular margarine	

Blend yolks and milk in saucepan; stir in sugar and butter. Cook over medium heat, stirring constantly, until thick and bubbling. Add vanilla.

Remove 1½ c. of this cooked mixture and add almonds to it. Cool; stir occasionally until of spreading consistency.

Sealing Frosting: Cool remainder of filling. Add 1½ to 2 c. sifted confectioners sugar and beat until of thin spreading consistency.

ORANGE/RAISIN FILLING

Golden raisins and orange candy teamed deliciously with almonds

½ c. sugar
2 tblsp. flour
2 c. light raisins, ground
1 c. water

1 c. finely cut orange gumdrops
1 c. finely chopped toasted almonds

Combine sugar and flour. Add to raisins in saucepan. Add water and stir to dissolve. Cook, stirring constantly, until thick.

Add gumdrops and cook 3 minutes.

Add almonds and cool thoroughly before using.

Sealing Frosting: Blend 2 slightly beaten egg yolks with ⅔ c. evaporated milk in saucepan. Stir in ⅔ c. sugar and ¼ c. butter or regular margarine. Cook over medium heat, stirring constantly, until thick and bubbling.

Remove from heat; add 1 tsp. vanilla and cool.

Stir in 1½ to 2 c. sifted confectioners sugar and beat to thin spreading consistency.

Bottom Tier: Trim crusts from the two 15½×10½×1″ cakes to make smooth straight sides.

Cut 9½″ square and 4″ square from each cake. Reserve the 4″ squares for top tier. (You'll have some scraps.)

Cut 9½″ square of cardboard and cover with foil. Place 9½″ square of cake on cardboard. Spread desired filling evenly over cake top. Place other 9½″ cake square on filling and press firmly.

Spread thin layer of Sealing Frosting over sides and top of this tier. Pull spatula over surface to make smooth straight sides.

Middle Tier: Trim crusts from the two 8″ square cakes to make 6½″ squares.

Cut 6½″ square of cardboard and cover with foil. Place 6½″

square of cake on cardboard. Spread with desired filling. Top with other 6½" square of cake. Center 6½" tier on bottom tier. Cover top and sides with Sealing Frosting.

Top Tier: Repeat procedure (using cardboard and foil) for two 4" squares. Center this on middle tier. Seal top and sides with frosting.

FLUFFY WHITE FROSTING

Looks like a white satin cloud

2 egg whites	¼ tsp. cream of tartar
1½ c. sugar	1 tsp. vanilla
⅓ c. water	

Combine all ingredients, except vanilla, in top of double boiler. Beat 1 minute on high speed with electric mixer.

Place over boiling water. Cook 7 minutes, beating all the time on high speed with electric mixer.

Remove from hot water. Turn frosting into bowl. Add vanilla; beat until of spreading consistency.

TO DECORATE CAKE

Let Sealing Frosting set before you apply Fluffy White Frosting.

Decide on placement of flowers before you apply final frosting.

Apply Fluffy White Frosting, starting with sides of bottom tier. Hold spatula perpendicular to tray and pull along carefully to make smooth sides and square corners. Apply to ledge of tier, building a ridge along outer edge. Repeat for each tier.

When frosting just begins to set, arrange flower design.

To Make Decorations

Select plastic flowers in pastel colors such as yellow or pink. For an orderly and attractive design, use no more than three varieties of flowers. Flowers that have definite form and petals that outline sharply show off best when dipped.

Wash plastic flowers in warm suds and rinse in clear water; dry. Cut individual flowers from stalk with a wire cutter, leaving a stem to hold when you dip it.

Dip plastic flowers in Dipping Frosting (recipe follows). Twirl in hand to distribute frosting evenly. Hold in hand a few minutes until frosting begins to set. Place on rack to dry. For thicker coating, you will probably want to dip again after first coating dries. When final coating is dry, snip off remaining stems.

Work out your desired arrangement for flowers before applying Fluffy White Frosting. Then when this final frosting is applied and just beginning to set, place flowers in desired spots.

DIPPING FROSTING

2 c. sugar
1 c. water
⅛ tsp. cream of tartar

1 to 1½ c. sifted confectioners sugar

Combine 2 c. sugar, water and cream of tartar in saucepan. Cook to a thin syrup (226° on candy thermometer). Remove from heat and cool to lukewarm (112°).

Add confectioners sugar gradually, stirring until smooth. Mixture should be of pouring consistency.

Place over warm water to keep frosting at right consistency for dipping. If too hot, plastic flowers will soften.

A little experimenting will determine the best consistency for coating. If you don't like appearance of flowers on first dipping, wash off frosting, pat dry with dish towel and redip.

GOLDEN PUNCH

This punch is on the tart side. It's refreshing, colorful, easy to fix

1 (6 oz.) can frozen orange juice concentrate
1 (6 oz.) can frozen lemonade concentrate
1 (12 oz.) can apricot nectar

2 c. pineapple juice
½ c. lemon juice
1 qt. lemon-lime carbonated beverage, or 1 qt. ginger ale
Sherbet

Reconstitute orange juice and lemonade as directed on cans. Combine in punch bowl with apricot nectar, pineapple juice and lemon juice.

Pour bottled carbonated beverage or ginger ale slowly down side of bowl. Drop scoops of pineapple, orange, lime or raspberry sherbet into punch. (Sherbet is not necessary, but it is decorative and delicious.) Makes about 3½ quarts without sherbet. With sherbet, punch makes about 30 servings. (You may want to double recipe.)

INDEX